Stuart Garner

The Teaching and Learning of Programming

Stuart Garner

The Teaching and Learning of Programming

The Use of a Technology Supported Part-Complete Solution Method

VDM Verlag Dr. Müller

Impressum/Imprint (nur für Deutschland/ only for Germany)

Bibliografische Information der Deutschen Nationalbibliothek: Die Deutsche Nationalbibliothek verzeichnet diese Publikation in der Deutschen Nationalbibliografie; detaillierte bibliografische Daten sind im Internet über http://dnb.d-nb.de abrufbar.

Alle in diesem Buch genannten Marken und Produktnamen unterliegen warenzeichen-, marken- oder patentrechtlichem Schutz bzw. sind Warenzeichen oder eingetragene Warenzeichen der jeweiligen Inhaber. Die Wiedergabe von Marken, Produktnamen, Gebrauchsnamen, Handelsnamen, Warenbezeichnungen u.s.w. in diesem Werk berechtigt auch ohne besondere Kennzeichnung nicht zu der Annahme, dass solche Namen im Sinne der Warenzeichen- und Markenschutzgesetzgebung als frei zu betrachten wären und daher von jedermann benutzt werden dürften.

Coverbild: www.purestockx.com

Verlag: VDM Verlag Dr. Müller Aktiengesellschaft & Co. KG
Dudweiler Landstr. 125 a, 66123 Saarbrücken, Deutschland
Telefon +49 681 9100-698, Telefax +49 681 9100-988, Email: info@vdm-verlag.de

Herstellung in Deutschland:
Schaltungsdienst Lange o.H.G., Zehrensdorfer Str. 11, D-12277 Berlin
Books on Demand GmbH, Gutenbergring 53, D-22848 Norderstedt
Reha GmbH, Dudweiler Landstr. 99, D- 66123 Saarbrücken
ISBN: 978-3-639-02547-7

Imprint (only for USA, GB)

Bibliographic information published by the Deutsche Nationalbibliothek: The Deutsche Nationalbibliothek lists this publication in the Deutsche Nationalbibliografie; detailed bibliographic data are available in the Internet at http://dnb.d-nb.de.

Any brand names and product names mentioned in this book are subject to trademark, brand or patent protection and are trademarks or registered trademarks of their respective holders. The use of brand names, product names, common names, trade names, product descriptions etc. even without
a particular marking in this works is in no way to be construed to mean that such names may be regarded as unrestricted in respect of trademark and brand protection legislation and could thus be used by anyone.

Cover image: www.purestockx.com

Publisher:
VDM Verlag Dr. Müller Aktiengesellschaft & Co. KG
Dudweiler Landstr. 125 a, 66123 Saarbrücken, Germany
Phone +49 681 9100-698, Fax +49 681 9100-988, Email: info@vdm-verlag.de

Copyright © 2008 VDM Verlag Dr. Müller Aktiengesellschaft & Co. KG and licensors
All rights reserved. Saarbrücken 2008

Produced in USA and UK by:
Lightning Source Inc., 1246 Heil Quaker Blvd., La Vergne, TN 37086, USA
Lightning Source UK Ltd., Chapter House, Pitfield, Kiln Farm, Milton Keynes, MK11 3LW, GB
BookSurge, 7290 B. Investment Drive, North Charleston, SC 29418, USA
ISBN: 978-3-639-02547-7

Contents

Chapter 1
Introduction

1.1 Introduction and Problem

Learning to write computer programs is not easy (e.g., du Boulay, 1986; Scholtz & Wiedenbeck, 1992) and this is reflected in the low levels of achievement experienced by many students in first programming courses. For example, Perkins, Schwartz & Simmons (1988, p.155) state that: "Students with a semester or more of instruction often display remarkable naivete about the language that they have been studying and often prove unable to manage dismayingly simple programming problems". Also, King, Feltham & Nucifora (1994, p.18) state that: "Even after two years of study, many students had only a rudimentary understanding of programming".

Jenkins (2002) suggests that the learning of programming is a perennial problem. Students struggle as they try to master the subject and it is not uncommon for a student's first experience of programming to be so negative and stressful that it leads to academic failure or withdrawal. In a study into the teaching and learning of first year programming, it was found that the main concerns were high failure rates, a low flow of students into higher degrees, and a perception of a wide variation of teaching skills (Carbone et al, 2000).

In many ways, this problem has become even greater over the last few years as many more students have enrolled into information technology and computer science type courses as the area of ICT (Information and Communication Technology) has expanded. In the past, computer programming was usually only studied by those considering becoming commercial programmers. However today a wider variety of students might be expected to develop programming code for such areas as macros within spreadsheets; multimedia applications; interactive web pages. Such students may be on business or e-commerce courses and not necessarily have the same aptitude to learn programming as the dedicated computer science students. Roussev (2003, p.1353) indicates that "programming has become an indispensable part of the IS component of the core curriculum at business schools".

Although the number and variety of students that attempt to learn to program has increased, high failure rates are a major problem and much of the literature provides many examples of new teaching approaches that have been used to try and overcome this problem (Bruce et al,

2004). A review of the literature on the teaching and learning of introductory programming reveals that there has been little, if any, research on how students go about learning to program (Bruce & McMahon, 2002). The review also points out that there have been many examples of innovative teaching practice implemented, but that these usually appear to have been developed independently of any research into the students' experience of learning programming. In practice, however, the ways in which teaching and learning takes place in the domain of programming have changed little and many students still find the learning of programming a very difficult process.

Additionally, there has been a rapid movement to the use of more student centred and flexible learning methods within the teaching and learning process (e.g., Nikolova & Collis, 1998). It can be argued that the instructional design for programming courses should take notice of these moves and possibly utilise some of these methods. Technological improvements have also been significant over the last few years enabling the production of engaging courseware that can help students studying in a flexible learning mode. Electronic scaffolds and supports can now be produced relatively easily to help students in their learning processes when they are studying on their own with limited access to a human tutor.

These issues and outcomes demonstrate that the teaching and learning of programming is still problematic today and is an area where new possibilities exist.

1.2   Purpose of the Study

A variety of methods and tools have been used to try and improve the teaching and learning of programming. Some have showed promise, however, many others remain to be successfully used. One strategy with particular promise that could help address the problem is known as the part-complete solution method (PCSM). Earlier studies demonstrated its potential (e.g., van Merrienboer, 1990b) but its success was never realised due to the absence of suitable electronic tools to support the process. With contemporary technology, many of these problems can now be overcome. In a course that utilises the PCSM, students are given programming problems together with part-complete solutions to those problems. For each problem, a student would study the problem and attempt to complete the part-complete solution that they had been given. Finally they would test the program to determine its correctness.

The purpose of this study was to investigate the production of a software tool to support the process of completing part-complete solutions to programming problems. It was believed that such a tool might help reduce the cognitive load that students experience during the learning process and reduce the need for students to be concerned about programming language syntax.

The tool was to be used in a variety of modes by students so that different types of part-complete exercises could be undertaken. The study was to investigate:

- The theoretical underpinnings to guide the design and development of such a tool;

- The usability of the tool and particularly the usability factors that might impact on student learning;

- How the tool would support and scaffold the process of learning programming;

- How the tool would impact on students' learning outcomes and achievements.

1.3   Significance of this Line of Inquiry

The study is significant as current practices in the teaching and learning of programming still leave a lot to be desired (e.g., Winslow, 1996). And yet the learning of programming is more important than ever and the complexities of many of the newer visual type languages have made its learning even more difficult. It is more important as a wider range of students are finding it necessary to learn programming. Examples include: finance and accounting students that have to create complex macros within spreadsheets using a language such as Visual BASIC for Applications; e-commerce students that have to produce complex web pages with embedded programming code using JavaScript; multimedia students that have to develop systems in languages such as Authorware; and of course computing and information systems students who have always had to learn to program in their courses using languages such as C, C++, Java and Visual BASIC.

The complexity of a visual language such as Visual BASIC makes the process of learning even more difficult than in the past. Students have always had to grapple with the syntax and semantics of a language in addition to learning the fundamental control and data structures together with basic programming algorithms. A language such as Visual BASIC compounds the difficulties as students also need to learn about objects and their properties together with the events that programming objects can respond to. It could be argued that a simpler, non visual language, should be used within an introductory programming course. However, in practice this is not possible as many courses of study at the tertiary level are already overcrowded with units and such an introductory programming unit has to use a commercial language that is being used in the marketplace.

The study is also of significance as it is important to investigate ways in which technology can support students who are learning programming in modes other than the traditional campus based mode. The move today is towards flexible learning where students may be studying away from a campus with little opportunity for face to face meetings with their tutors. This often creates serious difficulties for students of programming and the technological improvements of recent years may well provide support for such learners.

1.4   Structure of Thesis

This thesis reports the conduct of the study that was undertaken. It has been structured around 9 chapters that are illustrated in Figure 1.1.

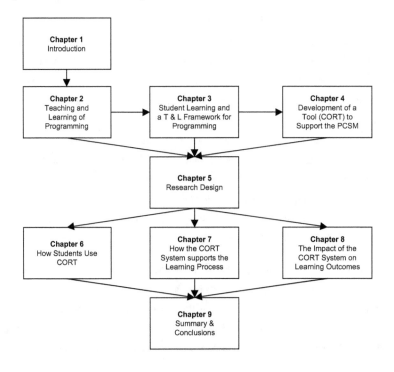

Figure 1.1: Structure of Thesis

Chapter 2 provides a review of the literature into the teaching and learning of programming and discusses: the difficulties that students have when learning to program; what constitutes expertise in the domain of computer programming; approaches to the teaching and learning of programming; approaches experimented with in the teaching and learning of programming; and tools used and experimented with in the teaching and learning of programming. It provides insights into the difficulties of learning to program and into some of the teaching and learning methods that might be of use in a model or framework to support the teaching and learning of programming.

Chapter 3 provides a review into how students learn that is particularly useful for the domain of programming. It looks at how expertise is developed; what is meant by knowledge; knowledge organisation; mental models and schema theory; cognitive load theory; and scaffolding. The literature is used to help inform the development of a conceptual framework of a system that could be used by students to aid their learning of programming.

Chapter 4 describes the design and development of a **CO**de **R**estructuring **T**ool (CORT) that was based on the teaching and learning framework that had been developed. The prototype of CORT and its subsequent testing with students are described, together with amendments that were made in response to student feedback.

Chapter 5 describes the research design that was used to investigate the use of CORT. Research methodologies in general are discussed together with the process by which the particular methodology was chosen for this project. The research questions are described together with the data collection methods that were used and the actual data gathering that took place.

Chapter 6 reports the findings from the usability study of CORT, with data on usability having been gathered from a detailed review of students' use of CORT. The usability factors of CORT which were found to be an issue for students are discussed together with the impact they had on student learning. Ten usability issues that were identified as potential impediments to learning are described. Finally, the apparent impact of these issues on the learning of the students is outlined and suggestions for the improvement of CORT in order to reduce the impact are put forward.

Chapter 7 describes an analysis of a qualitative inquiry that sought to investigate how the PCSM within the CORT system supported and scaffolded the learning process. The inquiry was carried out by observing students and particularly investigating the cognitive strategies that they used when attempting to solve problems with the CORT system.

Chapter 8 describes a quantitative inquiry which explored the impact of the PCSM within the CORT system on students' learning outcomes and achievements.

In Chapter 9, the study is summarised, the limitations of the study are discussed, and further areas of inquiry are proposed.

Chapter 2
The Teaching and Learning of Programming

This chapter explores the difficulties that students have when learning to program; what constitutes expertise in the domain of computer programming; approaches to the teaching and learning of programming; approaches experimented with in the teaching and learning of programming; and tools used and experimented with in the teaching and learning of programming.

2.1 Introduction

Programming is a complex body of knowledge and is defined to be (Hyperdictionary, 2005; WordReference.com, 2005):

"Creating a sequence of instructions to enable the computer to do something"

When programming, a student has to learn how to take a written description of a problem and put it into steps that a computer can perform (Lisack, 1998). While doing this, the student must recognise when the program needs to make a decision, and when the program requires a looping structure to perform some steps multiple times. With the new event-driven programming environments such as that provided for Visual BASIC .NET (Schneider, 2003), the complexity of the design process is magnified for some students because they must now separate the user's actions and decisions from the program's actions and decisions.

Because of its complexity, programming is a difficult subject for many students and developing expertise can be a long and painful process.

2.2 Difficulties of Learning to Program

Programming is a complex process involving many steps (e.g., Winslow, 1996). The process comprises:

- Studying a given problem statement / set of requirements and producing an algorithm, often in pseudo code, to solve that problem;

- Translating the algorithm into the programming code of a certain programming language; and

- Testing and amending the program until it meets the original set of requirements.

However, learning to program can be difficult and this presents great challenges to teachers to produce curricula and to use resources, including texts and tools, that help students in their learning process. Although learning to program is a key objective in most introductory computing courses, many educators have concerns over whether their students learn the necessary programming skills in those courses (McCracken et al, 2001). The challenge of learning programming in introductory courses lies in simultaneously learning: general problem solving skills; algorithm design; program design; a programming language in which to implement algorithms as programs; and an environment to support the program design and implementation (Fowler & Fowler, 1993). In addition, students need to learn testing and debugging techniques to validate programs and to identify and fix problems that they may have within their programs. Students are often exposed to concepts and topics that are completely abstract with no way of drawing upon their real world experience to help understand what they are being taught (Milne & Rowe, 2004).

The problem solving and program design skills that students attempt to gain include the development of appropriate schemata. Such schemata are also known as plans or patterns and are stereotypical sequence of statements, that expert programmers have knowledge of, to solve certain categories of problem. Three examples of such plans are shown in Figure 2.1.

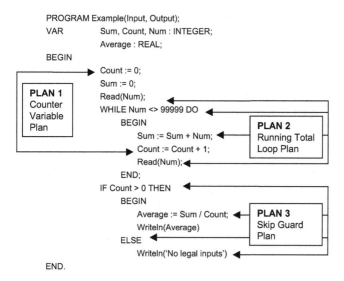

```
PROGRAM Example(Input, Output);
VAR         Sum, Count, Num : INTEGER;
            Average : REAL;
BEGIN
            Count := 0;
            Sum := 0;
            Read(Num);
            WHILE Num <> 99999 DO
                BEGIN
                    Sum := Sum + Num;
                    Count := Count + 1;
                    Read(Num);
                END;
            IF Count > 0 THEN
                BEGIN
                    Average := Sum / Count;
                    Writeln(Average)
                ELSE
                    Writeln('No legal inputs')
END.
```

PLAN 1
Counter
Variable
Plan

PLAN 2
Running Total
Loop Plan

PLAN 3
Skip Guard
Plan

Figure 2.1: Programming Plan Example

The following describes some of the particular difficulties that students meet.

2.2.1 General Problem-Solving Skills and Algorithm Design

In any programming course, students have to solve problems, the problems then being implemented in a programming language. This means that they have to acquire problem-solving skills involving understanding a problem to determine what is required and devising a plan or a sequence of steps for a solution (Milbrandt, 1995). This is probably the most difficult aspect of learning to program, and Rowe (1993, p.40) states that: "Many students who have an understanding of the major language features are not able to compose programs which contain groups of commands working in concert. ... the computer language is often the only topic addressed in computer texts and courses."

Deek, McHugh & Hiltz (2000, p.25) support this view and state: "The lack of basic problem solving competence and thinking skills is a prominent problem with novice programmers."

"The real problems that novices have lie in putting the pieces together, composing and coordinating components of a program" (Soloway, 1986, p.850). Also various studies have concluded that novices lack adequate mental models of the domain of interest; use general problem solving techniques rather than strategies dependent on the particular problem; tend to approach their designs through control structures; and use a line-by-line, bottom up approach to problem solutions (e.g., Winslow, 1996).

2.2.2 Program Design and Event Driven Languages

After students have attempted to solve a problem and designed an algorithm in, for example, pseudo code, a program has to be designed to implement the algorithm. The amount of work to do this depends to some extent on the degree of detail in the algorithm design. Students have to make decisions on how to break the algorithm down into various components such as procedures and functions and on the data structures that should be used. The particular difficulties that students have in this area include the concepts of variables, procedures, functions, and control structures (Rogalski & Samurcay, 1993).

These difficulties are compounded if a visual language, such as Visual BASIC, is to be used in the teaching and learning process. This is because the event driven nature of such languages adds to the already high cognitive load of the subject. Lisack (1998, p.604) states: "With the new event-driven environments, the complexity of the design process is magnified for some students".

Webb (1997, p.1) also supports this view and states:

> "Whether Mac or PC, the operating system now used employs a graphical/mouse interface with an underlying message passing system. Programs written on this platform inevitably need to interface with the operating system which generally requires the programmer to at least understand (if not be very familiar with) the operation of a message-passing (or event-driven) system. In addition, the construction of visual components such as dialog boxes and data entry components is a necessary part of the simplest program. Languages such as Delphi, Visual Basic, Visual C++ all facilitate the GUI interface, but increasingly these are now (in part, or variations on) Object Oriented languages. This in turn increases the complexity to the learning programmer, as an understanding of the fundamentals of object-oriented-programming becomes a requirement."

2.2.3 Language Notation

Students have to deal with the notation of the language being learnt including syntax and semantics (e.g., du Boulay, 1986; Fowler & Fowler, 1993; Lisack, 1998). Lisack suggests that learning a first computer language is much like learning a foreign language as there are new words, grammar rules and punctuation to learn and it requires a lot of practice. However, unlike learning a foreign language, programming requires greater attention to detail because each programming statement must follow the grammar rules exactly in order to be executed by the computer. Programming is precision intensive and 100% of the statements need to be correct for a program to work (Perkins, Schwartz & Simmons, 1988).

It was observed in introductory courses, using the BASIC programming language, that students had difficulties with certain statements (Martinez & Benko de Rotaeche, 1990) which included:

- Troubles using the instructions PRINT AT and PRINT TAB to place words or geometrical figures in a definite location of the screen (selection between type or character coordinates).

- Misuse of the instructions PRINT and INPUT.

- Bad interpretation of the meaning of the part ELSE in the conditional instruction IF..ELSE..ENDIF.

- Lack of comprehension of the use of cumulative variables.

- Incorrect identification and handling of the variable that determines the stop condition for loop construction.

- Confusion in connection with the instructions that should be inside a loop.

It was found that students quickly overcame their syntax errors but that these semantic type errors were more difficult for students to correct.

2.2.4 Pragmatics of Programming
The pragmatics of programming need to be learnt by students (du Boulay, 1986), these being the skills of specifying, developing, testing and debugging programs using the tools available. Students have to learn how to utilise the program development environment including: how

to enter and edit lines of code; how to compile and run programs; how to use the debug facility; and how to organise the files of their projects.

Recently the development environments have become increasingly sophisticated and complex. An example is that used with the common teaching language of Microsoft Visual BASIC (e.g., Schneider, 2003) which is now much more difficult for students to use compared to the original Visual BASIC environment of version one from 1991 (StartVBdotnet.com, 2005).

The process of debugging requires the programmer to diagnose and repair often obscure difficulties in a program and this means that sophisticated problem-solving skills are needed (Perkins, Schwartz & Simmons, 1988).

2.2.5 Cognitive Load on Students

The difficulties that students experience when learning programming are compounded as they have to deal with all of the above issues at once. It is suggested that students have a sense of information overload as well as a seemingly unstructured set of concepts to link together (Hagan & Lowder, 1996). Others also support this point of view stating that learning to program demands considerable cognitive resources and that should this load be excessive then any learning will be inhibited (Sweller, 1988; Sweller & Chandler, 1991; Sweller, van Merrienboer & Paas, 1998). The cognitive load has increased over recent years with the introduction of event driven programming languages and ever more sophisticated program development environments.

Such a cognitive load impacts upon novices' affective domains as many students feel unsure of what they are doing and hold in doubt their ability to make the machine do what they want it to do (Perkins et al, 1986). This can then become a threat to students' self-esteem and standing with peers and teachers.

2.2.6 Conclusions: Difficulties of Learning to Program

The range of difficulties that students experience when learning to program suggested that a teaching and learning approach that placed a minimal cognitive load on students whilst stimulating them to learn the "standard" plans that are the building blocks of common algorithms was required.

2.3   Approaches to the Teaching and Learning of Programming

In the previous section, the multitude of problems facing novice programmers were discussed. For many years teachers have explored ways to deal with this. In this section these methods are explored and discussed with a view to determining an approach that might provide promise for this study.

2.3.1   Common Approaches to the Teaching and Learning of Programming

Probably the most common pedagogical approach to the teaching and learning of programming that is still used in schools, colleges and universities today is that described by Linn & Dalbey (1985). It is:

- Learn the syntax and semantics of one language feature at a time;

- Learn to combine the language feature with known design skills to develop programs to solve problems (this expands the students' design skills and includes patterns and procedural skills such as planning, testing and reformulating); and

- Develop general problem solving skills.

This approach is also known as the syntactic approach (Tolhurst, 1993) with its focus on the function of individual commands and their specific syntactic construction. The individual commands are taught individually and each command's structure is explained together with how they are commonly used. Students are then encouraged to combine various commands to solve simple problems.

With respect to the above, good pedagogy requires the instructor to keep initial facts, models, and rules simple and only expand and refine them as students gain experience (Winslow, 1996). However, a perceived problem of this approach is that it does not encourage the development of appropriate programming schemata or plans. Winslow makes a very valid point when he states: "One wonders, for example, about teaching sophisticated material to CS1 (an introductory programming course) students when study after study has shown that they do not understand basic loops" (Winslow, 1996, p.21).

Many courses use this approach and try and deliver programming knowledge at too fast a pace for many students. Many instructors do not fully understand how difficult the subject is for many novices. Because a tutor has developed expertise themselves in programming, they often do not understand how students can find the subject difficult. Historically, there has been a shortage of information technology personnel in industry and this has meant that educational institutions have had difficulty in recruiting and retaining good staff. It has been suggested that those involved in the teaching of programming need to reconsider their approach to teaching, and that current theories on cognition may require the adoption of a more inductive, exploratory and interactive approach (Clear, 1997).

2.3.2 Expert, Spiral and Reading Approaches to the Teaching and Learning of Programming

van Merrienboer & Krammer (1987) distinguish three instructional design approaches to the teaching and learning of programming: expert, spiral and reading. The expert approach emphasises both algorithm and program design in a systematic top-down fashion and students are given non-trivial problems throughout a course. Students are expected to apply stepwise refinement to solving their problems and it is thought that this allows students to concentrate more on the semantic content of algorithms as less attention is needed to track the actions of lower level programming code. Critics of this method suggest that, because novices do not have the schemata that experts possess, they therefore have great difficulty in knowing how to break problem solutions down into small steps. This expert approach has similarities to problem based learning (PBL) in which authentic problems drive the learning (Barg et al, 2000), however this is not necessarily a very useful pedagogical approach as students do not necessarily know how to problem solve (Fincher, 1999).

The spiral approach is the parallel acquisition of syntactic and semantic knowledge in a sequence that stimulates student interest by the use of meaningful examples. It builds on and reinforces previous knowledge and develops confidence through successful accomplishment of increasingly difficult tasks. The approach is similar to that described by Linn and Dalbey (1985) with its emphasis on stepwise incremental learning. At the beginning of a course, students attempt very simple problems that emphasise syntactic and lower level semantic knowledge. Problems then become progressively more difficult and require serious algorithm design.

The reading approach emphasises the reading, comprehension, modification and amplification of non-trivial, well-designed working programs and an introductory programming course using this approach has four phases:

1. Students run and evaluate the strengths and weaknesses of working programs.

2. Students read and hand trace well structured working programs. Specific language features are learned by the study of these concrete programs.

3. Students modify and amplify existing programs. They are therefore introduced to design and coding.

4. Students generate programs on their own, developing design and structured coding skills.

The developmental approach is similar to the reading approach and was put forward by Marchionini (1985). It concentrates on the development of general concepts important for programming which are language independent, stressing those concepts rather than syntax; providing relevant and motivational examples and activities; proceeding from the concrete to the abstract depending on the age and learner experience; and using a sequence of increasingly complex activities that build upon and extend previously learned examples. Marchionini suggests a sequence of ten activities as shown in Table 2.1.

Table 2.1: Developmental Sequence of Programming Activities (Marchionini 1985, p.14)

Activity Type	Example
1. Use	Enter, run, alter inputs
2. Study	Read, describe the purpose, trace execution, predict output
3. Complete	Supply missing statements
4. Modify	Add formats for output, comments, alter to produce related outputs
5. Extend	Add features - related output, files, generalise
6. Test	Try all cases, assume naïve user role
7. Debug	Correct logic errors on-line and off-line
8. Design	State problem, describe output, input and procedures, draw flow diagrams, draw screen display
9. Code from design	Code a given algorithm
10. Develop	Design and write a complete program

2.3.3 Conclusions: Approaches to the Teaching and Learning of Programming

The reading or developmental approach would appear to have potential in introductory programming courses. It would not be expected, for example, that students should be able to construct essays without having first read other essays and books. Similarly it is unreasonable to expect that students should be able to learn programming without first studying existing programs. Most programming texts include worked examples for students to study. A variation on the reading approach is the schema based approach discussed by Tolhurst (1993). In this, the knowledge structures that represent the schemata of experts are explicitly presented to students in the hope that they will learn them and use them in solving problems.

The reading approach and its variations do not appear to be frequently used in mainstream programming education. The main reason is that it is difficult to motivate students to hand trace existing code that solves a given programming problem. Unless there is some form of assessment associated with this process, students tend to skip and gloss over it. However an advantage of using such a method would be that students would not be concerned about syntax and the cognitive load placed upon them would be low. For these reasons, the reading method helped inform the approach that was developed in this study.

2.4 Approaches Experimented with in the Teaching and Learning of Programming

Over the years many different approaches to the teaching and learning of programming have been experimented with by researchers. The literature concerning a variety of these approaches was reviewed to determine which might help inform the approach to be utilised in this study.

2.4.1 The Conceptual / Notional Machine

Pea (1986) researched the sort of conceptual problems that students have when programming and it was concluded that many novices, when writing programs, use the analogy of conversing with a human and this leads to three different classes of conceptual bug: parallelism, intentionality, and egocentrism. Parallelism bugs are those where students believe that different lines of code can be active at the same time. Intentionality bugs occur when students give programs the status of an "intentional being" which has goals and knows or sees what will happen elsewhere in itself. And finally, egocentrism bugs are fairly similar to intentionality bugs, students believing that the computer can do what it has not been told to in the program. For example, lines of code might be omitted because students have assumed that the computer can "fill in", as a human might, what the student wishes the program to do.

The above demonstrates that in general, novices have difficulty understanding how a computer executes the lines of code within a program. Because of these conceptual difficulties that students have, several researchers have investigated the use of a conceptual or notional machine to help students in their understanding.

A notional machine is the idealised model of the computer implied by the constructs of the language (du Boulay, O'Shea & Monk, 1981). It consists of a model of the execution of a programming language from which the user attempts to determine how the language works and thus builds their mental model of execution for the programming language they are learning (Rajan, 1992).

Some experiments that were carried out showed that novices who made use of a notional machine learned to program more effectively than those who did not (Mayer, 1981). The notional machine that was used comprised a diagram, which made the basic operations of the computer visible to the students, together with a textual description. Input was represented by a ticket window at which data lined up. Output was represented as a message notepad with one message written per line. Memory was represented as an erasable scoreboard in which there was a natural destructive read-in and a non-destructive read-out. Executive control was represented as a recipe or shopping list with a pointer arrow to indicate the line being executed. Mayer's model was static, however better cognitive support is provided by dynamic models of notional machines that allow users to (Ramadhan, 2000):

- Observe how program statements are executed in an animated way; and

- See hidden and internal changes in some conceptual parts of the underlying computer, such as memory space, and can relate program comprehension and debugging with the properties of the machine they are interacting with.

A conceptual model comprising computer graphics and animation to illustrate to students how a program was executed was used in a research project (Shih & Alessi, 1994). A warehouse analogy was used to represent variables and a small icon of a computer could move along a path and highlight each statement to be executed. A circular path with a gate was used to represent loops and the conditions for continuing and exiting, and a speech balloon emanating from the icon showed the evaluation of expressions. The study found that the practising of code evaluation by tracing worked examples, with the help of conceptual models, promoted conceptual understanding and facilitated the learning of evaluation skills and the transfer to generation skills. It also found that the ability to solve transfer problems was highly correlated with the quality of a student's mental model.

The research into notional machines and conceptual models suggests that the teaching of such a conceptual model to students, or the use of an animated model, aids students in their learning of programming. It does this by providing help in the students' construction of appropriate schemata and / or mental models thereby overcoming inappropriate mental models that they may possess. Various tools have been built to animate programs, some specifically for teaching purposes and some as debugging aids, and these are discussed later in a section on programming tools. It can be seen to be important to try and include an appropriate notional machine within any teaching and learning support tool for programming.

2.4.2 Intelligent Tutoring Systems

Intelligent Tutoring systems utilise artificial intelligence techniques in an attempt to provide more sophisticated support in the teaching and learning process (Deek & McHugh, 1998). Some of these systems have been built specifically for the programming domain with the aim of offering adaptive instruction to meet individual learner needs and being capable of the analysis of student responses to determine correctness. Some examples include:

- BIP (BASIC instructional program) (Barr, Beard & Atkinson, 1976) is a tutoring system for learning BASIC.

- PROUST (Johnson & Soloway, 1985) is a tutoring system for Pascal programming. This contains programming and pedagogical experts and comprises modules to determine: the location and content of bugs; what the students intend to do with their code; and to determine student misconceptions.

- ACT (Advanced Computer Tutoring) (Anderson et al, 1995) is a system that has been used in the domains of mathematics and programming. It distinguishes between declarative knowledge and procedural knowledge, the latter being represented by sets of production rules. Such a tutor can generate and follow the multiple possible solutions a student might attempt on any given problem and dynamically tailor instruction to each individual student and problem. It is claimed that the cognitive tutors observe student performance, identify strengths and weaknesses, and provide individualised, just-in-time instruction while students learn by doing. The ACT programming tutor supports the teaching of LISP and Prolog.

Such intelligent tutoring systems have never been accepted in mainstream education and Deek & McHugh (1998) suggested several shortcomings, including:

- Inadequate user interfaces;

- Large learning curves for the systems with the need for tutorial support to overcome the operational difficulties;

- Problems with knowledge bases that store "ideal" solutions to problems, these being intrinsically incomplete; and

- Reliance on a limited number of teaching paradigms.

There has been one initiative in the domain of intelligent tutoring systems that is of interest to this present study. An automated system for the planning and construction of programming tasks for introductory programming called CASCO has been designed although it is not clear if this has ever been implemented (van Merrienboer, Krammer & Maaswinkel, 1994). The generated tasks were to be in the form of completion assignments comprising an incomplete program; instructions to extend or change the program; explanations of new features that are illustrated by parts of the incomplete program; and questions on the working and structure of the program. The planning and construction of the completion assignments, as proposed in the introduction, could be based on a model in terms of programming plans, student profile, and problem database and could use a design that might be said to be in the "intelligent" tutoring domain.

2.4.3 Experiential and Situated Approaches to the Teaching and Learning of Programming

A distinction has been made between cognitive (meaningless) and experiential (significant) learning (Rogers & Freiberg, 1994). The former corresponds to academic knowledge such as learning vocabulary or multiplication tables and the latter refers to applied knowledge such as learning about engines in order to repair a car. The key to the distinction is that experiential learning addresses the needs and wants of the learner. Rogers lists these qualities of experiential learning: personal involvement, self-initiated, evaluated by learner, and pervasive effects on learner (Rogers, 2004).

Such an experiential model was employed in the design of a beginning programming class (Athey & Quick, 1997), and it required focus on a topic, action by the student to explore and learn the topic, support by the teacher, feedback from the teacher and other students, and a debriefing about what the student learned. This method appears to have had a mixed reaction from students, some suggesting that they preferred more structure in their classes and that they did not like the "trial and error" approach to learning new concepts. However students that had programmed before preferred the less structured, more self-paced approach.

Another approach takes the view that learning, as it normally occurs, is "situated" and is a function of the activity, context and culture in which it occurs (Lave & Wenger, 1990). It has two principles (Lave, 2004):

- Knowledge needs to be presented in an authentic context, i.e., settings and applications that would normally involve that knowledge; and

- Learning requires social interaction and collaboration.

This idea of situated learning has been further developed to emphasise the idea of cognitive apprenticeship which the focus is on authentic learning environments where the cognitive demands in the learning are qualitatively the same as the cognitive demands of the environment for which the instruction was preparatory (Duffy & Cunningham, 1996). Such an apprenticeship approach to the teaching and learning of programming is mentioned by Harvey (1992) who suggests that it is suitable for students with a high aptitude for programming and who enjoy the subject, and that they should be involved in solving serious problems in the same way that other students might be involved in the publishing of student newspapers. There is little in the literature to suggest however that this approach might be useful for low-ability students with little motivation for the subject.

There has been some research into using a virtual apprenticeship model with students learning programming (Chalk, 2002). A small set of on-line tools were used in a set of pilot studies by students who were learning programming. Results from the studies provided limited support for certain aspects of the apprenticeship model such as the use of shared tools and the usefulness of group work to help develop a shared identity.

2.4.4 Programming Plans

Expert programmers have the necessary schemata to easily perform familiar programming tasks and also to interpret unfamiliar situations in terms of their generalised knowledge (van Merrienboer & Paas, 1990). In the domain of programming these specific schemata are known as programming plans and they are learned programming language templates, or stereotyped sequences of computer instructions, that form a hierarchy of generalised knowledge. It should not be expected, for example, that students who are only exposed to tasks oriented around coding specific functions should gain an understanding of overall programming structure (Bruce et al, 2004). Research has taken place to identify various plans (e.g., Soloway, 1985; 1986) within programming languages and an example was shown earlier in Figure 2.1.

In the figure, three plans have been identified, these being: a running total loop plan; a counter variable plan; and a skip guard plan. Such plans are second nature to experienced programmers and can be extracted and applied to other problems almost automatically. Such plans have been categorised to be high-level, medium-level and low-level, examples being respectively: a general input - process - output plan; a running total loop plan as in the figure; and a statement to print the value of a variable. It is suggested that, within the programming domain, programming plans provide a hierarchy of increasingly context dependent strategies that may guide a process of "templating" in the creation of solutions to posed problems (van Merrienboer & Paas, 1990).

With respect to such plans, it has been suggested that the "disappointing reality" is that a "self-discovery" approach to learning programming does not work, students not being able to discover such plans themselves (Mayer, 1988). Mayer goes on to say that approaches that include direct instruction are required and this was taken up by Tsai who conducted research that included direct instruction of programming plans to students (Tsai, 1992). He found that learning improved for what he termed "low mindfulness students" as they were forced, through specific and continuous guidance, to induce effort expenditure in the mindful abstraction of such plans. However "high mindfulness students" were not as comfortable with this teaching and learning method as they indicated that they lost opportunities to invest mental effort by themselves.

Plans become more difficult to identify in long programs as they may be delocalised and spread throughout the programming code (Soloway et al, 1988). However, in the main, novices tend to deal with short programs and so the learning of such plans is most probably appropriate under such circumstances.

Research work has also been carried out with software design patterns (Clancy & Linn, 1999) and they have similarities to plans, templates and programming schemata. A design pattern has the following components: the pattern's name; its intent and applicability; its structure, components and collaborations; the results and trade-offs of applying it; sample code; examples of the patterns' use; and related patterns. A similar comment to Mayer's is made that novices do not infer patterns naturally.

The main implication that can be drawn from this research is that patterns or plans exist within programs and that these need to be learned by students who are learning to program in order to develop appropriate programming schemata. Self-discovery, by attempting to solve problems, does not necessarily work and any successful teaching and learning method would appear to need to promote the learning of plans.

2.4.5 The Use of Part-Complete Solutions in the Teaching and Learning of Programming

A lot of the work in the area of incomplete programming examples has been carried out by van Merrienboer and his colleagues (e.g., van Merrienboer, 1990a; van Merrienboer, 1990b; van Merrienboer & Paas, 1990; van Merrienboer & De Croock, 1992; van Merrienboer, Krammer & Maaswinkel, 1994). They argue that the traditional approach to the teaching and learning of programming is ineffective and that the "Reading" approach is a better one to follow. However, they also suggest that presenting worked examples to students is not sufficient as the students may not "abstract" the programming plans from them. "Mindful" abstraction of plans is required by the voluntary investment of effort and the question then arises as to how students can be motivated to study the worked examples properly. In practice, students tend to rush through the examples, even if they have been asked to trace them in a debugger, as they often believe that they are only making progress in their learning when they are attempting to solve problems.

One suggestion that has been put forward is that students should annotate worked examples with information about what they do or what they illustrate (Lieberman, 1986). Another suggestion is to use incomplete, well-structured and understandable program examples that require students to generate the missing code or "complete" the examples. This latter approach forces students to study the incomplete examples as it would not be possible for their completion without a thorough understanding of the examples' workings. An important aspect is that the incomplete examples are carefully designed as they have to contain enough "clues" in the code to guide the students in their completion. It is suggested that this method facilitates both automation, students having blueprints available for mapping to new problem situations, and schemata acquisition as they are forced to mindfully abstract these from the incomplete programs (van Merrienboer & Paas, 1990).

In one study, two groups of 28 and 29 high-school students from grades 10 to 12 participated in a ten lesson programming course using a subset of COMAL-80 (van Merrienboer, 1990b). One group, the "generation" group, followed a conventional approach to the learning of programming that emphasised the design and coding of new programs. The other group, the "completion" group, followed an approach that emphasised the modification and extension of existing programs. It was found that the completion group was better than the generation group in constructing new programs. It was found that the percentage of correctly coded lines was greater and that looping structures were more often combined with correct variable initialisation before a loop together with the correct use of counters and accumulators within the loop. It would appear that the completion strategy had indeed resulted in superior schemata formation for those students within that group. In addition, the completion group used superior comments in connection with the scope and goals of the programs, indicating that they had developed better high-level templates or schemata. It was noted in the study however that both groups were equal in their ability to interpret programs and that this might indicate that students in the completion group do not understand their acquired templates. It is then suggested that future completion strategies should include the annotation of the examples by students with details of what they are supposed to do and details of the templates (plans) that are being used.

A side effect of the research was also noted. The drop-out rate from the completion group was found to be lower than for the generation group, particularly for female students with low prior knowledge. This is important as other studies have concluded that females are more anxious and less confident than males with respect to computer skills (e.g., Staehr, Martin & Byrne, 2001; Werner, Hanks & McDowell, 2004). van Merrienboer (1990b) suggested that the generation of complete programs is perceived as a difficult and menacing task and that the use of the completion strategy may help reduce the anxiety for some of the less confident students.

Another study was undertaken in which 40 undergraduates, undertaking a short course in turtle graphics programming, were divided into completion and generation groups (van Merrienboer & De Croock, 1992), both learning activities and learning outcomes being investigated. The course was divided into four parts, each part having three modules. Each of the three modules was presented as an incomplete solution to the completion group and the group had to complete the solutions. The first two modules were presented as completed solutions to the generation group and the third module required the group to construct a solution from scratch.

In the area of learning activities, it was found that the generation group often had difficulties in finding or coding a solution to their programming problems as they had to undertake frequent searches for useful information or examples. It was also found that the completion group took far fewer notes about the programming commands and their syntax than the generation group. It was hypothesised that the reason was the incomplete programs provided to the completion group contained a lot of this information.

With regard to learning outcomes, it was found that students in the completion group had acquired better low and high-level programming templates and that the semantic correctness of their constructed programs was superior to the generation group. As with the previous study, there was no difference between the groups in their ability to comprehend programs, however both groups' levels of comprehension was found to be high.

The "degree" of completion of the solutions is an important aspect within the completion strategy and in some later work (van Merrienboer, Krammer & Maaswinkel, 1994) examples are given of completion assignments that might be used early and later in a programming course. In an early part of a course, an example may indeed be complete and include explanations and a question on its inner workings. In the latter part of a course, an example may be largely incomplete and include a question on its workings and an instructional task. Between these two extremes, examples will have varying degree of completeness and in all cases, the incomplete examples are acting as scaffolds for the students. A similar strategy was used in a study that investigated the effectiveness of fading within problem solving examples (Renkl et al, 2002). Problem solving and example study were combined as follows:

- A complete example was presented to students;

- An example was given to students such that one solution step was omitted; and

- More steps were omitted until just the problem to be solved was left, i.e. independent problem solving.

It was found that this method produced reliable results with students on near-transfer items, i.e. for similar problem types, but not on far-transfer items.

In summary, the research into the use of part-complete solutions and problem solving strongly suggests that this method of teaching and learning has great merit. In the learning of programming, the evidence suggests that the completion strategy is superior to the conventional generation strategy. By using the completion strategy:

- Students are better able to construct programs and abstract appropriate programming plans or schemata;

- There is a lower drop-out rate as students are not immediately faced with the daunting task of having to construct programs; and

- It results in a reduced cognitive load for students.

2.4.6 Cloze Procedure and Program Comprehension

The "cloze" procedure is associated with the use of part-complete solutions. The term is derived from "closure", a Gestalt psychology term referring to the human tendency to complete a familiar but not quite finished pattern (Cook, Bregar & Foote, 1984). The cloze procedure was first used to measure comprehension in English readability (Klare, 1974) and is still commonly used for this purpose (Instructional Strategies Online, 2001). However it has also been used in the teaching and learning of programming as a way of measuring student understanding of programs (e.g., Hall & Zweben, 1986; Thomas & Zweben, 1986; Kaijiri, 1998). Such program comprehension tests are constructed by replacing some of the "words" or tokens by blanks and requiring students to fill in the blanks during a test. The use of the cloze procedure in testing was found to correlate well with conventional comprehension, question - answer, type quizzes. It was also found to be much easier to create and administer (Cook, Bregar & Foote, 1984).

A number of researchers have experimented with the testing of program comprehension by omitting complete lines of code from programs and requiring students to fill in those lines (e.g., Norcio, 1980a; Norcio, 1980b; Norcio, 1981; Norcio, 1982; Ehrlich & Soloway, 1984). Norcio found that students were more likely to supply correct statements if they had been omitted within a logic segment rather than from the beginning of a segment. This is consistent with the chunking hypothesis (Miller, 1956) that specifies that the first element of a chunk provides the key to the contents of the entire unit. Ehrlich & Soloway (1984) looked at the differences between experts and novices in filling in missing lines of programming code within various programming plans and, as expected, found that the experts filled in the lines correctly taking into account the surrounding plan whereas novices had more difficulty.

In the various experiments in program comprehension using the cloze procedure, students had to fill in the lines of code without being given a selection of lines to choose from. In some work done in an area unrelated to programming, students were expected to create an essay using a file of statements, only some of which were relevant to the topic (Edward, 1997). The students were expected to copy and paste only the statements which they believed to be relevant and then to link them with their own text. It was suggested that learners would consolidate their understanding of the topics by having to actively evaluate all possible statements. The file of statements was acting as a scaffold to student learning.

Although previous research shows that the cloze procedure has mainly been used in measuring program comprehension, it appears that it could prove useful as a way of scaffolding student learning of programming when utilised with part-complete programming solutions. An incomplete solution to a programming problem could be given to a student together with a choice of statements that might be used in the solution. The student would then have to study the incomplete solution and the choice of statements and decide which statements to use and where to put them. If a software tool were to be used then the mechanism for placing the statements into the incomplete solution could be made to be very straightforward for the student and eliminate typing errors and therefore also syntax errors. Such a process could provide strong support for independent learning and encourage practice and rehearsal.

2.4.7 Conclusions: Approaches Experimented with in the Teaching and Learning of Programming

Of the variety of methods into the teaching and learning of programming that researchers have experimented with, three in particular appeared to be useful in helping inform the approach being considered for use.

Firstly the results of the work undertaken with programming plans suggested that students are not able to discover plans on their own and that some form of direct instruction is required. It is also suggested that such instruction should encourage effort expenditure by students.

Secondly the research into the use of part-complete solutions with novices supports a view that this approach could encourage such effort expenditure, encourage the abstraction of programming plans, and reduce the cognitive load on students.

Thirdly the research into the cloze procedure suggests that the use of part-complete solutions to problems could be scaffolded by the provision of sets of missing statements that had been removed from the solutions. Students could then be required to complete a solution to a problem by choosing lines of code from the corresponding set of removed statements and inserting them into the appropriate positions within the part-complete solution.

These three methods appeared to offer a way to provide support for an approach to be taken that would utilise a part-complete solution method (PCSM) in the teaching and learning of programming.

2.5   Tools Used in the Teaching and Learning of Programming

Having explored teaching strategies that might inform the PCSM, there are many possible ways to implement them. There is a need to examine tools to determine if any might be of use in informing the design of a tool for the PCSM. There have been many tools developed over the years that have been aimed at improving the teaching and learning of programming and two types that were of particular interest for this study were program visualisation tools and algorithm design tools.

2.5.1 Program Visualisation Tools

Several tools have been built to help students visualise program execution and in the main they are specific to particular programming languages. Program visualisations can be static or dynamic. A static visualisation shows the structure of a program as a static image whereas a dynamic visualisation allows a user to trace the flow of a program as it runs (Milne & Rowe, 2004). The dynamic visualisations are of interest to this study as they promote low-level models of programming and reinforce a model of program execution by explicitly showing how the execution of a statement affects the program state and environment in which the following statement is executed (Smith & Webb, 1998). Such visualisations can be of benefit to novice programmers as they help them develop understanding and mental models of how programs execute.

Various dynamic visualisation tools have been built, the most sophisticated, such as the Jinsight tool (De Pauw & Sevitsky, 1999), being aimed at experienced software developers rather than novice programmers. Such tools have also been developed for novice programmers. These are less sophisticated reflecting the difficulty of producing them and their non-commercial nature.

The BRADMAN visualisation tool (Smith & Webb, 1998, 1999, 2000) is a glass-box interpreter that helps students in their learning of the "C" programming language. In addition to the features of "standard" debuggers, it also contains a variables display; a verbal explanation of each statement as it is executed; and more visible input / output facilities. In an evaluation, it was found that a student group that had used BRADMAN performed significantly better than a control group at the manual interpretation of programs. Comments elicited from students were mainly positive, an example being: "It helped me understand programs that I could not normally understand" (Smith & Webb, 2000, p.29). Such a comment supports the view that visualisation aids the creation of appropriate mental models.

VINCE (Rowe & Thorburn, 1999, 2000) is also a tool to help in the teaching and learning of "C" programming. It has been written entirely in Java and is therefore accessible as an applet on a Web page. It appears to possess similar features to BRADMAN including a memory map so that variable contents can easily be inspected. In its evaluation, the use of VINCE did not change the students' perceptions of their programming ability relative to those in a control group, however their performance on a series of programming questions was better.

Jeliot 2000 is a program animation system intended for teaching Java to introductory computer science students at high school. Its goal is to help novices understand basic concepts of algorithms and programming like assignment, input / output and control flow, whose dynamic aspects are not easily grasped, just by looking at the static representation of an algorithm in a programming language (Levy, Ben-Ari & Uronen, 2003). An experiment with Jeliot showed that animation provides a vocabulary and a concrete model that can improve the learning of students who would otherwise have difficulty with abstract computer science concepts (Levy, Ben-Ari & Uronen, 2000).

The DISCOVER visualisation system differs from BRADMAN, VINCE and Jeliot as it animates a specific pseudo code language rather than a common commercial programming language. It supports a dynamic, graphical and concrete environment that allows users to relate program understanding and debugging to the dynamic behaviour of both language and machine (Ramadhan, 2000). In an experiment, results indicated that students who used the system had better conceptual programming knowledge and a better mental model of program execution than a control group.

Another tool that includes program animation is DIVITIC, a Dynamic Interactive Visualisation Tool in Teaching "C" (Chansilp & Oliver, 2002, 2004). This tool has a variety of characteristics including: syllabus/lecture notes; computer structure; animated examples; "C" compiler; "C" web-board; self-evaluation; FAQ pool; and "C" references & links. In an experiment, it was found that the element used most frequently by students was the animation tool and that less able students were assisted the most.

The visualisation tools that have been described support traditional procedural programming. The understanding of memory management in object oriented programming is particularly difficult for students (Milne & Rowe, 2002) and a three dimensional program visualisation tool for novice "C++" programmers, OGRE (Object-oriented Graphical Environment), has been built (Milne & Rowe, 2004). Formal and informal evaluations of OGRE indicated that it provided strong for students by helping them build appropriate conceptual models. Students commented that concepts became "more obvious" after an OGRE visualisation, or that they felt they could understand topics "more quickly".

The research that has been reported with respect to program visualisation tools has all demonstrated that low level animations of programming code can help students build their mental models of program execution. This facility appeared to be a useful element to consider in the design of a new system.

2.5.2 Algorithm Design Tools

Tools have been developed for novices that allow students to concentrate on the problem solving aspects and design of algorithms and some of these tools are able to generate the corresponding programming code (King, Feltham & Nucifora, 1994). Examples of such tools include DELTA (Kennedy, 1996) and Breeze (Webb, 1997). Such programs allow students to use a top-down design methodology to produce graphical representations of algorithms without having to be concerned about the syntax of a language. Processes can be described with natural language and this allows students to provide a much freer and yet complete description of a problem.

More recently, a flowchart interpreter system, FLINT, has been built that allows students to design algorithms by using flowcharts (Crews & Ziegler, 1998; Crews, Butterfield & Blankenship, 2000a; Crews, Butterfield & Blankenship, 2000b; Crews, Butterfield & Blankenship, 2002). The algorithms can then be animated revealing the logic flow and the content of memory variables. FLINT is not a program visualisation tool, as that category of tool animates programming code, but it is an algorithmic visualisation tool (Brusilovsky & Spring, 2004). FLINT's name has now been changed to "Visual" and is utilised in a popular mainstream introductory programming textbook (Crews & Murphy, 2004). Results of experiments revealed that beginning students made significantly fewer errors, had significantly more confidence in their answers, and spent significantly less time determining answers (Crews & Ziegler, 1998; Crews, Butterfield & Blankenship, 2000b).

Such algorithm design tools are generally used prior to the introduction of a programming language to students. This is done in the Crews & Murphy textbook, the first few chapters being dedicated to the "Visual" tool before Visual BASIC .NET is introduced. This can be problematic for some students as Kennedy (Kennedy, 1996) points out that there are trade-offs to be considered between the benefits gained by using such a tool against the time required to learn to use that tool. Students can become very frustrated if a tool that is being used to help them in their learning has a steep learning curve. This is especially true if they are then expected to stop using that tool in the latter part of a course and then learn to use the development environment of a particular programming language.

2.5.3 Conclusions: Tools Used in the Teaching and Learning of Programming

The work done with the visualisation tools that has been discussed demonstrated that animation and visualisation could help students construct appropriate schemata concerning program solutions. Although it was not planned that any tool to be built in this study should directly support such visualisation, the design of an overall system that would incorporate the PCSM was influenced by the visualisation research. This was because it was believed that it was important for students to be able to trace and animate their solutions in the integrated development environment of the programming language that would be used in the study.

Also, the findings by Kennedy (1996) indicated that tools to support the learning of programming can often have steep learning curves and are therefore unacceptable to many students. This suggested that the design of a tool to support the PCSM should be such that the tool would be very simple to use and therefore impose a minimal addition to the cognitive load that students in the study would experience in their learning of programming.

2.6 Programming Language

The actual programming language and the development environment that are used in the teaching of learning of programming can have a significant impact on the ease with which a novice can learn programming. Some of these languages are described in this section.

There has always been a school of thought that it is better to use pseudo code as a first "language" as this enables students to concentrate on solving problems without having to be concerned about syntax (e.g., Shackelford, 1998; Robertson, 2003). However, although this would appear to be pedagogically desirable, Ourusoff (2003, p.685) states that:

"... many have abandoned the goal as being impossible to achieve in practice. Relying entirely on pseudo-code, for example, has significant drawbacks: students lose interest if they don't see a program run, and unless one has a tool to translate pseudo-code into executable code, the resulting paper designs are error-prone and boring to students. Thus, most computer science programs have abandoned a language-independent approach to teaching programming."

Another approach has been to utilise mini-languages, these being small and simple languages to support novice programmers (e.g., Brusilovsky et al, 1994; Brusilovsky et al, 1997). Most of these languages control an actor, usually a turtle or robot, acting in a microworld. Such an actor can be physical, however usually a program model of a device is used. The mini-language is used to control the actor and it includes a small set of commands that the actor can perform, a basic set of control structures, a mechanism to create sub-programs, and a set of value-returning queries. Examples of such mini-languages include "Karel the Robot" (e.g., Pattis, 1995; Bergin et al, 1996; Rodger, 2002), "RoboPascal" (Carey, 1996), and LOGO (Lowenthal, 1998). It can be argued that using such languages can be very appropriate for school students as the manipulation of the actor provides a degree of motivation, however at the tertiary level students generally prefer to be using a "real" language that is used in the outside world. In a survey of languages used in introductory programming courses in Australian Universities (De Raadt, Watson & Toleman, 2002), there was no mention of such mini-languages being utilised.

Many universities and colleges use a first language that is also used in industry as it is perceived by them, and by students, as helping students gain industry specific skills. However an industry specific language is not necessarily one that is easy to learn by novices. For example, in the 1990s, many colleges replaced Pascal with "C" as a first programming language, and yet it is thought to be a more difficult language to learn (Gilbert, 1996). Johnson (1995, p.99) suggested:

> "The position of "C" as the de facto industry standard is the very reason why it should not be adopted as a student's first language. Consequently, students will be biased against all future languages as impractical and lack the motivation to come to grips with computer languages as a means for the communication of processes. One purpose of the first course in computer programming is to teach problem solving. Introducing "C" into the first course conflicts with this purpose because students end up solving the problems of "C" instead. The result is the teaching of debugging before they have anything useful to debug. Misplaced semicolons alone will, for many students, be the main experience they get. Excessive detail obscures concepts. The complexity of "C" slows the student's study of programming concepts. "C" should not be used as the first language in university study."

De Raadt, Watson & Toleman (2002) found that "C" was no longer the most popular introductory programming language used in Australia and that the top two were Java and Visual BASIC. Thirty-four percent of universities indicated that the most important reason for using a certain language in an introductory programming courses was its industrial relevance and the marketable skills that it gave students. It is interesting to note that a language's pedagogical benefits was not the most important reason for language choice.

Such commercial languages have very sophisticated integrated development environments (IDEs), such as that of Visual Studio .Net (Tsay, 2004) which supports a variety of Microsoft Languages including Visual BASIC .Net. Although such IDEs are too sophisticated for the requirements of novices, they do provide sophisticated trace and debugging facilities which allow users to step through programs line by line and to see the contents of variables and the truth values of conditions. These facilities can be used to help students gain an understanding of the notional machine thereby helping them develop their mental models. They are acting as a form of program visualisation and animation. Others (eg., Gibbs, 2002) have experimented with using simpler commercial languages such as the scripting language, JavaScript, however the disadvantage has been the absence of a good IDE with trace facilities.

In summary, introductory languages for students include pseudocode, mini languages, and commercial languages. Universities generally use commercial languages as it is believed that exposure to such languages make students more marketable in the work force. Most of these languages are large with sophisticated IDEs that impose large cognitive loads on students. However, these IDEs do have good program trace facilities that allow students to develop their mental models.

This study was concerned with the programming language to be used with novices, namely Visual BASIC. Visual BASIC has a sophisticated IDE that allows programs to be traced and the contents of variables to be visualised. Research on visualisation has shown the usefulness of such features and helped support a view that a tool to support the PCSM would benefit if it were part of an overall system that incorporated such visualisation features.

2.7 Chapter Summary

This chapter has reported a review of the literature concerning the difficulties that students face when learning to program; the various approaches to the teaching and learning of programming; some of the approaches experimented with in the teaching and learning of programming; and some of tools used and experimented with in the teaching and learning of programming.

The literature suggests that learning to program is difficult for many students and that many courses have high failure rates and dissatisfied students. Of the various methods of teaching and learning programming, strong support is provided for the "reading" approach to learning programming with its emphasis on the study and modification of worked examples.

The research has suggested that the various plans or schemata for programs have to somehow be abstracted from the various examples used with students. One way of helping students carry out mindful abstraction is to provide them with only incomplete solutions to programs. In such cases students' tasks are then to complete and / or modify those solutions. Such completion exercises are related to the use of the cloze procedure with the difference being that the cloze procedure has been used in the past to measure computer program comprehension whereas completion exercises are used in the learning of programming.

In regard to tools, research reveals that there have been many attempts to create tools to help in the learning of programming including program visualisation tools and algorithm design tools. The programming language used in the learning process also appears to affect the student learning experience as does the development environment of the language. Such environments are now much more sophisticated and helpful to students and, in many cases, can be used to step through solutions thereby illustrating the program flow and allowing the easy inspection of the contents of a program's variables. This helps develop a student's understanding of the notional or conceptual machine that is necessary to develop a student's mental model.

The literature review in this chapter has provided insights into the difficulties of learning to program and into teaching and learning methods that might be of use in a framework to support the teaching and learning of programming. It has provided strong support for making use of the part-complete solution method in the learning of programming. The cloze procedure would appear to have potential and could be incorporated into a tool to support the PCSM, by providing a set of possible lines of missing code from a part-complete solution.

Solutions that students would create by completing part-complete solutions would need to be tested and the section on programming tools suggested it would be useful to have tracing and visualisation as part of any system created. The literature also indicated that the design of such a tool should ensure that it would be easy to use by students and not have a steep learning curve. If this were not the case then the cognitive load imposed on students by the tool could interfere adversely with learning.

The following chapter reviews some of the general literature in the field of learning which, together with the insights from this chapter, could be used to provide a basis for the creation of a teaching and learning framework for programming from which a tool to support programming could be designed / formulated.

Chapter 3
Student Learning and a Teaching and Learning Framework for Programming

The previous chapter explored some of the existing research into the learning of programming and provided some information to guide aspects of the work. This chapter describes an inquiry into theories of teaching and learning appropriate to computer programming which could be used to develop a framework to guide the development of a part-complete solution method that could be used by students in their learning of programming.

3.1 Introduction

In the chapter, the following areas are discussed:

- Mental representation and the development of expertise;

- What is meant by knowledge;

- Knowledge organisation;

- Mental models and schema theory;

- Cognitive load theory; and

- Scaffolding.

3.2 Mental Representation

How we store information in memory, represent it in our "mind's eye", or manipulate it through the processes of reasoning have always seemed relevant to researchers in educational technology (Winn & Snyder, 1996). An understanding of how novices and experts represent knowledge is useful to inform the kinds of teaching and learning processes that might help students build their knowledge of programming.

The concept of "chunking" was introduced to describe how items that were to be remembered would be collapsed into single chunks, the suggestion being that the limits of short-term memory is around seven items (Miller, 1956). When more than seven items need to be learnt, they are learnt in groups (chunks) to keep to the short-term memory limit, before each group is stored in long-term memory. For example, the three letters "cow" would be considered three discrete elements by a young child learning to read, whereas they would be considered one chunk by a fluent reader.

The concept of storing knowledge within schemata is very similar to the use of chunks and the term was used as far back as 1932 (Bartlett, 1932). He dealt with the reconstruction of knowledge noting that learners recall the gist of information rather than verbatim information.

There are many descriptions of what a schema comprises. According to Paas & van Merrienboer (1994, p.123): "Cognitive schemata can be conceptualised as cognitive structures that enable problem solvers to recognise problems as belonging to particular categories requiring particular operations to reach a solution".

In other words, schemata can provide analogies to help people when they encounter new problem-solving situations. Within schema theory, declarative knowledge is encoded as an organised structure that is referred to as a schema and learning is based on one's existing schemata (Shih & Alessi, 1994) with new schemata being created or existing schemata being modified and refined. The schemata can be thought of as nodes within a semantic network, the nodes being linked together with varying degrees of strength.

Although there are many descriptions of what schemata are, most descriptions concur that a schema has the following characteristics (Winn & Snyder, 1996):

1. It is an organised structure that exists in memory and, together with all other schemata, contains the sum of a person's knowledge of the world (Paivio, 1974).

2. It exists at a higher level of abstraction than our immediate experience of the world.

3. It consists of concepts that are linked together by propositions.

4. It is dynamic and can change by general experience or through instruction.

5. It provides a context for interpreting new knowledge as well as a structure to hold it.

The memory representational ideas embodied in schemata have also been referred to as frames (Minsky, 1975) and as scripts (Schank & Abelson, 1977), however they all appear to encompass similar ideas.

Although schemata can be considered as a set of nodes linked together in a vast network, others consider that their organisation is more complex with various levels of schemata being organised hierarchically (e.g., van Merrienboer & Dijkstra, 1997; Sweller, van Merrienboer & Paas, 1997). For example, young children construct schemata for letters so that they can then classify the infinite number of shapes that can appear in handwriting. Higher order schemata can then include those low level schemata when children learn words and then phrases etc. Phrases can then be combined further, and an example of a very high level schema might be the representation of a passage from a Shakespearian Play. Many readers would be able to finish the sentence beginning with "To be or not to be" and the reason for that is the storage of that schema in their long-term memory.

In learning programming, the schemata that novices need build are sets of stereotypical programming plans such as those shown in Figure 2.1 of Chapter 2.

Another important area with respect to the mental representation of knowledge is that of mental models, the literature dating back to Craik (1943). This construct emerged from research in the field of human computer interaction and, like schemata, a mental model contains a person's knowledge of the world. Some researchers believe that mental models and schemata are synonymous, however, there are different conceptualisations of mental models. One suggestion is that mental models consist of propositions, images, rules of procedures and statements as to when and how they are used (Redish, 1994). Wilson and Rutherford (1989) conclude that knowledge structures such as schemata are hypothesised to represent background knowledge and that mental models would be the instantiation of such structures when they are used to plan actions, explain and predict external events.

The term envisionment is often applied to the representation of both the objects and causal relations in a mental model (Winn & Snyder, 1996). This is because visual metaphors are often used in any discussion of mental models as, when a mental model is used, a representation of it is seen in our "mind's eye". For example, envisioning an electrical circuit that contains an electric bell helps someone understand it (De Kleer & Brown, 1981). A mental model can be "run" like a film and watched in a person's "mind's eye", an example being that of a skier waiting at the start of a downhill "run". Such a skier can often be seen with their eyes closed moving their body as they "run through" the course in their "mind's eye", in effect running through their mental model.

Mental models are important in the domain of programming as it is important that learners develop good models of the way in which a computer executes programs. A lot of research has been done in the area of conceptual models of computers that can help induce good mental models within students (e.g., Mayer, 1975; Mayer, 1981; du Boulay, 1986; Milne & Rowe, 2004). Program and algorithm visualisations, such as those described in Chapter 2, help students in their development of such models. It was perceived as important that the planned design of the system to support the PCSM should include facilities to provide such help.

3.3 Mental Representation and the Development of Expertise

The knowledge that people have represented within schemata or mental models will change over time. When a student is studying a particular domain of knowledge it is important that the teaching and learning process is designed to help develop the schemata so that students move towards becoming experts in that domain. It is of course unrealistic to expect that students will have become experts after a particular course of work, however it would be expected that they have moved from being a novice in that given domain to being somewhere between novice and expert (Dreyfus & Dreyfus, 1986).

In order to help students "move along" the road to becoming a domain expert, it is necessary that we, as teachers, understand the nature of expertise. It is suggested that there are five stages that a person goes through in becoming an expert (Dreyfus & Dreyfus, 1986). These are: novice; advanced beginner; competent; proficient; and expert. When designing learning opportunities for students it is therefore important to know in which of the stages students are currently situated. The majority of students undertaking introductory programming courses are firmly in the novice stage, however they of course come to such courses with different levels of existing knowledge which means that they learn at different rates. Winn & Snyder (1996, p.125) suggest: "If we try to teach the skills of the expert directly to novices, we shall surely fail". It has to be recognised that the process of knowledge compilation and translation is a slow process (Anderson, 1983). Research on expertise suggests that people construct increasingly more accurate schemata as they gain more experience in a domain, experts being more likely to sort problems on the basis of structural features rather than surface features (Quilici & Mayer, 1996).

As the schemata are improved within a domain, so too do they become internalised requiring less conscious processing to activate them. In effect, the knowledge has become automatised such that relevant schemata can be activated automatically. Research into chess playing (Chase & Simon, 1973) showed that expert players recognise patterns of pieces on a board and therefore require less in-depth analyses of situations than less expert players. Such chess experts have a vast network of relevant schemata that they can activate automatically within a game. The importance of automaticity is that it frees up cognitive resources that can then be used within other parts of a problem. For example, in the domain of physics, a student who is tackling a motion problem may be able to automatically retrieve a schemata for an equation of motion such as "$s=ut + \frac{1}{2}at^2$" thereby freeing up their cognitive resources for the problem in question.

Looking at what is meant by expertise in programming is important as it has relevance to the discussion on the teaching and learning approaches that might be used to encourage the development of expertise. Expertise in programming has some extra dimensions to the five dimensions of novice through to expert (Tolhurst, 1993) and the characteristics are:

- They categorise problems according to deep structures;

- They think of problems in terms of the programming constructs required to reach a solution;

- They possess a large knowledge base in their domain; and

- They remember groups of instructions that represent structural components in programming.

In addition it has been found that (Chi, Glaser & Rees, 1982):

- Information remembered in a schema can activate higher level schemata;

- Experts' schemata contain additional procedural information;

- Experts' schemata contain much more explicit conditions of applicability to particular principles underlying a problem; and

- For an expert, solving a problem becomes a case of categorising a problem into one or more problem types and applying existing routines.

In contrast to experts, novices have the following characteristics (Tolhurst, 1993):

- They categorise programming problems according to surface structures;

- They tend to think of a solution to a problem in terms of the syntax of the language; and

- They recall single lines of code rather than groups or "chunks".

The above suggests that the pedagogy used in the teaching and learning of programming should attempt to enable novices to acquire some of the characteristics of expert programmers although it has to be recognised that it is a long process. Probably the best that can be hoped for is, that after a semester's course in introductory programming, students will have moved from novice to advanced beginner in the stages of expertise of Dreyfus & Dreyfus (1986). The "chain of cognitive accomplishments" (Linn & Dalbey, 1985) offers a description of the changing cognitive demands placed on students learning to program and comprises the following three links:

- The acquisition of syntactic and semantic primitives;

- The design skills used to combine language features to solve programming problems; and

- The development of capabilities to autonomously generalise the problem solving skills learned from one programming situation to another.

It would be hoped that an advanced beginner would have completed part of the second link and gained the necessary knowledge to be able to solve certain programming problems. However the types of problems that advanced beginners can solve are usually relatively straight forward and similar to others that they might have studied as worked examples. Linn and Dalbey (1985) suggest that the development of skills associated with the second link represents a major motivational and conceptual turning point in the acquisition of programming knowledge. Students have to incorporate "templates" of programming knowledge into their thinking and that repeated and unresolved failures impede progress and may also reduce the motivation to continue with programming.

Teachers need to use pedagogical methods that encourage the development of expertise in programming so that students can move through the stages as quickly as possible, whilst remaining motivated, within the time constraints of a course.

The literature has suggested that in order to develop expertise in programming, students need to build mental representations of programming plans or templates. It was believed that the planned PCSM system for this study could provide such support in an efficient manner because: students would not need to generate programs from scratch; and students would have fewer concerns about syntax because of the inclusion of sets of possible missing statements for each part-complete solution.

3.4 Mental Processes

The mental representations that we have stored as schemata are operated on by our mental processes. Mental representation and processing are of course intertwined as seen earlier in the discussion of the way in which mental models can be "run". However, for the purpose of this discussion, the two have been separated. Three kinds of mental processes can be categorised as information processing; symbol manipulation; and knowledge construction.

3.4.1 Information Processing

Information processing models of cognition describe the stages that information moves through in a person's cognitive system and the processes that operate on that information at each step. The description is in computer like terms and assumes that a system processes information sequentially from the time of input to the time of storage in secondary or long-term memory (Di Vesta, 1987). The mechanism consists of the sensory registers, the short-term or working memory and the long-term memory. This model can be traced back to Atkinson and Shiffrin (1968) who suggested that information is registered by the senses and placed into a short-term buffer. The information then needs to be "rehearsed" with so that it is related to existing knowledge and then has a chance of being moved to long-term storage. Rehearsal can be thought of as practice and is something that is usually needed within learning.

The main problem with this model was the recognition that working memory capacity was limited to around seven pieces of information and the model was modified to take into account the work on chunks (Miller, 1956), described earlier, and instructional design that attempts to induce such "chunking" is now commonplace. Another modification to the model that took place was to include the concept of schemata. It was recognised that the information passed from short-term to long-term memory was not a direct copy but a more abstract representation of its meaning. This modification stemmed from the work of Bransford and Franks (1971).

Originally information processing theory was considered to be data driven or bottom-up as information is firstly input to the sensory buffers. It has now matured to take into account that the way in which information is processed depends to a large part on what a person already knows, i.e. has stored already in long-term memory, and so information is processed in part in a top-down manner.

Many researchers distinguish between short-term and working memory as the latter is perceived as retaining information for longer periods than the former. It is suggested that a model is required that allows information to be held and manipulated while it is being processed, and the functions of working memory have been described as (Bower, 1975):

1. Providing the context for perception;

2. Serving a holding function for later retrieval;

3. Keeping a running account of immediately prior events that provide a reasonable context for occurring events;

4. Observing deviations in naturally occurring events, or in games such as chess, so that necessary adjustments can be made in the knowledge of procedural systems; and

5. Initiating and implementing plans for a given task within a given context.

3.4.2 Cognition as Symbol Manipulation

Many cognitive scientists believe that information is processed as symbols (e.g., Larkin & Simon, 1987). The idea is that humans mentally manipulate different types of symbols that are representations of objects in the real world. In the area of problem solving, it is thought that human reasoning takes place by applying rules to information that is encoded as a "production system" (Larkin & Simon, 1987). Such systems are sets of "If..Then" rules and they operate by testing the conditions of the rules and then taking specific actions when conditions are true. An example (Winn & Snyder, 1996, p117) is:

"If the sum of an addition of a column of digits is greater than 10 then

Write down the right-hand digit

Carry the digits to the left of the right-hand digit to the next column"

In this case, the symbols being manipulated are textual, however diagrams are often superior to text for solving certain problems. For example it is much easier to find answers such as "Is Raymond, Lisa's second cousin?" by using a family tree diagram rather than a large set of production rules. Production systems have been used in intelligent tutoring systems such as Anderson's ACT* that helps to teach LISP programming (Anderson, Farrell & Sauers, 1984).

3.4.3 Cognition as Knowledge Construction

During mental processing, people input information, process it by the mental manipulation of symbols and then possibly store the knowledge in long-term memory within schemata or modify existing schemata. The way in which the information is manipulated or processed depends upon our existing schemata, in other words on what we already know. We are therefore constructing knowledge and the newly constructed knowledge may well be different for different people as they all have different sets of existing schemata. This has led to constructivist learning theory which has now gained the attention and respect that was previously reserved for instructivist theories (e.g., Jonassen, 1991; Jonassen, 1994; Jonassen, 1995; Jonassen & Reeves, 1996; Ring & McMahon, 1997; Anderson, Simon & Rede, 2000).

"Constructivism is concerned with the process of how we construct meaning and knowledge in the world as well as with the results of the constructive process. How we construct knowledge depends on what we already know, our previous experiences, how we have organised those experiences into knowledge structures such as schemata and mental models, and the beliefs that we use to interpret the objects and events we encounter in the world" (Jonassen & Reeves, 1996, p.695).

The concept of constructivism is not new. For example the "perceptual cycle" suggests that what we know directs how we seek information; how we seek information determines what information we get; and how the information we receive affects what we know (Neisser, 1976). This also relates to the ideas of top-down and bottom-up processing of information described earlier. The constructivist learning theory places the learner at the centre of the knowledge acquisition process, not the environment. An example of how this revolution has impinged on higher education is the fact that educators now talk about "teaching and learning" rather than just "teaching" as they did in the past.

Some researchers have reacted against constructivism and suggest that some knowledge and skills have to be acquired and expressed in a uniform manner (e.g., Merrill, 1992; Ben-Ari, 2001). Merrill talks of idiosyncratic knowledge that is constructed by people that often defies expression to someone else, and he gives an example that idiosyncratic knowledge of how to fly a plane could lead to disaster! However, it can probably be concluded that a middle ground is necessary in many situations with environments provided to help students construct their own knowledge but with guidance provided where necessary, for example in the form of scaffolding. There are several stages that a person goes through in becoming an expert in any field, these being novice; advanced beginner; competent; proficient; and expert (Dreyfus & Dreyfus, 1986). The stage that a student is in can affect how well they are able to construct knowledge for themselves and it is claimed that learning by allowing students to construct knowledge only works for "advanced knowledge" that assumes that the basics have been mastered (Spiro, Jacobson & Coulson, 1992).

Learning programming in a constructivist environment can potentially be very effective as students can attempt programming problems thereby building and reconstructing their relevant schemata. However, care has to be taken with the instructional design. In a typical constructivist learning environment, students are active learners participating and interacting with the surrounding environment to create their own interpretations of reality. Without good guidance, student misconceptions of how programs are executed can cause problems later on in programming courses. For example, research on novice programmers has indicated that students can develop serious misconceptions of the underlying erasable nature of memory locations, where input data comes from, the differences in the way string and numeric data is stored etc (e.g., Bayman & Mayer, 1988; Pea, 1986). A lot of programming research that has looked at the use of conceptual models / notional machines in the teaching of programming

---

(e.g., du Boulay, 1986; Shih & Alessi, 1994) shows that in programming, especially with novices, there is a need for an agreed model of how computers execute programs for progress to be made in the learning of programming. Those students who have constructed a different model for themselves tend to have problems until that model has been rectified. It has been suggested that the model of a computer must be explicitly taught to programming novices and not left to haphazard construction and not glossed over with "facile analogies" (Ben-Ari, 2001).

3.4.4 Conclusions: Mental Processes
The mental processing that takes place during learning can become problematic for students when the domain of knowledge is particularly difficult and the instructional design is weak. This is generally true for the teaching and learning of programming as it is accepted that programming is a difficult subject and that often the instructional design has shortcomings. For the proposed design of the PCSM system, it was recognised that the embedded instructional design should impose a relatively low cognitive load on students. Cognitive load theory could therefore provide more direction on how this could be achieved.

3.5   Cognitive Load Theory
Cognitive load theory (e.g., Sweller, van Merrienboer & Paas, 1998; Sweller, 1999; Soloman, 2004) builds on the information processing model of mental processes described earlier and is very relevant to the research in this thesis. Its emphasis is on the size of working memory with its limitation of around seven chunks of material (Miller, 1956) and the idea that people can only deal with around two or three elements simultaneously. The degree of interactivity between the elements also affects the capacity of working memory.

Working memory is now thought to have part-independent processors (Baddeley, 1992) including a "visual / spatial scratchpad" for dealing with visual materials and a "phonological loop" for dealing with audio material. A central executive controls the above and working memory can be increased by the use of both processors.

In the earlier discussion on information processing, research into chess playing (Chase & Simon, 1973) showed that the main difference between novices and experts was the fact that the latter had thousands of board configurations, as many as 100000 (Simon & Gilmartin, 1973), stored in long-term memory within schemata. The consequence is that, unlike less-skilled players, experts do not have to spend as much time searching for good chess moves using their limited working memory. Similarly, research into problem solving (Carroll, 1994) confirmed that, compared to novices, experts have knowledge of an enormous number of problem states and their associated moves. Such states are within long-term memory and such research indicates that human problem solving comes from stored knowledge and not from complex reasoning within working memory. It is suggested that humans are poor at complex reasoning unless most of the necessary elements are already in long-term memory, working memory being incapable of highly complex interactions using novel elements (Sweller, van Merrienboer & Paas, 1998; Sweller, 1999). In the domain of programming, studies have shown that experts remember algorithms or plans whereas novices remember lines of code. This means that novices who are attempting a problem must engage in complex chains of reasoning using their working memory. During this process it is likely that working memory will be overburdened, the cognitive load being too great.

Ways in which cognitive load can be reduced for novice problem solvers are therefore very important. In the schema theory of model representation, a schema can be anything that can be treated as a single entity or element such as a mathematical formula or a particular programming algorithm. Schemata have the function of storing knowledge and reducing the burden on working memory.

Experts in a domain of knowledge can process information relevant to their domain automatically, novices however having to process information consciously (Schneider & Shiffrin, 1997; Tindall-Ford, Chandler & Sweller, 1997). An example of such automatic processing is that of the expert driver who can drive their car without apparently thinking, whereas a learner driver has to consciously think of several things at the same time such as depressing the clutch and shifting to a new gear, observing the road ahead, moving the steering wheel etc. Any instructional design for a domain has to therefore not only encourage the construction of sophisticated schemata but also encourage the automatic processing of those schemata. This is important because of the limited capacity of working memory that can only deal with a few schemata at the same time. The ease with which information can be processed in working memory is the main thrust of cognitive load theory. In programming, the instructional design should encourage the construction of schemata concerning programming plans together with the ability to automatically incorporate the relevant plans in solutions to given programming problems.

Working memory may be affected by intrinsic cognitive load and extraneous cognitive load (Sweller, 1994). In recent research, a further distinction is made with the inclusion of germane cognitive load (Sweller, Van Merrienboer & Paas, 1998).

3.5.1 Intrinsic Cognitive Load

Intrinsic cognitive load is determined by the mental demands of the task (Chandler & Sweller, 1996). Some material has very low cognitive load and an example is the learning of the basic vocabulary of a foreign language. Each element or schema is independent from the others with no interactivity and subsequently the required mental processing, or intrinsic cognitive load, is low. Tasks that have low element interactivity can be learnt serially rather than simultaneously. Tasks with a high degree of element interactivity have a heavy intrinsic cognitive load and an example is the learning of the grammar of a foreign language as all the words in phrases need to be considered, that is processed, at once.

Programming is a domain with a high intrinsic cognitive load and this needs to be recognised in any instructional design. The intrinsic cognitive load cannot be reduced, however good instructional design can help reduce the extraneous cognitive load.

3.5.2 Extraneous Cognitive Load

Extraneous cognitive load is generated by the instructional format used in the teaching and learning process and poor design leads to a high extraneous cognitive load. If a high extraneous cognitive load is combined with a high intrinsic cognitive load then this can lead to working memory overload. This is often what happens with novice programmers when the instructional design is poor. For example, new programming topics such as loops might be introduced too early in a course at a time when students had not grasped some of the basic concepts such as variables, assignment statements, data types etc. Students might be expected to generate solutions to difficult programming problems with little guidance from their tutor.

The important point is that when the intrinsic cognitive load of the material is high, then it is incumbent on the instructional designer to think very carefully and ensure that the extraneous cognitive load is as low as possible. A lot of research has been done in looking at ways of reducing extraneous cognitive load (e.g., Chandler & Sweller, 1991; Sweller, 1994; Marcus, Cooper & Sweller, 1996; Tindall-Ford, Chandler & Sweller, 1997; Kalyuga, Chandler & Sweller, 1998). These include: integrating diagrams and text so as to reduce the "split-attention" effect; goal-free problem solving; and the use of worked examples in problem solving.

3.5.3 Germane Cognitive Load

More recently, the concept of germane cognitive load has been introduced into cognitive load theory (Sweller, Van Merrienboer & Paas, 1998). It is thought that if the instructional design is such that the extraneous cognitive load is kept to a minimum, then there may be some unused working memory available. This could then be used by learners, with appropriate instructional design, to engage in conscious processing that helps in the construction of schemata in the particular domain of interest (Gerjets, Scheiter & Catrambone, 2004). This conscious processing is the germane cognitive load. An example is the use of part-complete solutions in the learning of problem solving (e.g., van Merrienboer, 1990b; van Merrienboer & De Croock, 1992; Paas, 1992; Atkinson, Renkl & Merrill, 2003).

3.5.4 Conclusions: Cognitive Load Theory

The studying of complete worked examples in programming by students can be seen as one way of reducing the extraneous cognitive load. When students have to complete a part-complete worked example then they have to attempt to "mindfully abstract" the relevant schemata from the example in order to understand it. That is, they have to consciously process it and this increases the germane cognitive load. Cognitive Load Theory provided support for the use of the PCSM in this study and Figure 3.1 shows the relationship between the various cognitive loads in the domain of programming.

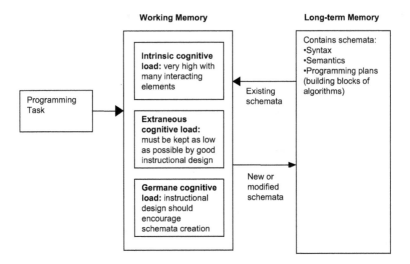

Working Memory

Long-term Memory

Programming Task

Intrinsic cognitive load: very high with many interacting elements

Extraneous cognitive load: must be kept as low as possible by good instructional design

Germane cognitive load: instructional design should encourage schemata creation

Existing schemata

New or modified schemata

Contains schemata:
•Syntax
•Semantics
•Programming plans (building blocks of algorithms)

Figure 3.1: Cognitive Architecture for the Domain of Programming

3.6 Problem Solving

Cognitive load theory indicates to us that it is important to reduce extraneous cognitive load and this can be done by improving instructional design. To understand how this should be done in the specific domain of programming, it is useful to review some of the research that has taken place in problem-solving methods in other domains.

Polya, a famous mathematics educator, suggests four problem-solving steps (Polya, 1957): understanding the problem; devising a plan; carrying out the plan; and looking back. It is suggested that devising a plan is a difficult step for learners as they lack any experience in solving problems. Polya also suggests that analogy pervades all our thinking and that the key to problem solving techniques is to try and make use of a related problem that you already know about. A similar strategy states that if learners cannot solve a given problem then they should try to solve an easier, related problem (Schoenfeld, 1985). That is, learners should look for known solutions to related problems.

However, when students do not know a similar problem to the one that they are attempting then they usually attempt to solve a problem by a "weak" method such as means-ends analysis (e.g., Sweller & Cooper, 1985; Sweller, 1988; Ward & Sweller, 1990; Sweller, 1994). A student using such a strategy attempts to reduce differences between each problem state encountered and the goal state by using the problem solving operators of the domain which, in the case of mathematics and science are the rules of those two domains. Experts however can usually solve problems using their existing schemata and automated rules. It is suggested that although means-ends analysis is an efficient strategy for achieving a problem goal, it actually interferes with learning as schemata acquisition is hindered due to the heavy cognitive load being placed on working memory. That is, the extraneous cognitive load is high with many interacting elements having to be processed in working memory simultaneously including considering and making decisions about the current problem state, the goal state, differences between states, and problem solving operators that can be used to reduce such differences. It has been proposed that alternatives to conventional problem solving can be more effective, these focussing attention on problem states and their appropriate moves (Ward & Sweller, 1990). One such method is to use worked examples with students. Ward and Sweller suggest that such a method facilitates learning and subsequent problem solving to a greater extent than actually engaging oneself in the solution process.

3.6.1 Use of Worked Examples in Problem Solving

Several researchers have experimented with the use of worked examples in place of conventional instruction and found strong advantages. In the domain of algebra, it was proposed that students would learn better by studying worked examples until they had "mastered" them rather than attempting to solve problems as soon as they had been presented with, or familiarised themselves with, new material (Sweller & Cooper, 1985). In a research project (Sweller & Cooper, 1985), students studied worked examples and teachers answered any questions that the students had. Students then had to explain the goal of each problem together with the steps involved in the solution and then complete similar problems until they could be solved without errors. It was found that this method was less time-consuming than the conventional practice-based model and that students made fewer errors in solving similar problems than students who were exposed to the conventional practice-based model of instruction. There was no significant difference between the "worked example" group and the "conventional" problem solving group when they attempted to solve novel problems and it was therefore concluded that learning was more efficient and yet no less effective when this worked example method was used.

Research by Anderson, Fincham & Douglass (1997) also indicates that exposure to worked-out examples is critical when learners are in the initial stages of learning a new cognitive skill in well structured domains such as computer programming.

Other researchers had similar findings. Zhu and Simon (1987) found that a three year mathematics course could be completed in two years by emphasising worked examples. Ward and Sweller (1990) found that under conventional classroom conditions, a heavy use of appropriately structured worked examples facilitated subsequent problem solving in a variety of areas in physics. They also found however that worked examples had to be carefully constructed to avoid splitting student attention between diagrammatic and text materials. Similar findings were made in the domain of geometry (Paas & Van Merrienboer, 1994) where it was found that students learnt better if they studied worked examples rather than attempting problems themselves and then looking at the problem solutions. The suggestion was made that if students try and solve problems before studying the solutions, i.e. the worked examples, then they may perform less well because they have included their failed solutions in their schemata.

The evidence from the literature provides support for the extensive use of worked examples in the learning of problem solving and their use is an example of "scaffolding" learners in their endeavours to become competent problem solvers.

3.6.2 Scaffolding and Problem Solving

A scaffold is a temporary support for student learning that is available until the student can perform independently of that support. The support can fade away as the internal capacity of a student develops (Atkinson, Renkl & Merrill, 2003). Scaffolding is described as: "... controlling those elements of the task that are initially beyond the learner's capability thus permitting them to concentrate upon and complete only those elements that are within their range of competence" (Wood, Bruner & Ross, 1976, p.9). As students gradually gain control of the task, they take over more of the responsibility and the scaffolding is gradually removed.

Scaffolding is connected with the theories developed by Vygotsky who stated that problem solving tasks and other skills could be placed into three categories: those performed independently by the student; those that cannot be performed even with help; and those that fall in between, the tasks only being able to be performed with the help of others (Vygotsky,

1978). This last type of task falls into what is known as the zone of proximal development (ZPD) and is the area in which an individual's optimum learning can occur. Scaffolding can be provided in the ZPD for students.

Good teachers have always provided scaffolding for students, however technology now provides instructors with new opportunities to provide scaffolding and this is especially important within flexible learning. For example, hypermedia can support the acquisition of new vocabulary when words on a page are linked to separate pages with definitions and examples. Another example of scaffolding is provided by Linn (1992, p.125) who describes a method of programming instruction that involves scaffolds comprising of templates. Templates are reusable abstractions of programming knowledge that students can use and study to help them construct appropriate schemata. Each template describes the programming knowledge associated with an action such as "do something a certain number of times", or "select from alternatives". Linn's templates have different representations of an action including programming code, pseudocode, verbal descriptions, diagrams, and possibly dynamic illustrations. Many such templates were created in her study to help scaffold student learning in the domains of both pascal and LISP programming and they were linked together using hypermedia.

3.6.3 Conclusions: Problem Solving

When the research describing learning supports is taken in its entirety, it supports the notion that a technology supported PCSM could support problem solving by the provision of appropriate scaffolds. The worked examples would in effect be the part-complete solutions provided for students. Scaffolding would be provided by the set of possible lines of code from which appropriate lines could be selected for insertion into part-complete solutions. Levels of scaffolding could be adjusted by:

- Reducing or increasing the number of lines of code removed from a solution;

- Including extra "distracter" lines of code, that are incorrect but similar to the correct lines, in the set of lines of code that a student might choose from to complete a solution;

- Requiring students to key-in certain lines of code from scratch; and

- Informing students of the positions in a solution from which lines of code were removed.

3.7 Higher Order Thinking

The solving of problems requires the application of higher order thinking with students utilising their cognitive skills to plan and structure a solution to a given problem and then to reflect on that solution. Hopefully, any learning environment that students experience when learning to solve problems in a given domain of knowledge would encourage higher order thinking.

Higher-order thinking essentially means thinking that takes place in the higher-levels of the hierarchy of cognitive processing and Bloom's Taxonomy is the most widely accepted arrangement of this sort in education (Bloom, 1956). The taxonomy can be viewed as a continuum of thinking skills starting with knowledge-level thinking and moving through to evaluation-level of thinking. Bloom's taxonomy comprises: knowledge, comprehension, application, analysis, synthesis, and evaluation. Thinking strategies may be conceived of as problem solving approaches, decision making skills, conceptualising, classifying and interrelating categories (Glaser, 1984).

Learning environments designed to foster problem solving are based on a view that learners need mastery of various categories of skills (McLoughlin, 1997), such as

- Flexible acquisition of a domain specific knowledge base;

- Heuristic methods (i.e., techniques for problem identification and analysis); and

- Metacognitive skills (i.e., knowledge of ones own cognitive strategies, self-monitoring and regulation).

There has been a debate as to whether it is possible to teach general thinking skills as a set of generic skills or whether thinking is more often context free (Nickerson, Perkins & Smith, 1985). Nickerson et al suggest that the evidence points to thinking being more often context bound rather than context free and that "packaged" thinking skills programs are not the best way to foster higher order thinking. This is also supported by McLoughlin (1997) who believes that higher order thinking necessarily involves procedural knowledge (knowing how) and declarative knowledge (knowing that). She suggests that declarative knowledge must be available for consideration and that procedural knowledge are the cognitive strategies applied to planning, performing and evaluating the task in question. Also, metacognitive processes enable students to control and monitor their own performance. Her model is shown in Figure 3.2.

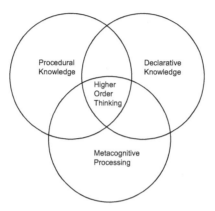

Figure 3.2: Elements of Higher Order Thinking (McLoughlin, 1997, p.34)

In the context of solving programming type problems, the declarative knowledge is the syntax and semantics of the language and the procedural knowledge is the knowledge of how to solve a given problem. The metacognitive processing is then the reflection by a student on the solution that they have created. However, thinking is hard work (French & Rhoder, 1992) and strategies to encourage higher order thinking should focus attention, minimise anxiety, and maintain motivation (Jones et al, 1987). The proposed system to support the PCSM would appear to encourage higher order thinking by:

- Its use of the part-complete solution method which both reduces cognitive load, thereby minimising anxiety, and focuses attention on solutions; and

- Its maintenance of student motivation as solutions are created more quickly with a consequential reduction in times that feedback is received on the correctness of solutions.

3.8 Summary and Conclusions

The review of the literature has revealed a number of important elements germane to this study. It has been revealed that in learning it is necessary for learners to develop their cognitive schemata and mental models and that experienced problem solvers have numerous patterns stored which they can then use to apply to new problems and situations (Chase & Simon, 1973).

Also, in order to help build their cognitive schemata, it has been seen that learners have to mentally process their mental representations or cognitive schemata. This can be done using a model such as "information processing" (Di Vesta, 1987) which describes the stages that information goes through in a person's cognitive system. Constructivism suggests that the construction of knowledge by learners is dependent upon their existing schemata or what they already know. For example in the domain of programming some learners may already have well developed schemata in mathematical problem solving that will help them in their construction of programming knowledge. This indicates that learning should be student centred with students being able to progress at their own pace (Jonassen, 1995).

Cognitive load theory (e.g., Soloman, 2004) suggests that in problem solving domains, it is necessary to keep the extraneous cognitive load to a minimum as the domain itself has a very high intrinsic cognitive load. It has been shown that it is possible to have some germane cognitive load imposed on learners thereby ensuring that they have to actively engage with the material that they are studying. One method of doing this is to utilise learning materials that require learners to have to complete solutions to part-complete solutions that they have been given. Such part-complete solutions can vary in their degree of completeness and such materials act as scaffolds to support student centred learning so that learners are then within Vygotsky's zone of proximal development (Vygotsky, 1978).

The acquisition of problem solving skills was also seen to be an example of higher order thinking (Bloom, 1956) and there is evidence to support the notion that such thinking is context bound involving both declarative and procedural knowledge with learners applying metacognitive processes to control and monitor their own performance (Nickerson, Perkins & Smith, 1985). In the context of solving programming type problems, the declarative knowledge is the syntax and semantics of the language and the procedural knowledge is the knowledge of how to solve a given problem. The metacognitive processing is then the reflection by a student on the solution that they have created.

Specifically with respect to programming, it has been shown that there are various teaching and learning methods in existence including expert, spiral, reading (van Merrienboer & Krammer, 1987); syntactic and developmental (Marchionini, 1985); and schema based

(Tolhurst, 1993). Of these, the method that appeared to match best with cognitive load theory is the reading method utilising part-complete solutions to programming problems.

There was also support in the literature for developing the mental models of learners with respect to the notional or virtual machine (Shih & Alessi, 1994). Some of that research showed that novices who made use of a notional machine learned to program more effectively than those who did not (Mayer, 1981). Conclusions reached showed that the use of an animated model aids students in their learning of programming. Such a model provides help in the students' construction of appropriate schemata and / or mental models thereby overcoming inappropriate mental models that they may possess.

3.9   A Proposed Learning Framework

From the literature review, it was possible to propose a framework of learning attributes that could provide support for learning in problem solving domains of knowledge such as programming. The set of attributes and their rationale are shown in Table 3.1.

Table 3.1:   Proposed Learning Framework for Encouraging the Development of Appropriate Schemata in Problem Solving Domains

Learning Attribute	Rationale for Attribute
1. Support for student centred learning.	Different learners gain expertise in problem solving at different rates and it is therefore important that the learning environment supports independence (e.g., Vygotsky, 1978; Jonassen, 1995; Jonassen, 1996).
2. Support for the creation of appropriate schemata and mental models.	The learning environment should support the creation and amendment of appropriate schemata that pertain to problem solving and also support the mental processing that needs to take place during this process (e.g., Paas & Van Merrienboer, 1994; Winn & Snyder, 1996).
3. Support for the reduction of extraneous cognitive load.	The learning environment would need to reduce the extraneous cognitive load as problem solving domains tend to have high intrinsic cognitive loads (e.g., Kalyuga, Chandler & Sweller, 1998; Tindall-Ford, Chandler & Sweller, 1997).
4. Support for the increase of germane cognitive load.	To promote problem solving skills, cognitive load theory suggests that a learning environment should encourage learners to mindfully abstract appropriate problem solving patterns (e.g., Paas, 1992; Sweller, Van Merrienboer & Paas, 1998).
5. Support for the promotion of reflection and higher order thinking.	The development of problem solving skills in a specific domain of knowledge requires support for higher order thinking with learners being encouraged to reflect on their solutions to given problems (e.g., Glaser, 1984; McLoughlin, 1997).

The literature had suggested that a technology supported part-complete solution method (TSPCSM) would be appropriate in the development of a learning environment for the domain of programming as it would be able to support most of the learning attributes of the learning framework. Table 3.2 shows how environmental elements needed for learning computer programming might be incorporated into a form of TSPCSM.

Table 3.2: Elements of a TSPCSM Environment to Support the Learning of Programming

Environmental Element	Support from the TSPCSM
1. Support for student centred learning.	The completion method supports active learning with students having to engage with learning materials.
2. Encouragement of the development of appropriate schemata and mental models.	Provision of appropriate programming schemata in the form of stereotypical programming plans.
3. Reduction of extraneous cognitive load.	Visually simple interface. Provision of appropriate examples and exercises.
4. Manipulation of germane cognitive load.	Removal of lines of code from complete programs varies the germane cognitive load on learners.
5. Promotion of reflection and higher order thinking.	Reduction of the amount of lower order thinking that is required and encouragement of more higher order thinking as students reflect on their solutions.

At this stage of the study a teaching and learning framework for programming that included these environmental elements was developed and is described in the next section.

3.10 A Teaching and Learning Framework for Programming

The design of the proposed teaching and learning framework was influenced by an instructional design framework put forward by Oliver (1999). Oliver's framework is heavily influenced by his belief that constructivism best describes how learning takes place and the framework permits the critical constituent elements of technology based learning to be described. It comprises three critical elements: course or unit content; learning activities; and learner supports as shown in Figure 3.3.

The teaching and learning framework for programming was to be supported by technology and include sets of learner activities and supports. For these reasons Oliver's instructional design framework appeared appropriate to use.

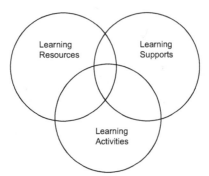

Figure 3.3: Instructional Design Framework (Oliver, 1999, p242)

The overall design of the teaching and learning framework for programming is described in the following sections with reference to this instructional design framework's three elements: learning activities, learning supports, and learning resources.

3.10.1 Learning Activities

Learning activities play a fundamental role in determining learning outcomes (Wild & Quinn, 1997). The activities determine how learners will engage with the various materials and need to provide meaningful contexts for learning.

The main form of activities that were selected comprise a set of programming problems and their part-complete solutions that need to be completed by a learner. It was proposed that for each activity, students would be provided with a programming problem and a part-complete solution. The completion of a part-complete solution by students would involve:

- Selecting appropriate lines of code from a set of possible lines and placing them in the "correct" locations within the corresponding part-complete solution;

and / or

- Keying-in appropriate lines of code.

After "completing" a program, that program would be tested in the programming environment of the particular language being used which, in the case of this research, would be Visual BASIC (VB). Feedback to students would be provided by the VB environment. The program may work as expected or the VB debug tools might have to be used so that students could try and determine the causes of any errors. Such errors would be corrected by amending the solution and this would be done by: replacing some of the lines of code that had been used to complete the program with different lines of code; and / or moving lines of code within the program; and / or amending lines of code that had been keyed in.

3.10.2 Learning Supports

Learning supports describe the guides and feedback provided to learners that are responsive and sensitive to learner individual needs (McLoughlin & Oliver, 1998). In "traditional" settings supports have often been provided by actively involved teachers (Laurillard, 1993) whereas in technology based learning environments, supports are often technology based "scaffolds" to help learners during their knowledge construction process (Roehler & Cantlon, 1996). In programming, an example of such a support is the facility that some programming editors have to help complete lines of programming code for the user as they are keyed-in. The best forms of supports are scaffolds that provide help at the point of need but which fade as the learner progresses.

In the proposed teaching and learning framework, some learning activities act as learning supports and so the boundary between activities and supports is somewhat blurred. Several learning supports were proposed, some of which were designed to be directly supported by the TSPCSM.

The first support would be provided by the set of possible lines of code that is given to a learner to be used in the completion of a part-complete program. It was recognised that the level of this support could be varied by providing one of the following methods:

Method 1. All of the lines of code that are missing from the program are provided as options.

Method 2. All of the lines of code that are missing from the program, together with some extra lines of code that are not needed to complete the program, are provided. These extra lines act as "distracters".

Method 3. Some of the lines of code that are missing from the program might be provided, however some other missing lines must be keyed-in by the learner.

The important variable that affects which of the above methods might be used for a given problem would be the degree of difficulty of that problem. For example, if a problem was relatively simple then method 2 might be used, whereas method 1 might be used with a more difficult problem. Fading would not be straight forward as the programming problems in the latter part of a programming course are usually more difficult than earlier ones and it might therefore still be necessary to use method 1 supports for some of the problems. It was proposed that a mechanism would be provided to allow the easy manipulation of the missing lines of code from a part-complete solution.

The second support would be a facility to easily move missing lines of code into a part-complete solution and then to manipulate lines within that solution. Such a support has not been available in previous work with respect to the completion method and yet this is seen as important in helping reduce extraneous cognitive load.

The third support would be the provision, for each programming problem, of a screen image of the problem interface. The interface would be the output "form" or window that is displayed to a user of a program when it is executed and includes the various objects such as buttons and text boxes. The screen image would also be annotated with the internal names of the objects (i.e. the object names that are used within the programming code) thereby reducing the split-attention effect (e.g., Chandler & Sweller, 1991). This particular support might also be considered a learning resource, the boundary between supports and resources being blurred for some entities.

The fourth support would be the environment of the programming language itself. Many such modern programming environments, or integrated development environments, provide sophisticated facilities to help programmers debug their programs. These include the tracing, or step by step execution, of code and the ability to display the contents of variables. The language that would be used in this research was Microsoft's Visual BASIC which has excellent debugging facilities that can be used by novices in their learning of programming.

Other supports that would be provided include the "conventional" ones such as the provision of a tutor, other students, and a textbook. When campus based students require help in solving a programming problem, they might directly seek such help from their tutor or fellow students. With a flexible, technology based course that support would most likely be provided by email. Learners also look to their conventional textbook which, in addition to providing content, can also be considered to provide support.

3.10.3 Learning Resources
Learning Resources can be thought of as the materials which are provided to help students construct their knowledge and meaning with respect to a domain of knowledge. Traditionally these resources have been available in the form of books and lecture notes and the move to flexible technology based systems has led to a lot of content being made available electronically. It has been estimated that many such systems are too content-oriented with 90% of planning and development being in content creation (Dehoney & Reeves, 1999).

The emphasis of this current research was the exploration of the completion method of programming and it was decided that the content would be provided by the existing programming textbook (Schneider, 2000) and the lecture notes of the lecturer. It was recognised that on-line content and resources would be very useful to learners and was something that might be explored in the future. Typical content for programming courses includes descriptions of language syntax; data and control structures; descriptions of algorithms; descriptions of how to solve certain categories of problem; and example programs.

3.10.4 Summary of the Teaching and Learning Framework for Programming
The various components of the proposed framework were developed from the elements identified for a TSPCSM environment shown in Table 3.2 and from the instructional design framework proposed by Oliver (1999). Figure 3.4 summarises the structure of the proposed framework and also those features that would be supported by a technological tool. In the proposed framework, some of the elements overlap so that, for example, some resources might be considered supports.

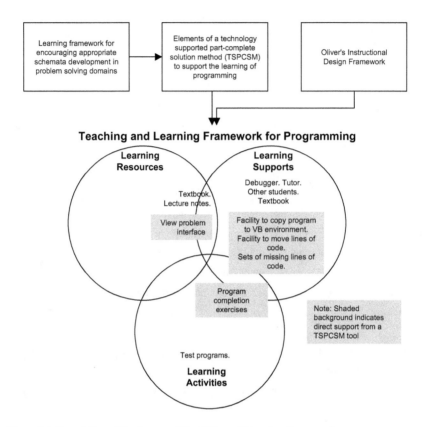

Figure 3.4: Description of the Proposed Teaching and Learning Framework

With these design principles in mind the next phases of the study were planned and these included strategies to:

- Design and develop a learning system that would implement the framework, a key component being a technology supported tool to support the PCSM;

- Test the usability of the system with students; and

- Empirically test the system with students to determine its support for learning and its effect on learning outcomes.

Chapter 4 describes the design and development of the technology supported tool to support the PCSM.

Chapter 4
Development of a Tool to Support the PCSM

The previous chapter proposed a teaching and learning framework for programming together with high level design specifications for a tool to support novices using the part-complete solution method to learn programming. This chapter describes: the development of a prototype of the tool; the trials of the prototype that took place with students; and the amendments that were made to the prototype in response to student feedback.

4.1   Initial Design of the Tool to Support the PCSM

The support tool for novice programmers that was to be designed was given the name CORT, this being an acronym taken from **CO**de **R**estructuring **T**ool. CORT was designed to provide learning activities to students in the form of part-complete programming problems and a number of learning supports to help scaffold their learning.

4.1.1 Functional Requirements of CORT

The learning supports and activities to be provided by CORT are shown in Figure 3.4 of Chapter 3 and the specific functional requirements that were planned for CORT, together with their rationale, are listed in Table 4.1.

Table 4.1: Functional Requirements of CORT

Requirement	Rationale for Requirement
1. A mechanism for learners to view and print out a programming problem statement.	Problem statements need to be presented to students and a Print facility will enable them to work away from the computer.
2. A mechanism for learners to view and print out a part-complete solution to a problem together with a set of possible lines of code that might be used to complete that program.	This requirement is fundamental to the PCSM that CORT supports. Providing a facility to print the lines of code will permit students to work away from the computer.
3. A mechanism for learners to view an image of the Visual BASIC (VB) form that is to be used in the solution to a problem. This image should have the various objects such as buttons, textboxes and picture boxes annotated with their internal names that are used within the program.	This learning resource was identified in the teaching and learning framework of Figure 3.4.
4. A mechanism for learners to be able to easily move a line of code from the set of possible lines into any position within the part-complete solution.	This requirement is fundamental to the PCSM that CORT supports.
5. A mechanism for learners to be able to easily move complete lines of code up and down within the part-complete solution.	This requirement will permit students to move lines of code into different positions within a part-complete solution should they determine that certain lines have been positioned incorrectly.
6. A mechanism for learners to be able to easily	Indentation and alignment of lines of code within

Requirement	Rationale for Requirement
indent and outdent lines of code within a part-complete solution.	control structures are important in computer programs (e.g., Baecker, DiGiano & Marcus, 1997; Miara et al, 1983) as an aid to program comprehensibility.
7. A mechanism for learners to be able to insert blank lines before or after existing lines of code in a part-complete solution.	"White space" is often used in computer programs to aid readability and a mechanism is needed to insert blank lines.
8. A mechanism for learners to be able to remove blank lines of code from a part-complete solution.	A mechanism is needed to remove blank lines should they have been inserted incorrectly.
9. A mechanism for learners to be able to remove a line of code from a part-complete solution.	This requirement is fundamental to the PCSM. If a distracter line of code is incorrectly inserted into a part-complete solution then a facility is needed to remove it. Such distracter lines are needed for the Method 2 learning support of the Teaching and Learning framework that was described in Chapter 3.
10. A mechanism for learners to be able to invoke a text editor so that a part-complete solution can be edited thereby allowing lines of code to be keyed-in.	The Method 3 learning support requires students to add their own lines of code to a part-complete solution and hence a mechanism to facilitate this is needed.
11. A mechanism for learners to be able to copy a part-complete or completed solution and paste it into a programming environment such as that provided with VB.	This requirement is one of the learner supports of the Teaching and Learning framework described in Chapter 3.
12. A mechanism for learners to be able to copy the code within a programming environment and paste it back into CORT.	This requirement is needed in order that programming code can be amended within CORT after having been tested and possibly changed within the Visual BASIC development environment.

4.1.2 Design issues

The design of the user interface of CORT took into consideration three issues that are fundamental to interface design: development, usability, and acceptance (Marcus, 1992).

In the first area, development, the design and production tools that were available needed to be determined together with the support that they would give for rapid prototyping. As CORT was to have some quite complex functionality, it was decided that a programming language would be required in its development in order to build the necessary features. Prototypes were to be produced and the Visual BASIC (VB) programming language was chosen as it is one of the best available to support such prototyping. VB can only be used to produce programs for Personal Computer (PC) environments however, given that the students in the research would be learning the VB language which itself only runs on PCs, this was not seen as a constraint.

In the second area, usability, it is suggested that two important issues are legibility and the ability to convey a clear conceptual model (Marcus, 1992). The need for an interface to create a coherent mental model in the mind of the user of the functions and structure of a computer product or system are perceived as important (Ring, 1996). Ring expands on this to state that a primary goal in interface design is to create an interface that facilitates the mapping of the interface designer's model onto the user's model and that the quality of the interaction depends upon the mental model that the user has constructed of the system. To this end, a checklist was useful during the design of the CORT interface (Marcus, 1992):

- Easily grasped metaphor and idea or image that captures the essence of the system;

- Appropriate organisation of data, functions, tools, roles, and people in a task-oriented cognitive model;

- Efficient navigation schema in the cognitive model, that is, the action relationships that enable reading and writing of these data, functions, tools, roles, and people;

- Quality appearance characteristics (the size, shape, colour, orientation, location, etc.) of each visual element on the screen; and

- Effective interaction sequencing (the logical protocols for the visual elements) and their relation to hardware input/output devices.

The third design area to be considered was user acceptance. Any program or system that has been developed has to be accepted by its users. Commercial software usually goes through a set of acceptance tests (Schneiderman, 1998) such as:

- Time for users to learn specific functions;

- Speed of task performance;

- Rate of errors by users;

- User retention of commands over time; and

- Subjective user satisfaction.

An acceptance testing phase was planned that could adequately deal with all of these elements in a manner which recognised the intended use of the product.

4.1.3 Interface Design

The most important functional requirements of the set of requirements that was developed for CORT were those to support the completion method of learning to program. An interface design for CORT was inspired by the common use within certain programs of two parallel windows containing lists of items. In such programs, users can move items quickly and easily between the two windows thereby adjusting the contents of the lists. An example of such an interface taken from an email program is shown in Figure 4.1.

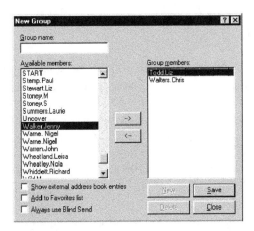

Figure 4.1: Parallel Window Interface

With reference to Figure 4.1, to move an item to the right-hand window, the item in the left-hand window is highlighted and then the button with the right-hand arrow is clicked. The item is then removed from the left-hand window and appears in the right-hand window. Items can also be moved back from the right-hand window to the left-hand window.

With this style of interface in mind, it was thought that such a mechanism could be used in the CORT interface. An initial interface design was produced such the right-hand window would contain the part-complete solution to a programming problem and the left-hand window would contain programming statements that might be used to complete the program. Programming statements could then easily be moved to and from the program in the right-hand window. It was thought that this met one of the main criteria suggested by Marcus (1992) in connection with interface design, i.e. that an easily grasped metaphor or idea should be used. Many computer users are now used to building and amending lists by utilising two parallel windows. The idea is used in several programs, in addition to the above, including the Microsoft Office suite in which toolbars can be customised using such a mechanism.

4.1.4 CORT Prototype Program

An initial prototype of the CORT program (version 1) was created to try and meet the planned functional requirements. Version 1 was built by the researcher using Microsoft Visual Basic Version 6 as this is a powerful Windows programming language that lends itself to the easy creation of Windows interfaces. It was also decided to use an evolutionary prototyping in conjunction with evolutionary design, with the prototype being used in the final system and not having to be thrown away (Hawryszkiewycz, 2001). The initial version of CORT took approximately 100 hours to build and debug and comprised over 1400 lines of code.

The descriptions below provide a discussion of the first version of CORT from the learner's viewpoint.

4.1.4.1 CORT Prototype: Learner's Standpoint

1. Starting CORT
A learner runs the CORT program and two empty parallel windows are displayed. S/he then clicks on the [] button and an open dialogue appears allowing the learner to browse and select a text file with the file extension "txt".

This file contains a part-complete solution and possible lines of code for that solution.

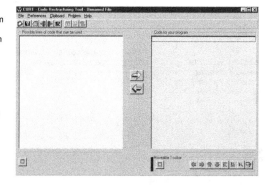

2. Loading a CORT activity

After opening the appropriate file, the right-hand window is loaded with the part-complete solution to a problem and the left-hand window with lines that can be used to complete the solution.

These windows can be expanded and contracted horizontally so as to view the complete lines by clicking the corresponding  button.

3. Viewing the problem description

A learner may have been given a hardcopy of the problem description but can also view that description by clicking the 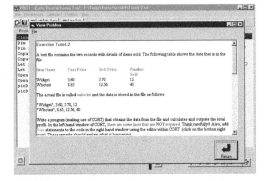 button. From here the learner can select **File > Print** to print the problem description. The window is closed by clicking the **Return** button.

4. Viewing the problem interface

A learner can click on the 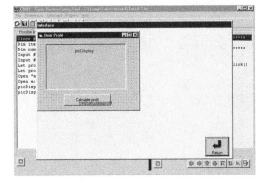 button to view the problem interface. This is a screen image showing the expected output "form" for the problem that the learner is attempting. This image is annotated with the internal VB object names.

In this example there is a picture box, **picDisplay**, and a command button, **cmdCalculateProfit**.

5. Moving code between windows

A line of code can be moved from the left to the right by: highlighting the line in the left-hand window; highlighting the line in the right-hand window after which the line from the left is to be placed; and clicking the  button.

Several lines of code can be highlighted in the left-hand window and moved in one operation. Lines can also be moved back into the left-hand window.

6. Rearranging / manipulating lines

Lines of code can be rearranged in the right-hand window by moving them up or down. Lines can also be indented or outdented.

Blank lines can be inserted before or after an existing line of code and blank lines can be deleted.

7. Adding extra lines of code

Lines of code can be keyed-in by learners using a simple text editor. This can be invoked by clicking on the button. After editing the program, the editor is closed by clicking the **Return** button and the changes are reflected in the original right-hand window.

8. Opening Visual BASIC
When a learner is ready to test their solution, they can click on the 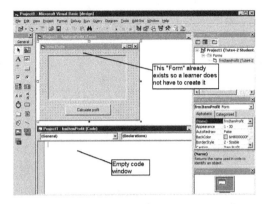 button and the code from the right-hand window is pasted into the Windows Clipboard. They then run VB and open a file that contains the VB output "form" but does not contain any code.

This figure shows an example VB "form" with an empty "code" window.

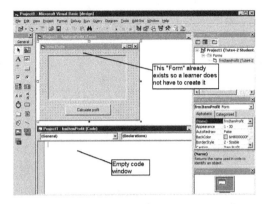

9. Pasting the code into VB
A learner now pastes the contents of the Windows Clipboard into VB's empty code window by clicking the button. The program can then be run and / or traced in VB.

After testing a program in VB, a learner can if necessary switch back to CORT and amend the solution, recopy the code and repaste it into VB. This is an iterative process that is carried out until the program works to the learner's satisfaction.

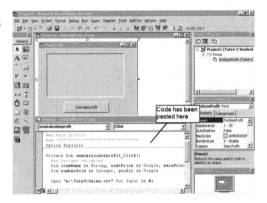

10. Copying code back into CORT
Learners may have changed code within the VB environment. The VB code can then be copied to the clipboard within VB and pasted back into CORT so that the code in the two environments is synchronised.

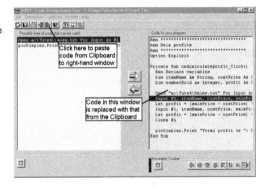

4.1.5 CORT Prototype: Testing with Students

After the development of the first version of CORT, a trial was set up with students in order to gain some initial feedback on its usability, particularly with respect to the interface, and to remove any errors that still existed within the program. The trial was undertaken by fifteen students who were studying a second year introductory programming unit using Visual BASIC within an undergraduate Information Systems course at an Australian university. The students were a mixture of Australian and International students with basic computer literacy but little or no programming experience. Each student had the use of a computer workstation within a computer laboratory and each workstation had both Visual BASIC and CORT Version 1 installed.

The trial lasted for a period of 3 hours. In the first 30 minutes, the researcher walked the students through the solving of a simple problem using CORT. During the next 2 hours and 15 minutes, the students were asked to attempt 4 CORT problems. In this period, the researcher observed all of the students for varying amounts of time and discussed a variety of issues with them that they might have been experiencing. During the last 15 minutes of the trial, an open discussion took place between the researcher and the students in order to determine any further issues that might not have emerged during the period of observation.

Data from observations and discussions were analysed and four main problems emerged with respect to CORT usage. Solutions were then identified and changes made to CORT as follows.

Problem 1
Students often did not realise that the problem descriptions could be printed out.

Solution
The facility to print out the problem descriptions was made more explicit by making the line menu description clearer.

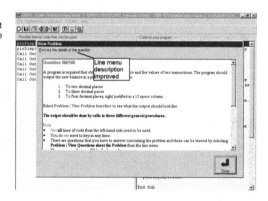

Problem 2

Some students suggested that the two parallel windows were rather narrow and that more of the lines of code could be seen without having to expand a window.

Solution

The buttons that allow students to move lines between windows were placed on the moveable toolbar, thereby increasing the width of the windows.

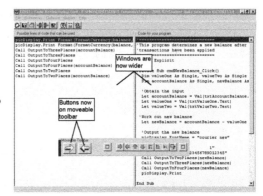

Problem 3

Some students suggested too few lines of code could be viewed in a window.

Solution

A facility to change the font type and size was included.

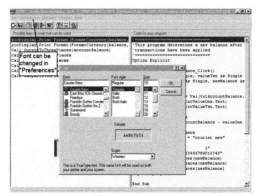

Problem 4

Some students had indicated that the facility to expand and contract a window by clicking on a button was slow and cumbersome.

Solution

The facility to expand and contract the windows was changed so that it could be invoked by double clicking within the appropriate window.

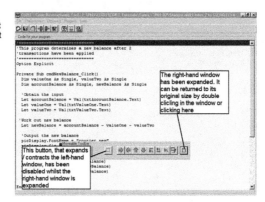

Other changes were made to the original CORT prototype to take into account a raft of other forms of student feedback:

- The problem description window was changed to display automatically after a CORT part-complete solution file is loaded. This enabled students to immediately view the problem statement without having to invoke the facility from a menu item.

- A menu item that allowed the printing out of the contents of the two windows was added to enable students to work on the initial development of a problem solution away from the computer.

- The facilities to view information about a problem were also made available within the line menu in addition to the toolbar buttons of the CORT prototype. This ensured that all of the facilities that were available from buttons were also available from the textual line menu, thereby enabling students to invoke facilities in two different ways.

- The two parallel windows were made to automatically resize when the main form is resized within Microsoft Windows. This enabled students to resize the main CORT window and still view the code in both parallel windows.

- A "Save As.." facility as well as a "Save" facility was added, thereby enabling a CORT file to be saved with a different name.

Other changes to the prototype that were made took into account some observations by the researcher:

- The file extension of the main CORT file corresponding to a CORT part-complete solution was changed to "pcs", this being an acronym for "part-complete solution". This file originally had the file extension "txt" in the prototype and this caused some confusion for students as some of the programming problems utilised text files for input and these too had file extensions of "txt".

- The automatic alphabetical sorting of the lines of code in the left-hand window was removed. Such lines of code are selected and used by students to complete a part-complete solution in the right-hand window. For some CORT problems, it was believed that it would be useful to group sets of similar lines of code together in the left-hand window, and the automatic sorting of lines had not permitted this facility. For example, a "correct" line of code to be used in a solution could be grouped with other similar, yet incorrect lines of code, thereby requiring students to study the lines and select the one they believed to be correct.

4.2 CORT Files

The changes made to the CORT prototype resulted in CORT Version 2. At the same time the files structures were finalised. Each CORT problem was built with a set of files and these are shown in Table 4.2.

Table 4.2: Required Files for Each CORT Problem

File Type	File Extension	File contents
Rich Text file	prb	Description of the problem to be solved.
Text file	pcs	The part-complete solution together with the possible missing lines
Graphical image	gif	Annotated screenshot of the VB interface for the problem solution
Text files	frm and vbp	The VB files for the problem solution without the necessary lines of code.

For example, consider a CORT problem given the number **00010**. The required files for this question are shown in Figure 4.2. The main names of each file are identical however the file extensions are different. By keeping the main filenames the same, CORT "knows" which files should be accessed after the initial part complete solution, **00010.pcs**, has been opened within CORT by a learner.

00010.frm
00010.gif
00010.pcs
00010.prb
00010.vbp

Figure 4.2: CORT Files

4.2.1 Creation of Part-Complete Solutions for CORT

CORT was intended to be utilised with students who were learning programming with Visual BASIC. This required the researcher to be able to create programming problems and part-complete solutions to those problems in Visual BASIC. The procedures for creating a CORT problem are as follows, the example being for a problem that is numbered **00110**.

1. Creation of a problem / activity

A programming problem is devised and keyed-into MS Word. This is then saved as a rich text file and given the file extension ".prb".

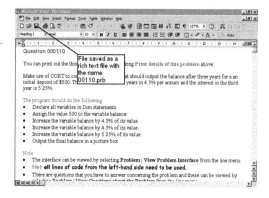

2. Solution put into CORT

The problem is solved in VB and the solution is saved with the name **00110Solution.vbp**. The code is then copied and pasted into the right-hand CORT window by clicking the button.
The VB code is then deleted from the VB program and saved as **00110.vbp**.

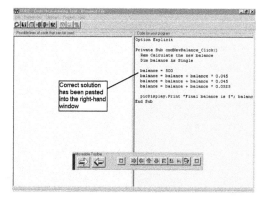

3. Adding extra lines of code

The CORT editor is now invoked and extra, incorrect lines, are added if necessary. The requirement to do this depends upon the CORT method being utilised.

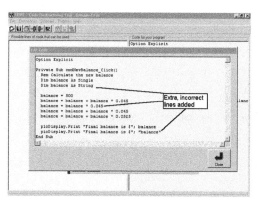

4. Removal of lines of code from the solution

Certain lines together with the incorrect lines are moved to the left-hand window by highlighting them and clicking 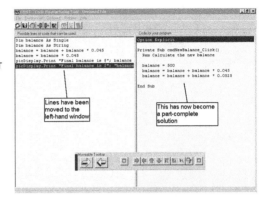. The CORT file is now saved with the name **00110.pcs**.

5. Creation of VB "Form" interface

The output "form" that is within the VB file **00110.vbp** is copied using an image copying program and pasted into a graphics editing program such as PaintShop Pro.

The VB objects are then annotated with their VB internal names. This file is saved as a "gif" file and given the name **00110.gif**.

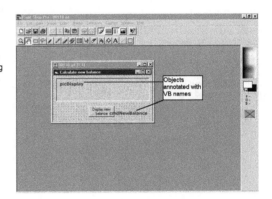

4.3 Summary

Following the development and testing of the functional requirements for CORT Version 2, the tool was utilised in a study that sought to explore:

• The use of CORT by students;

• The support for learning provided by the PCSM within CORT; and

• The impact of the PCSM within CORT on learning outcomes.

The detailed research design is described in the following chapter.

Chapter 5
Research Design

This chapter discusses the design of the research that investigated: the use of CORT by students; the ways in which a technology supported part-complete solution method supported the learning process; and the impact that CORT and part-complete solutions had on learning outcomes. It begins by discussing research methodologies in general and the process by which a particular methodology was chosen for this project. It then describes the research questions, the data collection methods that were used, and the actual data gathering that took place.

5.1   Research Methodologies

Research is a systematic investigation to find answers to a problem (Burns, 1994) and philosophers of science and methodologists have been engaged in a long-standing epistemological debate how best to conduct research (Patton, 1990). According to Patton, this debate has centred on the relative value of two fundamentally different and competing inquiry paradigms. The first paradigm is logical-positivism which uses quantitative and experimental methods to test hypothetical-deductive generalisations. The second and competing paradigm is phenomenological inquiry which uses qualitative and naturalistic approaches to inductively and holistically understand human experience in context-specific settings. Its purpose is to develop an understanding of individuals and events in their natural state, taking into account the relevant context (Borg & Gall, 1989).

In the past educational research generally followed the first paradigm above of traditional objective scientific method, however there has been a strong move towards the second paradigm of a more qualitative and subjective approach since the 1960s.

The main strengths of quantitative research methods are thought to lie in precision and control: precision through quantitative and reliable measurement; and control through the sampling and design (Burns, 1994). Also, hypotheses are tested through a deductive approach and the data collected can be subjected to statistical analysis. However, Burns also points out some of the limitations of quantitative research including: the denigration of human individuality and the ability to think; and that quantification can become an end in itself rather than a humane endeavour seeking to explore the human condition.

According to Cohen and Manion (1994) other criticisms levelled at positivist social science that uses quantitative methods include:

- It presents a misleading picture of the human being in that it is conservative and ignores important qualities;

- It fails to take account of our unique ability to interpret our experiences and represent them to ourselves; and

- Findings of positivistic social science are often said to be so banal and trivial that they are of little consequence to those for whom they are intended.

In contrast to quantitative research, qualitative research stresses the validity of multiple meaning structures and holistic analysis. It is based upon a recognition of the importance of the subjective, experiential "lifeworld" of human beings. Qualitative research can be considered particularly relevant as there can be little meaning, impact or quality in an event isolated from the context in which it is found (Eisner, 1979). One of the main advantages of this approach is that it makes possible distinctive insights into the field under investigation. However, some of the limitations of the qualitative research method pointed out by Burns (1994) include: the problem of adequate validity and reliability because of its subjective nature; and the time required for data collection, analysis and interpretation.

Bogdan and Biklen (1992) describe several characteristics of qualitative research that are particularly useful for this research study. These are that qualitative research: has the natural setting as the direct source of data and the researcher is the key instrument; is descriptive; is concerned with process rather than simply outcomes or products; tends to use inductive data analysis; and is concerned with "meaning".

Writers in the domain of qualitative research display a variety of perspectives. For example Tesch (1990) lists forty-five approaches to qualitative research and Patton (1990) suggests ten approaches. Merriam (1998) describes five types of qualitative research commonly found in education, these being the basic or qualitative study, ethnography, phenomenology, grounded theory, and case study. Merriam suggests that although these types can be distinguished from each other, they all share the essential characteristics of qualitative research:

- The goal of eliciting understanding and meaning;

- The researcher as primary instrument of data collection and analysis;

- The use of fieldwork;

- An inductive orientation to analysis; and

- Findings that are richly descriptive.

Merriam's common types of qualitative research in education are summarised in Table 5.1.

Table 5.1: Common Types of Qualitative Research in Education (Merriam, 1998, p.12)

Type	Characteristics	Example
Basic or Generic	• Includes description, interpretation, and understanding; • Identifies recurrent patterns in the form of themes or categories; • May delineate a process.	Meaning-making in transformational learning.
Ethnography	• Focuses on society and culture; • Uncovers and describes beliefs, values, and attitudes that structure behaviour of a group.	A study of twenty successful Hispanic high school students (Cordeiro and Carspecken, 1993).
Phenomenology	• Is concerned with essence or basic structure of a phenomenon; • Uses data that are the participant's and the investigator's first hand experience of the phenomenon.	The role of intuition in reflective practice (Mott, 1994). Practices inhibiting school effectiveness (Aviram, 1993).
Grounded Theory	• Is designed to inductively build a substantive theory regarding some aspect of practice; • Is "grounded" in the real world.	A framework for describing developmental change among older adults (Fisher, 1993).
Case Study	• Is intensive, holistic description and analysis of a single unit or bounded system; • Can be combined with any of the above types.	A comparative case study of power relationships in two graduate classrooms (Tisdell, 1993).

The main aims of the inquiry were to investigate:

1. The use of CORT by students.

2. The ways in which the part-complete solution method (PCSM) within the CORT system supports the learning process.

3. The impact that the PCSM within the CORT system has on learning outcomes.

From the previous discussion, it was determined that a qualitative approach would be best suited for exploring 1 and 2 above as it was unclear how CORT would be used by students and how a technology supported part-complete solution method might support learning. A quantitative approach was deemed appropriate for exploring question 3 as it was only concerned with learning outcomes. The validity and reliability of the findings in answering research questions 1 and 2 could also be supported by the collection of appropriate quantitative data. The use of complimentary quantitative and qualitative methodologies is supported by several writers (e.g., Reichardt and Cook, 1979; Mercurio, 1979; Miles and Huberman, 1994), however it should be recognised that the main research thrust of this project was to be qualitative.

5.2   Selection of a Research Methodology and Data Collection Methods

While a qualitative methodology appeared to be the best fit for the needs of this research, the term "qualitative" is very general and there are many qualitative methodologies to choose from. Crotty (1998, p.1) makes the following important observation:

> "Research students and fledgling researchers-and, yes, even more seasoned
> campaigners-often express bewilderment at the array of methodologies and
> methods laid out before their gaze. These methodologies and methods are not
> usually laid out in a highly organised fashion and may appear more as a maze
> than as pathways to orderly research. There is much talk of their philosophical
> underpinnings, but how the methodologies and methods relate to more
> theoretical elements is often left unclear."

Crotty (1998) suggests that in any research project, the methodologies and methods that will be employed need to be chosen together with the justification of that choice. This leads to four specific questions that need to be considered with respect to a research project:

- What methods should be used?

- What methodology governs the choice and use of methods?

- What theoretical perspective lies behind the methodology in question?

- What epistemology informs this theoretical perspective?

Crotty argues that these four elements are basic to any research process. Together they govern the choice of:

- *Methods*: the techniques or procedures used to gather and analyse data related to some research question or hypothesis.

- *Methodology*: the strategy, plan of action, process or design lying behind the choice and use of particular methods and linking the choice and use of methods to the desired outcomes.

- *Theoretical perspective*: the philosophical stance informing the methodology and thus providing a context for the process and grounding its logic and criteria.

- *Epistemology*: the theory of knowledge embedded in the theoretical perspective and thereby in the methodology.

These four basic elements are interlinked and inform one another as shown in Figure 5.1.

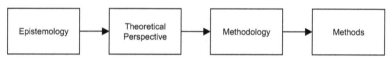

Figure 5.1: Four Basic Elements of Research (Crotty, 1998, p.4)

A representative sample of the four elements is shown in Table 5.2. Crotty further argues that the lists shown are by no means exhaustive.

Table 5.2: Basic Elements of Research (Crotty, 1998, p.5)

Epistemology	Theoretical perspective	Methodology	Data Collection Methods

• Objectivism
• Constructivism
• Subjectivism (and their variants)
	• Positivism (and post-Positivism)
	• Interpretivism
	  • Symbolic interactionism
	  • Phenomenology
	  • Hermeneutics
	• Critical inquiry
	• Feminism
	• Postmodernism
	• etc.
		• Experimental research
		• Survey research
		• Ethnography
		• Phenomenological research
		• Grounded theory
		• Heuristic inquiry
		• Action research
		• Discourse analysis
		• Feminist standpoint
			• Sampling Measurement and scaling
			• Questionnaire
			• Observation
			  • Participant
			  • Non-participant
			• Interview
			• Focus group
			• Life history
			• Narrative

		research	• Visual ethnographic methods
		• etc.	• Statistical analysis
			• Data reduction
			• Theme identification
			• Comparative analysis
			• Cognitive mapping
			• Interpretative methods
			• Document analysis
			• Content analysis
			• Conversation analysis
			• etc.

The application of these four research elements to the current study yielded the following analyses and decisions.

5.2.1 Epistemology

One particular view of cognition that emerged from the literature review was that of constructivism (e.g., Jonassen 1991, 1994, 1995; Jonassen and Reeves, 1996; Ring and McMahon, 1997). Constructivism is the theory that guided this research as newly constructed knowledge may well be different for different people as they all have different sets of existing schemata and how people construct or amend schemata is dependent upon their existing schemata and mental models. The literature suggests that a framework of learning for a complex problem solving domain, such as programming, should help students construct appropriate mental models and also encourage the building of appropriate domain schemata. Hence the epistemology chosen for this research project was that of knowledge construction.

5.2.2 Theoretical Perspective

While there are many theoretical perspectives, the appropriate perspective appeared to be interpretivism-phenomenology. In interpretivism, understanding the meaning of a process or experience constitutes the knowledge to be gained from an inductive, theory-generating mode of inquiry (Merriam, 1998). Phenomenological inquiry focuses on the question: "What is the structure and essence of experience of this phenomenon for these people?" (Patton, 1990, p.69) where the phenomenon for example might be an emotion, a job, or a program. Phenomenologists believe that it is important to know what people experience and how they experience the world. In this research project, the phenomena include students using the

CORT program itself, and students attempting different types programming completion problems.

Patton suggests that a phenomenological perspective can mean either or both of the following:

1. A focus on what people experience and how they interpret the world. This could be done by interviewing without the researcher actually experiencing the phenomenon.

2. A methodological mandate to actually experience the phenomenon being investigated. This would imply the use of participant observation.

The use of an interpretivism-phenomenology theoretical perspective appeared to provide the most appropriate lens for the planned inquiry.

5.2.3 Methodology

There are many methodologies available for an interpretivism-phenomenology theoretical perspective and several are listed in Table 5.2. The main intention of this research project was to investigate how students use CORT and part-complete solutions when learning programming. It was thought that observation and participation by the researcher had potential as a major method of collecting data and that an action research methodology might be suitable for the study.

Action research is defined by Burns (1990, p.252) to be: "The application of fact-finding to practical problem solving in a social situation with a view to improving the quality of action within it, involving the operation of researchers, practitioners and laymen."

Whyte (1989) indicates that action research explicitly and purposefully becomes part of the change process by engaging people in a program in studying their own problems in order to solve those problems. Zuber-Skerritt (1992, p.14) presents a useful working definition of action research which includes the following:

"If yours is a situation in which

- *people reflect and improve (or develop) their own work and their own situations*

- *by tightly interlinking their reflection and action*

- *and also making their experience public not only to other participants but also to other persons interested in and concerned about the work and the situation (i.e. their (public) theories and practices of the work and the situation)*

and if yours is a situation in which there is increasingly

- *participation (in problem-posing and in answering questions) in decision making*

- *learning progressively by doing and by making mistakes in a "self- reflective spiral" of planning, acting, observing, reflecting, replanning, etc.*

then yours is a situation in which action research is occurring".

The above working definition suggested that an appropriate methodology for this research project was action research, with students attempting to reflect and improve upon their knowledge of programming and also to make that knowledge public to the researcher acting as a participant-observer. The researcher was the practitioner exploring his practice of helping students learn programming.

A quasi-experimental design framework was planned for use within the action research methodology. The design was deemed to be quasi-experimental as it was not possible to achieve "randomisation" of exposures which is essential if true experimentation is to take place (Cohen and Manion, 1994). Best and Kahn (1998, p.175) state in connection with such designs, that "because random assignment to experimental and control treatments has not been applied, the equivalence of groups cannot be assured". In a quasi-experimental design, it is possible to have control over the "who and to whom of measurement" but have little control over the "when and to whom of exposure". Such a design is perceived as a compromise (Kerlinger, 1970) and this is often the situation in education as the complete random selection of subjects is often very difficult. Since equivalence among students within the groups could not be guaranteed, a quasi-experimental design appeared the best alternative.

As the research involved students, it appeared appropriate that the action research methodology should make use of several case studies. A case study is defined as an intensive, holistic description and analysis of a single entity, phenomenon, or social unit (Merriam, 1998). According to Patton (1990), a case can be a person, an event, a program, an organisation, a time period, a critical incident, or a community. In the context of the current research, the cases involved people (students) using CORT over certain time periods of time.

Since a principal aim of this study was to explore if CORT could enhance learning outcomes, a quantitative element was planned for the study. This was to enable the achievements of a control group to be tested against those of an experimental group to determine if any significant differences could be attributed to the use of CORT.

5.2.4 Data Collection Methods

Several data collection methods were considered for use within the chosen quasi-experimental action research methodology. In order to help improve internal validity, it was planned that the research study would use a variety of methods and also make use of some quantitative techniques.

The problem of internal validity concerns whether researchers actually observe or measure what they think they are observing or measuring (Burns, 1994). For example, participant observation is considered to have high internal validity as it is conducted in natural settings that reflect the reality of the life experiences of participants.

A common way to improve the internal validity of a study is triangulation. It is defined as "the use of two or more methods of data collection in the study of some aspect of human behaviour" (Cohen and Manion, 1994, p.233). Patton (1990, p.187) has a more general definition as he states that "it is a combination of methodologies that are used in the study of some phenomena or programs so as to strengthen a study design".

The following discusses the various methods that were considered for use in the study.

5.2.4.1 Observation

This is a basic ethnographic approach that involves the observation, organisation and interpretation of data. One of the advantages of this method is that it makes it possible to record behaviour as it occurs (Burns, 1994). Burns suggests that there are four possible research stances for the person who is participating in a research study: the complete participant, the participant-as-observer, the observer-as-participant, and the complete observer.

The advantages of observation include (National Science Foundation, 1993, 1997):

- They provide direct information about behaviour of individuals and groups;

- They permit a researcher to enter into and understand situation/context;

- They provide good opportunities for identifying unanticipated outcomes; and

- They exist in a natural, unstructured, and flexible setting.

However, disadvantages include (National Science Foundation, 1993, 1997):

- They are expensive and time consuming;

- Observers may need to be content experts; and

- The behaviour of participants may be affected.

The research stance of participant-as-observer appeared to have potential as a major data collection method in this study. An aim of the research was to determine CORT's usability and its support for student learning, and observation of students using CORT seemed to be an appropriate method to use. It was thought that the method might enable the researcher to understand the variety of ways different students use CORT and to probe students when certain unanticipated actions were observed.

5.2.4.2 Interviews

This method is a major tool in qualitative research (Burns, 1994) and provides a way of providing corroboration of data from alternative sources (Eisner, 1991). Accounts derived from interviews can be studied for themes and this data reported as narrative containing direct quotations (Burns, 1994). Three types of question can be asked in interviews: closed items, open-ended items, and scale items.

The advantages of interviews include (National Science Foundation, 1993, 1997):

- They usually yield rich data, details and new insights;

- They permit face-to-face contact with respondents;

- They provide an opportunity to explore topics in depth;

- They enable the interviewer to experience the affective as well as cognitive aspects of responses; and

- They allow the interviewer to explain or help clarify questions, increasing the likelihood of useful responses.

However, disadvantages include (National Science Foundation, 1993, 1997):

- They are expensive and time-consuming;

- An interviewee may distort information through recall error, selective perceptions, or a desire to please an interviewer; and

- Flexibility can result in inconsistencies across interviews.

It was thought that the use of interviews in this study could enable the clarification of certain issues that might emerge during observations of students using CORT.

5.2.4.3 Questionnaires

The simplest and cheapest method of surveying a group is to use a questionnaire. The questionnaire, like the interview, is another descriptive survey method, surveys being the most common data collection method within educational research (Burns, 1990). According to the National Science Foundation (1993), not only are questionnaires useful for obtaining information about the opinions and attitudes of participants in a study, but they are also useful for the collection of descriptive data, for example personal and background characteristics (race, gender, socio-economic status) of participants.

The advantages of questionnaires include (National Science Foundation, 1993; Burns 1990):

- They enable data to be gathered from the whole population of participants thereby helping to validate the data collected by observation and interviews;

- They are inexpensive; and

- They can be completed anonymously.

However, disadvantages include (National Science Foundation, 1993; Burns 1990):

- Unlike interviews, further probing questions cannot be asked dependent on responses given to previous questions; and

- There is no control for misunderstood questions, missing data, or untruthful responses.

In this inquiry, it was thought that questionnaires might provide a way of collecting student background data and data concerning how they utilised CORT when different problems were attempted.

5.2.4.4 Document Studies
Documents are an important source of data in many areas of investigation and include records, reports, printed forms, etc. A document can be defined as "any written or recorded material that was not prepared specifically in response to a request of the inquirer" (Lincoln and Guba 1985, p.277).

The advantages of document studies include (National Science Foundation, 1997):

- They are available locally and are inexpensive;

- They are grounded in the setting and language in which they occur;

- They are useful for determining value, interest, positions, political climate, public, attitudes, historical trends or sequences; and

- They are unobtrusive.

However, disadvantages include (National Science Foundation, 1997):

- They may be incomplete;

- They may be inaccurate and of questionable authenticity; and

- The analysis may be time consuming.

In this inquiry, it was thought that document studies had potential to be used in gathering data concerning students' previous achievement levels.

5.2.4.5 Performance Assessment

The most common form of performance assessment is the test in which an individual's knowledge, depth of understanding, or skill is measured (Borg, Gall and Gall, 1993). Most tests are either norm-referenced (measuring how a given student performed compared to a previously tested population) or criterion-referenced (measuring if a student had mastered specific instructional objectives and thus acquired specific knowledge and skills) (National Science Foundation, 1993).

The advantages of performance assessment include (Borg, Gall and Gall, 1993):

- They are inexpensive and easy to administer;

- They are easy to use and often require less time than some other methods;

- The whole population can be tested; and

- They provide "hard" data.

However, disadvantages include (Borg, Gall and Gall, 1993):

- Because they are timed, a slow worker is disadvantaged; and

- If as student is ill or tired, they may perform below their capacity.

One of the aims of this inquiry was to investigate the impact of the CORT system on student learning outcomes and the use of student performance assessment seemed to be an appropriate method to collect such data.

5.2.5 Overall Research Process for the Study

Applying the four basic elements of research of Crotty (1998) to this inquiry suggested that the overall research process should be that shown in Figure 5.2.

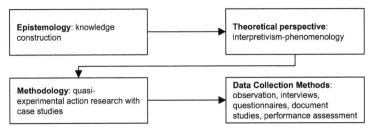

Figure 5.2: Overall Research Process for the Study

5.3 Research Questions

The wording of the research questions determines the focus and scope of the study. Morse (1998) suggests that as qualitative research is often tenuous, especially in the early stages, the research questions should be as broad as possible so that the study is not prematurely delimited. By making the research questions explicit, a researcher is helped to channel their energy in the "right" directions and to focus their data collection (Miles and Huberman, 1994).

The aims of the research were to determine the ways in which students made use of CORT and to what extent student learning is supported when using the technology supported part-completion method of learning to program. To achieve this, the study sought to explore the following questions:

1.   How did students use CORT?

2.   How did the PCSM within CORT support the learning process?

3.   What impact did the use of the PCSM within CORT have on learning outcomes?

5.4 Research Design

5.4.1 Background

The investigation was planned to take place over a period of one semester at a university, a semester being 14 teaching weeks. The unit that the students were to take was an introductory programming unit for students within a school of Management Information Systems. Students are expected to gain fundamental programming knowledge in this unit including the three basic control structures, built-in functions, user-defined functions, event and general procedures, text file processing, and array processing. An example of an outline for this unit is included in Appendix 1.

The traditional way of delivering this unit is to have a two hour lecture, in which basic knowledge is introduced to the students together with methods of solving standard problems, and to have a one hour computer laboratory. In a laboratory, students are given programming problems to attempt to solve using Visual BASIC. If a student requires help then they usually ask fellow students or their tutor.

The students had to enrol in one of four computer laboratories. Two of the laboratories were to use the CORT program and the other two laboratories were to have "conventional" programming exercises without CORT. In order to reduce possible bias, at the time of enrolment, the students did not know whether they would be in the CORT or non-CORT group.

5.4.2 Subjects

The students who were the subject of the research comprised 16 females and 33 males, this being a typical composition for this unit of study. There were 21 younger students whose ages were less than 21, and 28 older students. 26 of the students had moderate computing experience and the remaining 20 had extensive computing experience.

The CORT (experimental) group had 5 females and 19 males while the non-CORT (control) group had 11 females and 14 males. The CORT group had 12 younger and 12 older students, whereas the non-CORT group had 9 younger and 16 older students.

The uneven division of numbers between the different groups was due to the students selecting computer laboratories according to times that were convenient to them and not being directed to specific laboratories by the researcher. The students were given an opportunity to change groups, however all chose to remain in their initial groups.

5.4.3 Data Collection Plan

A data collection matrix has been used to summarise the methods of data collection; data required; and the ways in which the data were to be analysed, for each of the research questions. The data collection methods that were used and the data collection matrix are shown in Tables 5.3 and 5.4 respectively. There were several data collection methods used, some data being used to triangulate other data rather than to prove particular points.

Table 5.3: Data Collection Methods

a	Observation	d	Document study: University record system
b	Interviews of students	e	End-tests
c	Questionnaires		

Table 5.4: Data Collection Matrix

Research Question	Method	Data Required	Analysis
1. How students use CORT.	a, b, c	List of usage statistics. Descriptions of preferences concerning CORT. Examples of student perceptions of the level of difficulty of using CORT. Interview data.	Mapping of usage patterns. Identification of trends in the preferred ways of using CORT. Identification of trends in the levels of difficulty of using CORT.
2. How does a technology enabled part-completion method support the learning process.	a, b, c	List of support types provided by CORT. List of levels of support provided by CORT. List of cognitive strategies used by students. Interview data.	Exploration of change in types of assistance and levels provided by CORT over time. Influence of CORT on student cognitive strategies. Identification of trends.
3. What impact did the use of CORT and part-complete solutions have on learning outcomes.	c, d, e	Data from university record system. Initial questionnaire on computing knowledge and experience. Post tests and formal assessment.	Statistical analysis to determine if there are any significant differences between the test results.

All of the data were collected over a period of one semester and the data collection schedule is shown in Table 5.5.

Table 5.5: Data Collection Schedule

	Initial questio-nnaire	Document study of student records			Student interviews								
Week No.	1	2	3	4	5	6	7	8	9	10	11	12-14	15
	Consent forms	Observation of students within laboratories. Solutions to programming problems. Student problem questionnaires.											End tests

5.4.4 Student Consent to the Research

As part of the university research ethics policy it was necessary to have the research accepted by the university ethic's committee and to obtain approval from every student in the study. It was necessary to create two different student consent forms, one for a CORT group and one for a non-CORT group. The forms are shown in Appendices 2 and 3 respectively.

5.4.5 Initial Questionnaire: Computing Knowledge and Experience

It was important that certain background details of the students should be gathered so that any comparisons that were to be made between students could take their background into account. These details were planned to be gathered in the form of a "computing knowledge and experience" questionnaire and this can be found in Appendix 4 and the questions and their rationale are shown in Table 5.6.

Table 5.6: Initial Questionnaire: Computing Knowledge and Experience

Question	Rationale
Question 1 What is your Gender? • Male • Female	Differences in learning programming using a technology supported part complete solution method may emerge between males and females.
Question 2 Which of the following age ranges are you in? • 20 years or under • 21 years to 30 years • 31 years to 40 years • 41 years or over	Differences in learning programming using a technology supported part complete solution method may emerge for different age ranges.
Question 3 How would you rate your current computing expertise? (Tick one box only) • **Limited**: you have not used computers very much at home, school or university. • **Moderate**: eg. you use computers for email, Web browsing, word processing etc. You have a limited knowledge of Windows. • **Extensive**: eg. you use computers for email, Web browsing, word processing, spreadsheeting, database (eg "Access"). You can change a program's preferences or options. You have a good knowledge of Windows with the ability to create folders, zip files, use the Control Panel etc Comments: ____	This question was asked as it was possible that computing expertise may be a factor that affects the ease with which students learn the CORT program.

Question	Rationale
Question 4 What is your previous computer programming experience? (Tick one box only) • **None** • **Limited**: eg. You have done a programming course at school, you have taught yourself to program, you have used and amended scripts for the Web. • **Moderate**: eg. You have done a formal programming course, you have written some large computer programs. Comments: ___	This question was asked as it was possible that students who are not novice programmers may well have different learning experiences to novices when CORT is utilised.
Question 5 What is your science and maths knowledge? (Tick one box only) 1. **Limited**: eg. you have no passes in science and maths at TEE. 2. **Moderate**: eg. you have at least one pass at TEE in a science subject such as physics or chemistry (not biology) and / or at least one pass in a TEE maths subject. 3. **Extensive**: for example you consider yourself good at science and maths and have achieved high scores in two or more TEE science (do not include biology) and maths subjects Comments: ___	In this question, TEE refers to the tertiary entrance examination that is taken by students within Western Australia. This question was asked as it was thought that mathematical knowledge may be a factor in a student's learning of programming.

5.4.6 Student Information from University Record System

In order to obtain useful data concerning student background and past performance, a document study was proposed of the university's student record system. Student records are stored electronically within an Oracle database and contain data concerning the average marks in units of study to date together with students' previous semester's average marks.

5.4.7 Programming Problems

Programming problems were carefully designed in order to cover the objectives of the unit syllabus. They were different for the CORT and non-CORT groups as it was important for the integrity of the research that there was no collusion between any of the students in the different groups. However, although each week's problems were different for the groups, they were of a similar nature and degree of difficulty to try and ensure that students would have the same learning opportunities and that comparisons could be made in the performances of the groups.

The programming problems were to be given to the student groups over a period of ten weeks. It was planned that there would usually be two problems assigned each week and that students would be expected to finish them in their own time if they could not be completed in the laboratory. In an attempt to ensure that students would try hard to complete the assigned work, it was decided that the students would be required to hand-in their solutions on disk in week 12 of the unit and the work assessed.

The files that would be required for each CORT problem were to be placed on a disk drive on a local server and the CORT students would be required to copy them to their floppy disks at the beginning of each computer laboratory session. The required files are shown in Figure 4.2 in Chapter 4.

For each problem, it was planned that the problem description would be available from within CORT in electronic format and that it would also given be to students in the form of a hardcopy. After reading a problem description, students would view the part-complete solution within CORT as described in Chapter 4, and attempt to complete the program and test their solution within Visual BASIC.

The students in the non-CORT group were to be given floppy disks at the beginning of the semester that contained all of the programming problems in electronic format. Hardcopies of the problems were also to be given to the students and it was planned that students would save their solutions to disk.

5.4.7.1 An Example of a CORT Problem
The problem shown in Figure 5.3 concerned string processing.

A program is required that obtains, via a textbox, a telephone number. Examples of numbers that might be entered are:

    08 9275 5623
    09 7612 4296

The numbers are always of the same structure but may have leading or trailing spaces entered too. The program should output, on separate lines, the three parts of the number, Eg:

    STD Code: 08
    Exchange: 9275
    Number: 5623

Note
- Not all lines of code from the left-hand side need to be used.

- You will need to key-in a line to determine the "last part" of the number.
- There are questions that you have to answer concerning the problem and these can be viewed by selecting Problem | View Questions about the Problem from the line menu.

Figure 5.3: Example of a CORT Problem

This is an example of a method 3 type CORT problem, the three possible methods of using CORT having been described in chapter 3. A method 3 type problem may have some lines of code available in the left hand window of CORT, other lines having to be keyed-in by the student.

5.4.7.2 An Example of a Non-CORT Problem

The similar problem to the above that was designed for the non-CORT students was an amended version of a textbook question (Schneider, 2003) and is shown in Figure 5.4.

Write a program to generate a rent "receipt". The program should request the person's name, amount received, and the current date in three different text boxes and output a receipt to a picture box. Example input data might be:

    Jane Smith
    645.50
    04/08/01

The format of the receipt can be determined from the following which is the receipt for the example data:

    Received from Jane the sum of $645.50
    Year: 01

Figure 5.4: Example of a Non-CORT Problem

The output from the solution to the non-CORT problem does not contain enough data to be a "real" receipt and the reason for this was to try and ensure the problem required similar functionality in its solution to that of the CORT question.

5.4.7.3 Weekly CORT Problem Summary

A summary of the weekly CORT problems that were designed is shown in Table 5.7. The table shows the problem structures; the CORT method that was utilised; the number of lines in the part-complete solution; the number of lines removed from the original solution; the number of extra lines added to act as distracters; and the number of lines that had to be keyed-in. Comments are also included that explain the reasons for the particular CORT method used. Similar problems to the CORT problems were developed for the non-CORT students. These were taken from the unit textbook or were created by the researcher. The CORT method details are shown again to help the reader understand the table:

Method 1. All of the lines of code that are missing from the program are provided as options.

Method 2. All of the lines of code that are missing from the program, together with some extra lines of code that are not needed to complete the program, are provided. These extra lines act as "distracters".

Method 3. Some of the lines of code that are missing from the program might be provided, however some other missing lines must be keyed-in by the learner.

Table 5.7: Weekly CORT Problem Summary

Week No.	Problem No.	Problem Information	CORT Method	No. lines in part-complete solution	No. lines removed from original solution	No. of extra lines (distracters)	No. of lines to key-in	Comments
2	2	Change a screen object's properties dynamically	2	6	3	3	0	There was only one problem in the first laboratory session. Method 2 was used as the problem was very simple and a similar one was planned to be discussed with the students.
3	3	Simple process and output. All variables numeric.	1	4	13	0	0	Several new concepts were to be introduced to students and CORT method 1 was therefore planned.
3	4	Simple process and output. All variables numeric. The processing was slightly more difficult than in problem 3.	2	4	5	4	0	The problem type was similar to that of 2. The scaffolding was reduced by using method 2.
4	5	Simple input, numeric processing and output.	2	9	6	11	0	Screen input and output formatting were to be introduced. Many distracter lines were added for these two areas.
4	6	Simple input from a text file, process and output.	1	6	10	0	0	Input from text files was planned to be introduced and students usually experience difficulty with this topic. Method 1 was therefore used.
5	7	Use of integer arithmetic functions to determine the notes and coins for a wage	2	22	13	6	0	The order of the lines in the final program is crucial for success in this problem. The distracters used

Week No.	Problem No.	Problem Information	CORT Method	No. lines in part-complete solution	No. lines removed from original solution	No. of extra lines (distracters)	No. of lines to key-in	Comments
		packet.						incorrect integer functions.
5	8	Use of simple string handling functions.	3	11	17	5	1	This was the first problem in which method 3 was used, students having to key-in a line of code. This method was used as the problem was straight forward.

Week No.	Problem No.	Problem Information	CORT Method	No. lines in part-complete solution	No. lines removed from original solution	No. of extra lines (distracters)	No. of lines to key-in	Comments
6	9	Use of general procedures with parameters.	1	18	16	0	0	This used method 2 as students have great difficulty with procedures. The task was also difficult as there were four procedures in the part-complete solution and the students had to determine which lines should be moved into which procedures.
6	10	User defined functions.	2	17	8	2	0	User-defined functions is a difficult topic. Method 2 was used as the number of lines removed from the solution was relatively small and only 2 distracters were used.
7	11	"IF" statements.	1	11	6	0	0	Method 1 was used because a new control structure had been introduced and the solution required a nested "IF" statement.
7	12	"CASE" statement.	3	17	14	0	10	Method 3 was used because the lines to be keyed-in were very similar as they were part of the "CASE" statement. The number of lines to be keyed-in was relatively large and so no distracters were used.
8	13	"WHILE" loops.	1	24	9	0	0	Method 1 was used as this is a difficult topic. Also, for the first time it was planned that the students had to add an object to the interface and change its properties, this adding to the cognitive load.
8	14	This problem also used a "WHILE" loop and input data from a text file.	3	14	13	4	4	Method 3 was used as students had already used "WHILE" loops in problem 13 and Input from text files was to have been covered in week 4. Students were also required to add an object to the interface.
9	15	Array Processing. The solution required data to be loaded from a text file into a one-dimensional array and then output in columns.	3	15	9	2	1	Although array processing is difficult, method 3 was used. The cognitive load was kept low as only one line had to be keyed-in and there were only two distracters.

Week No.	Problem No.	Problem Information	CORT Method	No. lines in part-complete solution	No. lines removed from original solution	No. of extra lines (distracters)	No. of lines to key-in	Comments
9	16	Array Processing. This was a more difficult array processing problem than 16.	1	17	11	0	0	Method 1 was used as this was a difficult problem.
10	17	Array Processing: sorting and searching.	2	64	17	2	0	The solution required a large number of lines of code, this being 81. Method 2 as opposed to method 3 was therefore used to reduce the cognitive load. The missing lines were from two specific procedures and it was planned to inform students which set of possible lines to use for which procedure.
11	18	Text file processing. A text file had to be created by the program from data entered via an input form. The program then processed the newly created to produce two new files.	3	41	14	9	9	Although this problem was complex, method 3 was used as the lines that had to be keyed-in were for one particular procedure and were similar to one of the other procedures in the program. As with problem 17, there were also missing lines from two specific procedures and it was planned to inform students which set of possible lines to use for which procedure.

5.4.8 Individual Problem Questionnaires

It was planned to collect data from students concerning the problems that they attempted and to this end a short questionnaire was designed. It was planned that a questionnaire would be completed electronically for every problem that was attempted. The planned questions for the CORT students and the rationale for their choice are shown in Table 5.8 and the original questionnaire is shown in Appendix 5.

Table 5.8: CORT Problem Questions, Response Choice, and Rationale

Question and Response Choice	Rationale
Question 1 Approximately how long did it take to complete the problem? **Possible Responses** • less than 15 minutes • 16 to 20 minutes • 21 to 25 minutes • 26 to 30 minutes • 31 to 35 minutes • 36 to 40 minutes • 41 to 45 minutes • more than 45 minutes	It was thought that responses to this question help determine if there were any differences in time required by different groups to achieve certain learning outcomes. This was to be used for research question 3.
Question 2 What help / resources did you use in solving the problem? **Possible Responses** • none • tutor • fellow student • Schneider textbook • other: please give details _____	CORT and the part-complete solution method are used to help support student learning, thereby reducing extrinsic cognitive load, whilst applying a certain amount of germane cognitive load. These 2 questions were designed to determine the type of help and to estimate the amount of help that students required in addition to that provided by CORT. It was planned to use the data to try and determine if there were any differences in the type and amount of help required by different groups to achieve certain learning outcomes. This was to be used for research question 3.
Question 3 How much help did you use in solving the problem? **Possible Responses** • none • little • moderate • extensive	
Question 4 What features of CORT did you use? **Possible Responses** • view problem description • view problem interface • changed font in preferences • expand - reduce left-hand window • expand - reduce right-hand window • insert blank line before • insert blank line after • remove blank line(s) • CORT code editor	This was used for research question 1 which aimed to determine how students used CORT.

The problem questionnaire for the non-CORT students was the same as that of the CORT students with the exception that the fourth question was omitted. It was hoped that useful comparative data concerning time taken and help required would be obtained by having identical questions in the questionnaires.

5.4.9 Observation

It was planned that this would be a major data collection method in the inquiry providing data for both research questions 1 and 2. It was planned to use the "participant-as-observer" approach with details of observations recorded onto microcassette tapes. It was hoped that during the observations, patterns and trends in the usage of CORT and the part-complete solution method would emerge together with evidence of reflection and higher order thinking. The researcher would act as the observer and would prompt students to try and make their thinking explicit when certain courses of action were undertaken.

It was also planned that two students would be observed throughout the semester in which the inquiry would take place enabling longitudinal data to be captured, and six further students would be observed for shorter periods of time.

5.4.10 Interviews

The purpose of the planned interviews was to gather further data concerning CORT and the part-complete solution method that might not have emerged during the periods of observation. The questions that were planned to be asked and the rationale for their choice are shown in Table 5.9. All the students that were to be observed were to be interviewed together with several other CORT students. Responses to the interview questions were to be recorded on interview pro-formas.

Table 5.9: Interview Questions and Rationale

Interview Question	Rationale
Question 1 Have you in the main moved lines to the right-hand side in a thoughtful manner or did you use trial and error. Has your strategy changed for different problems?	This was used for research question 2. The aim of the part-complete solution method is that students will have to think in completing the solutions to problems. However it was thought that some students might just use a trial and error approach to solving a problem.

Interview Question	Rationale
Question 2 When testing a program in Visual BASIC, what did you do if the program did not work? **Follow up:** • Where did you get help from? Book / student / tutor. • Would you like to see instant help on lines of code, possibly by e-movies? • If you used Debug in Visual BASIC, did this help in your understanding?	This was used for research question 2 and concerned the learning supports provided to students when testing and refining code. It was hoped that this would help gather data concerning: • How well CORT helped students debug a problem. • How well Visual BASIC helped students debug a problem. • What the other sources of help that were used by students to help them debug programs.
Question 3 Does CORT provide too little or too much help? (ie what is the perceived degree of scaffolding) **Follow up:** • How did CORT help: with easy / difficult problems; with problems in the earlier / latter parts of the unit.	This was used for research question 2 and was aimed at gathering data concerning the amount of scaffolding provided in the way of part-complete solutions. Of particular interest was how much the method (of the three possible CORT methods) of the part-complete problem helped students and also how the method should be varied as the course progressed through the semester.
Question 4 Which method of CORT problem helps your understanding most? • Method 1: all lines provided. • Method 2: too many lines provided • Method 3: too few lines provided (and you need to type some in)	This was used for research question 2 and concerned learner reflection and higher order thinking. It was thought that the method of the CORT problem that students believed helped them most in their understanding would have caused them to think and reflect to the greatest extent during the problem solving process and yet still provide enough scaffolding for them to solve a problem.
Question 5 What do you like / dislike about the CORT environment? How could CORT be improved?	This was used for research question 1 and concerned learner preferences in the CORT environment.
Question 6 How easy / difficult do you find CORT?	This was used for research question 1 and concerned the perceived level of difficulty of using CORT.

5.4.11 End-Tests

Research question 3 concerned the impact of CORT on learning outcomes and ends tests were created in order to collect appropriate data. Two tests were created, the first was a program completion test that required students to complete part-complete programs, and the second was a "conventional" final exam for the unit.

5.4.11.1 Program Completion Test

A semester comprises 14 "face-to-face" teaching weeks and the program completion test was planned to be administered to students in week 15. The test, which can be seen in Appendix 6, had 8 program completion questions and an example of the type of question used is:

The Problem

A program is required that requests a whole number of inches and converts it to feet and inches. Note that 12 inches equals 1 foot. There are several lines missing from the program and possible lines of code are given to you. You do not have to use all the possible lines to complete the solution.

You are required to write out the letters of the lines of the existing code and the numbers of the missing lines in the correct order.

Part-complete Program

```
   Option Explicit
   Private Sub cmdConvert_Click()
     Dim inches As Single, feet as Single
A.   picDisplay.Print "Number of feet = "; feet
B.   picDisplay.Print "Number of inches = "; inches
   End Sub
```

Possible lines of code

```
1. Let feet = inches \ 12
2. Let feet = inches Mod 12
3. Let inches = inches \ 12
4. Let inches = inches Mod 12
5. Let inches = Val(txtInches.Text)
```

The type of question created for this test was similar to the type of problem that the CORT students would have attempted during the semester in the computer laboratories. An aim of this test was to determine if the CORT students would perform better at such code reading and completion tests than the non-CORT students who would have undertaken their learning of programming in a "conventional" manner.

5.4.11.2 Final Exam for the Unit

This final exam can be seen in Appendix 7 and it comprised two sections, A and B. Section A had 10 compulsory short questions, each of which was worth two marks. These questions were designed to test student understanding of existing programming code. An example of a Section A question is:

The Problem

What will be the output of the following program when the command button is clicked?

```
Private Sub cmdDisplay_Click()
  Dim num As Integer
  num = 10
  Call DisplayMult(num)
  num = 5
  Call DisplayMult(num)
  num = 2
  Call DisplayMult(num)
End Sub
```

```
Private Sub DisplayMult(num As Integer)
  If num <= 3 Then
      picOutput.Print 3 * num;
    Else
      If num > 7 Then
         picOutput.Print 7 * num;
         End If
  End If
End Sub
```

Section B had two long questions, only one of which had to be attempted by the students and which was worth 20 marks. The questions were designed to test the students' ability to develop or generate a program. An example of one of the questions follows:

The Problem
A file called "marks.txt" contains names and test marks for students. Names can appear more than once. A program is required that accepts a name as input, via a textbox, and outputs the average of the marks for that student and that student's highest mark.

The name entered should not be sensitive to the case of the letters. For example, if the text file contained the following and the name entered was "brenda", then an average of 40 would be output together with the highest mark of 63.

```
"Alf", 56
"Brenda", 63
"Gladys", 45
"BRENDA", 34
"Adnams", 44
"brenDA", 23
```

If the name does not appear in the file then a message "Name not in file" should be output.

Note that an array is not required.

For the above:

(a)   Create a task / object / event (TOE) chart.
(b)   Draw an interface sketch naming all objects.
(c)   Write detailed pseudo code or Visual BASIC code, including details of variables and their types.
(d)   Draw up a test table showing the input data, expected output and the reasons for each test. Make sure that the tests that you suggest would thoroughly test the program.

5.5   Summary

This chapter has discussed research methodologies and contrasting quantitative and qualitative techniques. It emerged from this discussion that the main methodology to be used in this research study would be qualitative.

The basic elements of research as outlined by Crotty (1998) helped inform the overall research process for the study. The process chosen was a quasi-experimental action research methodology using case studies.

The specific research questions for the study were specified together with the proposed instruments to be used in data collection. There were several instruments in order to ensure internal validity of the study.

The analysis of the data collected is described in the next three chapters, each chapter discussing outcomes and findings in relation to each of the 3 research questions.

Chapter 6
How Students Use CORT

6.1 Introduction

This chapter discusses aspects of the usability of CORT, with data on usability gathered from a detailed review of students' use of CORT as part of the main study. The students in the study were learning programming via the part-complete solution method and in order to determine how CORT influenced learning, it was necessary to determine if the way the CORT software was designed and developed hindered the students in any way. The chapter describes the usability factors of CORT which were found to be an issue for students and the impact they had on student learning. The chapter also explores the ways in which these issues were, or were not, overcome and the amount of time it took students to learn the functional features of CORT and to become comfortable and fluent in its use.

This chapter describes and discusses ten usability issues that were identified as potential impediments to learning. It discusses the apparent impact of these issues on the learning of the students and provides suggestions for the improvement of CORT in order to reduce the impact of these issues.

6.2 CORT Usability

CORT was designed with the aim of being simple and intuitive to use. In all instances where students were observed using CORT, they appeared to develop familiarity with the application reasonably quickly. A prototype had been designed and tested (described in chapter 4) and this had led to some small revisions and amendments to the prototype. This revised prototype was then utilised with students in this second stage of the study.

In the second stage of the study, CORT was used over a period of 10 weeks during the semester, beginning in week number 2 and finishing in week number 11. Each week, students were given a hardcopy describing one or two programming problems to solve. They then executed the CORT program from the usual Windows **Start** button and the CORT interface would appear with two empty windows as shown in Figure 6.1.

Figure 6.1: Initial CORT Interface

Students then opened a CORT file with the file extension ".pcs", which is short for part-complete solution, and the right-hand window was populated with a part-complete solution and the left-hand window was populated with possible lines of code to complete the solution. The problem statement was initially displayed to the students in a window that is smaller than and overlays the windows of the part-complete solution as shown in Figure 6.2. Students were then required to solve the programming problem presented by moving lines of code until the desired algorithm was completed.

Figure 6.2: CORT Problem Statement

Observations of the students throughout the study revealed a number of usability factors that were seen to hinder some students as they worked to solve the part complete solution. Across the period of the main study, these usability factors appeared to be of three main forms:

- Operation of the problem files;

- Manipulation of the lines of code; and

- Editing the lines of code.

The following sections describe the problems students were observed to face in each of these areas and discuss the impact these problems appeared to have on the successful completion of the part complete solutions themselves.

6.2.1 Operation of the Problem Files

There were four different types of difficulty observed among some of the learners in relation to the operation and application of the files associated with CORT. Some students were observed in initial stages of their use to have difficulty opening the part complete solution files. Several were observed to have difficulty viewing problem statements and in the same vein, a small number of students were observed to have trouble initially viewing problem interfaces. Later in the unit, a majority of students were seen to have some difficulties in viewing the contents of data files that were being utilised in file-handling problems.

6.2.1.1 Opening a CORT Part-complete Solution File

Initial observations revealed several students having difficulty opening a ".pcs" file so as to populate the two windows with a part-complete solution and possible lines of code to complete the solution. The students indicated that they normally opened Windows' files from within Windows Explorer by double clicking on a file name so that the program associated with that particular file type would execute and then automatically load the file. This mechanism had not been built into CORT. The problem vanished quickly as students learned the correct procedures. The difficulty was only observed in the first week and after that time students were able to open the files without hesitation. The findings suggested the need for such a file association to be built into CORT. The small number of students who experienced the problem and the speed with which the problem was overcome indicated that this issue did not negatively influence the use of CORT in any major way.

6.2.1.2 Viewing a Problem Statement

The learning environment was designed with the intention that students would read each problem statement from the hardcopy that was given to them at the beginning of each laboratory session. However in the major study it was clear that most students preferred to read the problem statement on the screen. When questioned these students indicated that they were very used to reading text on screen and to them it was preferable. Some students also indicated that they often misplaced hard copies. However the CORT design did not allow the two windows with the programming code statements to be viewable at the same time as the window with the problem statement. This was seen to be a difficulty for those students wishing to read the problems on the screen. When interviewed these students indicated that all three windows should be available simultaneously. In the study the students adapted quickly to having to use the hardcopy form for problems and this limitation of the program was noted. In terms of impeding learning, this problem appeared to have minimal impact. Students adapted quickly to the conditions and this aspect of usability was judged to have only minimal impact, and was seen as a minor irritation.

6.2.1.3 Viewing a Visual BASIC Program's Interface

After viewing and reading a problem statement a student would close the front "View Problem" window. It was thought that students would then view the problem interface, as shown in Figure 6.3, to help them in their understanding of what the required output from the completed program should look like. This function is invoked by either selecting:

Problem > View Problem Interface

from the line menu or clicking on the 🔲 icon.

Figure 6.3: Visual BASIC Problem Interface

However data collected indicated that many students did not use this function in the early weeks of the semester and three students did not use the function at all. This can be seen by the data in Figure 6.4 which was collected from the individual problem questionnaires. It shows the number of students who viewed the problem interface against the CORT problem number. The graph shows that the number of students who viewed the problem interface grew steadily as the course progressed and experience was gained. Towards the end of the course usage appeared to stay steady.

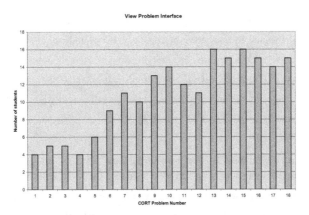

Figure 6.4: Graph Showing the Utilisation of the "View Problem Interface" Function

An example of this function's usefulness for learning is shown by a question that a student asked the researcher in connection with question 13 in week 8. He asked the researcher if the output from his program solution was correct. The researcher suggested to the student that he should view the problem interface that showed the expected output and, after doing this, the student commented that this function of CORT was very useful to his understanding of the problem requirements and also as a way of giving him feedback to the correctness of his solution. He stated that he wished that he had known about it earlier in the semester.

Those students who did use the function on a regular basis commented on its usefulness and they particularly liked the fact that the object names were shown on the interfaces. An example of an object name is **cmdMakeRed** in Figure 6.3.

The overall impression of this limitation in the main study was that student lack of knowledge concerning this function was evident only in the early weeks. It was seen to have a minor effect on some students' use of CORT as the function provided a way of clarifying the problem description and also giving feedback as to the correctness of a student solution. The students quickly learned the feature and for the large part of the study were able to use it when required.

6.2.1.4 Display of text files

A majority of students were observed having difficulties viewing the contents of text (data) files which were utilised with certain problems in the latter part of the unit. For example, in problem 14 which was given in week 8, a text file was provided for students. This was stored within a folder together with all the other files required for that particular problem. The list of these other files is shown in Figure 4.2 of chapter 4. All the other files in the folder are utilised by being either loaded from within CORT or from within Visual BASIC. However there was no simple mechanism available within CORT to display the contents of such a text file and this concerned several students who did not know how to display the contents of such files from within Windows.

Overall the difficulty that students were observed to have when viewing text files was minor and quickly overcome. It was perceived to be a small problem that did not affect or impede learning, however a future improvement to CORT would be to have a built-in system to view such files.

6.2.1.5 Summary

In overall terms, there was only a small number of students who were observed to experience problems with the file aspects of the CORT program described above. In the main, the problems were due to a lack of experience with the program and its features. In all instances, the students who were seen to experience difficulties with the interface overcame the problems within the first few weeks of the course and proceeded to use CORT unimpeded by the problems. The small number of problems and their speed of solution suggested that these limitations were minimal and not likely to contribute in any negative way to the learning supports offered by CORT.

6.2.2 Manipulation of the Lines of Code

There were three different types of difficulty observed among some of the learners in relation to the manipulation of lines of programming code in the two code windows. At times, some students were observed to have difficulties viewing lines of code that were longer than one of the window's widths. Some had trouble in the movement of lines of code between the code windows, and finally there were students who had problems moving lines into position in the right-hand window.

6.2.2.1 Expansion / Contraction of the Line Manipulation Windows

The left and right-hand windows were of such a width that longer lines of code could not be fully viewed on the screen as they are truncated on the right. There is no sideways scroll facility in CORT and in order to view such lines, the windows would be expanded in width as shown in Figure 6.5.

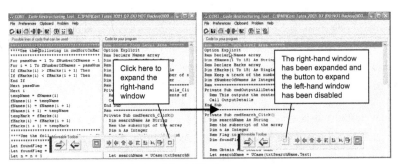

Figure 6.5: Expansion of the Right-hand Code Window

Figure 6.6 is a graph which shows the number of students throughout the study who used the expansion and contraction of the line manipulation windows. The graph reveals low levels of usage in early weeks leading to much higher levels of usage as the course progressed. The usage figures in the graph support the observations made that indicate that many students did not recognise that this facility existed early in the unit. They were observed to move lines into the part-complete solution even though some lines could not be fully read.

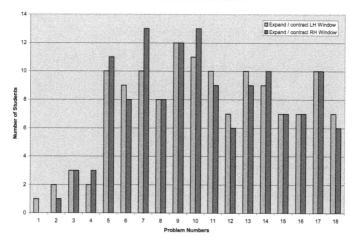

Figure 6.6: Graph Showing the Utilisation of the "Expansion / Contraction" Function

When students did discover this function then they used it frequently. However, the expansion of a code window did appear to unsettle some students. For example, one student made the comment that he felt uncomfortable about a window disappearing completely off the screen when one of the ▢ buttons was clicked. He suggested that it would be preferable to have a facility such that a vertical bar between the windows could be dragged to the left or right thereby increasing the width of one window whilst decreasing the width of the other. Such vertical "splitter bars" are common in many Windows programs.

Although the viewing of longer lines of code was an initial problem with CORT, most students soon became familiar and comfortable with the viewing functions and it appeared that there was no lasting detrimental affect on learning as a consequence of this shortcoming. However the use of a standard Windows "splitter bar" is seen as a preferable mechanism and this would appear to be a sound improvement which could be made to the CORT system.

6.2.2.2 Moving Lines of Code between Windows

The ease with which lines of code can be moved between the code windows is fundamental to the usability of CORT. Students were initially observed to have some difficulty in knowing which left and right arrow button to use in order to move lines between the windows. Figure 6.7 shows part of CORT's toolbar and the larger left and right buttons were the ones to use for this function, the smaller buttons having the function of indenting / outdenting the highlighted line(s) in the right-hand window. Students also indicated that it would have been useful to be able to drag and drop lines between the windows.

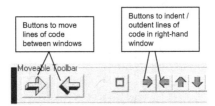

Figure 6.7: Toolbar Arrow Buttons

Many students were observed to be unsure where a line would be inserted in the right-hand window when it was moved from the left. CORT inserts a highlighted line from the left directly below the highlighted line on the right. However, when a CORT file is initially loaded, the highlighted lines are the first ones in the two windows as shown in Figure 6.8. Often students were observed to select a line from the left to move to the right, click on the large right-hand arrow on the toolbar and this would result in that line being placed after the first line in the right-hand window. They would then move the line into what they thought was the correct position by utilising the up and down arrow buttons.

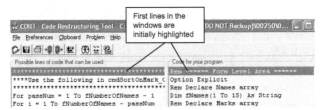

Figure 6.8: Code Windows After Initial File Load

It was also observed that some students were unsure of how a line of code could be inserted into the position before the first line in the right-hand window. This had to be done by inserting the line into position 2 and then moving it to the top with the up arrow button.

Several lines could be highlighted in the left-hand window and then moved to the right in one process, however most students were unaware of this.

The fact that lines could be placed anywhere in the part-complete program in the right-hand window caused unanticipated errors with programs that had more than one procedure. This was because students would sometimes move lines into the right-hand window and place them outside of the existing procedure structures, as shown in the example of Figure 6.9. When such a program was eventually tested in the Visual BASIC development environment, an error message would be output.

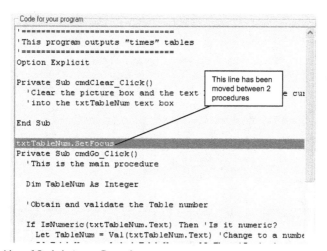

Figure 6.9: Line of Code between Procedures

This type of error does not usually appear when students develop programs directly in Visual BASIC as the intelligent editor automatically places dividing lines between procedures as shown in Figure 6.10.

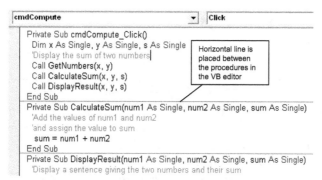

Figure 6.10: Procedures in Visual BASIC Editor

There is a facility within CORT, available from buttons on the moveable toolbar, to allow users to insert blank lines into a part-complete solution, however it was observed that most students were initially unaware of this.

It was also observed that students were uncomfortable with the fact that lines moved back from the right-hand window to the left-hand window were placed at the bottom of the existing lines. For example, a student may have moved a line from the left-hand window into a certain position in the right-hand window as shown in Figure 6.11.

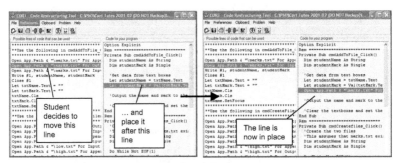

Figure 6.11: Line of Code Moved into Right-hand Window

The student may then have a change of mind and decide to return the line back to the left-hand window. This would be done by clicking the large left-hand arrow key and the result would be as shown in Figure 6.12 resulting in the original line being placed at the bottom of the lines in the left-hand window.

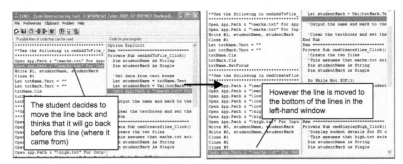

Figure 6.12: Line of Code Moved Back into Left-hand Window

Several students also suggested that it would be useful for the lines that had been moved into the right-hand window to be highlighted in some way so that they were easy to identify. They indicated that his would help them in the reselection of those lines in order to move them back to the left-hand window if necessary.

A further suggestion was that there should be a separate window which would act as a "waste bin" for discarding the extra "distracter" lines that were included, but not required for the correct solution, in CORT method 2 or 3 type problems. Students indicated that this would help them concentrate on what they believed were the correct lines of code to be included in the solution.

The movement of lines of code between the code windows could be considered as the most important function of CORT as this is the mechanism for directly building the solution to a given problem. It is therefore not surprising that it was observed that the mechanism raised several usability issues with students. It is recognised that the mechanism could be improved upon, however overall, students appeared to quickly become familiar with the mechanism suggesting that it had little negative impact on their learning.

6.2.2.3 Moving and Manipulating Lines within the Right-hand Window
After lines of code had been moved into the right-hand window, students were required to move them up or down into positions that they considered to be correct. This is done by clicking on the up and down arrow buttons on the toolbar with a line moving by one position for each mouse click. It was observed that students often found this tedious in situations where a line had to be moved a long way up or down in the right-hand window. When interviewed, some students indicated that they had a "work-around" for such situations and that they would move a line back to the left-hand window and then move it directly into the correct location in the right-hand window. Most students suggested that it would be better to be able to "drag and drop" a line into the correct position rather than use the up and down arrows.

It was also observed that a majority of students did not realise that more than one line could be highlighted in the right-hand window and that the block of lines could then be moved into position using the up and down arrow keys.

The overall impression concerning the line manipulation function for the right-hand window was that, although students found the mechanism rather slow and tiresome, it did not hinder them from being able to move the necessary lines of code into position relatively quickly. It had been observed that students used this function intuitively from the beginning of the study although most did not take advantage of the ability to move blocks of code lines up and down within the right-hand window.

6.2.2.4 Summary

The manipulation of the lines of programming code between the two code windows and within the right-hand window of the part-complete solution is fundamental to the use of CORT. Overall the students quickly overcame the minor usablity problems and were able to rapidly move and position lines of code into and within the right-hand code window. The observations revealed that the problems did not affect to any great degree the student support for learning provided by this aspect of CORT's functionality.

6.2.3 Editing the lines of code

6.2.3.1 The CORT Editor

Some of the CORT problems were of the "method 3" type in which it was necessary for students to key-in some lines of code that were missing from the part-complete solution, and a text editor was provided for this purpose. The first such problem was given to students in week 4 and it was problem number 8 in the study. The other problems that required the use of the editor were 12, 14, 15 and 18. Figure 6.13 is a graph which shows the number of students who utilised the CORT editor for each problem number. The graph indicates that the initial usage of the editor for the first mode 3 problem, which was problem number 8, was relatively low. However the usage of the editor was high for the other mode 3 problems. This data supports the observations that several students did not initially know that the CORT editor existed and therefore added the necessary lines directly in the Visual BASIC editor. However after learning of the existence of the CORT editor, the majority of students used it extensively with the later problems. An anomaly in the data is revealed for problem number 17. The graph indicates that 10 students made use of the editor for this problem even though use of the editor was not required as it was a mode 2 type of problem. However this particular problem was found to be particularly difficult by some students and many therefore resorted to changing lines of code in the editor.

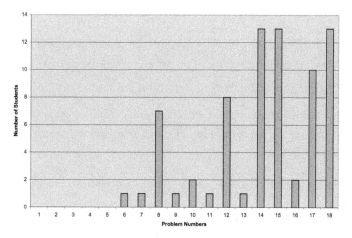

Figure 6.13: Graph Showing the Utilisation of the CORT Editor

The functions of the CORT editor included a facility to copy and paste lines of code using the normal [CTRL + C] and [CTRL + V] key combinations however it was observed that several students did not know about this feature.

When invoked, the editor is displayed in a relatively small window as shown in Figure 6.14. Some students when interviewed indicated that they disliked the fact that when the window size was increased, the area in which the text is displayed remained at the original size and did not increase proportionally.

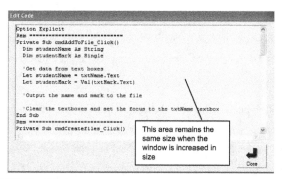

Figure 6.14: CORT Editor Window

Students who had knowledge of the existence of the CORT editor and yet still preferred to use the Visual BASIC editor gave the following reasons during interviews:

1. Horizontal lines are displayed between procedures in the Visual BASIC editor. Students had stated that they sometimes felt overwhelmed when the same program was viewed in the CORT editor.

2. The Visual BASIC editor makes use of colour which helps understanding. Keywords are shown in blue, comments are shown in green, and lines with syntax errors are shown in red.

3. The Visual BASIC editor gives syntax help in various situations. For example, if the picturebox object name **picResult** is keyed-in then a list of possible methods is listed as shown in Figure 6.15.

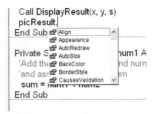

Figure 6.15: Visual BASIC Syntax Help

However some students did suggest that such a list of possibilities could be quite long and actually cause confusion.

A problem that was observed for some students who used the Visual BASIC editor rather than the CORT editor was that, if they did not copy the code that they had amended in Visual BASIC back into CORT, then the code in CORT ended up being different to that in Visual BASIC.

The observations and interviews provided ample evidence to suggest that students tended to find the editor functions of CORT easy to use. However some of the basic editing features such as copy and paste were not intuitive for students and could be improved upon. Figure 6.13 indicates that despite its limitations, most students made good use of the editor with the problems that it was required for and there was no evidence to suggest any difficulties experienced by students which impacted negatively on this aspect of learner support.

6.2.3.2 Copying and Pasting Code to Visual BASIC

Students were required to copy code from the right-hand window in CORT to the Windows Clipboard and then paste the code into the Visual BASIC code window of the integrated development environment (IDE) for testing purposes. It was only necessary for students to either click on the button or select the appropriate command from the line menu in CORT in order to copy the code. However it was observed that many students would highlight all of the lines in the right-hand window of CORT before selecting the copy function. This was probably because this is the way lines are copied in most other Windows programs.

A problem did arise in the pasting of the Clipboard contents into the Visual BASIC code window. In the early part of the semester, most students copied the lines from the code window of CORT into the Clipboard before invoking the Visual BASIC development environment. From within Visual BASIC the students would load the appropriate Visual BASIC files for the problem that they were attempting, these files containing the Visual BASIC interface for that particular problem. It was found that the opening of the Visual BASIC development environment had the effect of clearing the Windows Clipboard and so the students had to go back to CORT and reselect the "Copy to Clipboard" function.

It was also observed that some students had not read the instructions properly in the early part of the study and did not realise that it was necessary to load the Visual BASIC files that contained the Visual BASIC problem interface for each CORT problem they were attempting. They therefore created the Visual BASIC interface themselves in a new Visual BASIC project and pasted the lines of code into the code window. This often resulted in unanticipated errors as the interfaces that they created would often contain objects with names that did not match the object names in the program code. Hence the programs would not run and would often output obscure error messages.

Overall, although the mechanism for copying the code from CORT to Visual BASIC was not seamless, the majority of students quickly became familiar and comfortable with it. The mechanism provided a minor annoyance to some students, however no lasting negative impacts on learning were observed or reported.

6.2.3.3 Code Indentation

Good programmers understand the importance of aligning lines of code correctly within programming control structures and yet this is an area that many novices struggle with.

Buttons have been provided within CORT, as shown previously in Figure 6.7, to allow a line of code that has been moved into the right-hand code window to be aligned correctly with respect to the control structure in which it has been placed. Most editors of integrated development environments such as that of Visual BASIC automatically align a line of code that is being keyed-in with the line immediately above it. However, when a line of code in CORT is moved to the right-hand window it is positioned as shown in Figure 6.16.

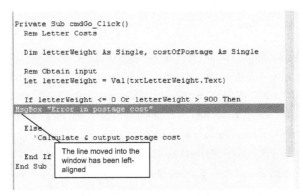

Figure 6.16: Position of Line After Addition to Right-hand Window

It was observed that the majority of students in the early weeks of the study did not indent and align these lines of code that they had moved and this caused them some difficulty in initially understanding and identifying the control structures that were within their programs. However, most students soon recognised the usefulness of code alignment and made extensive use of the indent / outdent facility. The impression was that all students found the indent / outdent facility very easy to use and that it was a useful support.

6.2.3.4 Summary
In overall terms, the editing of lines of code in CORT and the copying of code to Visual BASIC for testing purposes caused initial problems with a small number of students. The CORT editor was purposely created to be as simple as possible so that not too great a cognitive load would be imposed upon students and to this end it appeared to meet this specification. Whilst recognising that improvements to the editor and the copy / paste mechanism of lines of code to Visual BASIC are desirable, the observations and interviews that took place suggested that there was little detrimental affect on student learning.

6.3 Summary of Usability Elements

The overall impressions gained from the usability study was that that the majority of students quickly became comfortable with the basic functionality of CORT and that it met the original requirements of providing a sound technological support for students in their learning of programming via the part-complete solution method. The usability study identified three main areas where CORT was seen to provide some initial problems for some users in terms of utility and functionality. These were:

- Operation of the problem files;

- Manipulation of the lines of code; and

- Editing the lines of code.

In all cases, the actual impediments these difficulties posed for learning tended to be minimal with students quickly overcoming difficulties through their experiences and continued use. The majority of the problems were seen to disappear within the first few weeks of the course and where the interface problems lingered, successful workarounds were found by all students.

The small learning curve of CORT suggested that the extraneous cognitive load imposed upon students by CORT's usability was quite minimal, leaving students with more unused working memory available to concentrate on solving the part-complete problems.

From the usability study, the following changes emerged as means by which the usability of CORT could be improved upon in future versions:

- Associating the CORT part-complete solution file extension of "pcs" with the CORT program so that the CORT program automatically opens when such a "pcs" file is double-clicked on within Windows Explorer.

- Allowing a CORT problem statement window to be open at the same time as the CORT line manipulation windows.

- Changing the current expansion / contraction mechanism of the line manipulation windows by providing a vertical "slider" between the windows. Such a slider is used in many Windows' interfaces and can be moved left or right by the mouse in order to increase or decrease the width of the windows.

- Permitting the dragging and dropping of lines of code between the windows (the large left and right arrow buttons would be removed).

- Disallowing the placement of lines of code between procedures in the right hand window.

- Having a menu appear in the right-hand window (when the mouse is right-clicked) to allow blank lines to be inserted.

- Having the lines that have been moved to the right hand window appear in a different colour to others (in order to distinguish them from the original lines of code in the part-complete solution).

- Allowing lines to be moved back to the left hand window and to be placed in their original positions.

- Having a "waste bin" window into which lines that were thought not to be required could be placed.

- Improving the functionality of the CORT editor to:

  - Place horizontal lines between procedures;

  - Use colour for keywords in a similar way to the Visual BASIC editor; and

  - Give some basic syntactical help when keywords are entered without the complexity of the Visual BASIC editor.

- Providing a mechanism to automatically indent and align lines of code in the right hand code window of CORT.

- Providing a function within CORT to display a text file that might be needed for a problem

- Improving the mechanism by which a Visual BASIC file is loaded and the CORT code is copied into Visual BASIC. This mechanism should be seamless to the user.

Chapter 7
How the CORT System Supports the Learning Process

7.1 Introduction

This chapter is an analysis of the research data with respect to the second research question which sought to investigate how the part-complete solution method (PCSM) within the CORT system supported the learning process. This was done in a qualitative way by observing students and particularly investigating the cognitive strategies that they used when attempting to solve problems with the CORT system.

Investigating student cognitive strategies and student engagement with learning materials, or in this case the CORT system, is a sound strategy to determine how well those materials support the learning process. Not all materials do provide support. For example, Sweller, van Merrienboer & Paas (1998) found in an experiment that some students did not adequately engage with their learning materials and were therefore not able to make the most effective use of those materials. This suggests that those students did not gain adequate support from the materials with which they had been attempting to engage with.

When students engage well with learning materials in a learning environment, then higher order thinking is encouraged and it is more likely that they will construct relevant knowledge in the domain that they are attempting to learn (Oliver & Herrington, 2001).

7.2 Analysis of Student Solution Methods using CORT

In this investigation into CORT's support for the learning process, a total of eight students in the CORT group were observed whilst they attempted programming. The students were observed in the following way. The same two students were observed during nine computer laboratories, and each of three pairs of students was observed for three computer laboratories. The students were not necessarily observed during all of their problem solving attempts. This was because a student might have been absent or, in weeks when there were two problems to attempt, a student may have spent all of the laboratory time on the first problem. Table 7.1 shows: the students; the weeks in which they observed; and the problem numbers that they were observed attempting. Student names have been omitted in order to ensure anonymity and full details of the research design have been described previously in Chapter 5.

Table 7.1: Student Observation Details

Student	Week Numbers of Laboratory	Problem Numbers Observed
Student A	2 – 5, 7 - 11	2 – 7, 11, 17, 18
Student B	2 – 5, 7 - 11	2 – 8, 11 – 18
Student C	2 – 4	2 – 4
Student D	2 – 4	2 – 5
Student E	5, 7, 8	7, 9, 10, 13
Student F	5, 7, 8	7, 8, 11, 13
Student G	9 – 11	15, 17
Student H	9 – 11	15, 17, 18

7.2.1 Levels of Cognitive Strategy with the CORT System

The forms of learner cognitive strategy were tabulated and levels were identified from the forms of student activities observed. This determination of levels provided a discrete set for analyses and inquiry.

From the observations of student activities that took place by the researcher, five distinct levels of cognitive strategy were identified with respect to CORT. These ranged from the lowest level of cognitive strategy where a student demonstrated no planning and randomly moved lines from the left hand window into a part-complete solution, through to the highest level where a student demonstrated thorough planning and testing of a problem solution. These levels were classified by the researcher and are described in Table 7.2.

Table 7.2: Classification of Levels of Cognitive Strategy

Level of Cognitive Strategy	Solution Method
1	Unplanned and random. For example a student: • Does not read through the part-complete solution. • Chooses a line of code at random from the set of lines in the left-hand window and then moves it to a random position in the right-hand window. • Tests their code in an unplanned and random manner. • Does not trace code in the Visual BASIC debugger.
2	A low level of consideration in their approach. For example a student: • Partially reads a part-complete solution. • Chooses a line at random and then moves the line with some thought to a position in the right-hand window. • Identifies a subset of lines in the left-hand window, chooses a line to move from that subset and moves it to a random position in the right-hand window. • Demonstrates little planning in their testing. • Does not trace code in the Visual BASIC debugger.
3	Some levels of consideration in their approach. For example a student: • Thoroughly reads a part-complete solution. • Identifies a subset of lines in the left-hand window and then chooses a line to move from that subset. • Moves the line with some thought to a position in the right-hand window. However this is done at a micro level such that they move the line to be adjacent to lines which look similar, e.g. the line $n = 1$ is in the right hand window and therefore they move $n = n + 1$ to be close to this line • Tests and traces their program several times.

Level of Cognitive Strategy	Solution Method
4	High levels of consideration and some evidence of strategy. For example a student: • Thoroughly reads and studies a part-complete solution. • Carefully selects lines of code. • Carefully and thoughtfully places the lines into the part-complete solution. • If a part-complete solution has more than one procedure, they work on one procedure at a time in the right hand window. • Shows some evidence of testing the part-complete solution in a strategic manner, making extensive use of the Visual BASIC debugger.
5	Deliberate approach. For example a student: • Thoroughly reads and studies a part-complete solution and the lines of code in the left-hand window. • Demonstrates initial planning. • Carefully selects lines of code and thoughtfully places the lines into the part-complete solution. • If a part-complete solution has more than one procedure, they work on one procedure at the time in the right hand window. They might thoroughly test that procedure that they have completed the code for before they work on completing the code for other procedures. • Tests the part-complete solution at appropriate points to check their hypotheses about the lines and the way the program should behave.

7.2.2 Support Types Identified and Scaffolded by the CORT System

The students were observed to use CORT in a number of different ways in response to the difficulties they experienced while attempting the programming problems. The use of CORT helped scaffold the students to various degrees and this section describes a classification of support types and an explanation of how estimates were made of the scaffolding provided by CORT. The types of support provided by CORT were categorised as syntactical, semantic, structural, and algorithmic. These categories are standard forms within programming environments (e.g., Soloway, 1986; Winslow, 1996). Examples of the types are shown in Table 7.3.

Table 7.3: CORT Support Types

Support Type	Example
Syntax	A choice of two lines is available: Let txtName.ForeColor = vbRed Let txtName.ForeColor = Red A student initially chooses the second line which is syntactically incorrect and uses CORT to identify the error.
Semantic	A choice of two lines is available to place a string literal into a variable. Let personName = "Bill" Let personName = Bill A student initially chooses the second line which is semantically incorrect and uses CORT to identify the error.
Structural	**Example 1**: A student places variable declarations statements (DIM statements) in incorrect positions and uses CORT to identify the errors. **Example 2**: A student initially places lines of code in between (outside of) procedures and uses

Support Type	Example
	CORT to identify the errors.

Support Type	Example

Algorithmic	In solving an algorithm to determine the average of a set of numbers, a line of code is placed in the wrong position. For example:
	Do While Not EOF(1)
	    Input #1, number
	      Let total = total + number
	Loop
	Let count = count + 1
	Let average = total / count
	In the above, the incrementing of the variable **count** should be within the loop. The CORT system helps the student identify the error.

In addition to determining the types of support that the CORT system provided for students for the problems that they attempted, it was important to determine the degree of assistance that CORT offered. Table 7.4 shows this classification of the scaffolding levels provided by CORT and their meanings.

Table 7.4: Classification of Levels of Scaffolding

Scaffolding Level	Meaning
1	The CORT system provided little help in solving the problem, but did help identify the errors.
2	The CORT system provided some help in solving the problem.
3	The CORT system provided a lot of help in solving the problem.

The following section describes the programming problems that were attempted by the students and, for each problem, discusses how the CORT system was used by the students in their problem solution. The CORT method that was used is also indicated. A summary of the problems was shown in Table 5.7 of Chapter 5 and the three methods were described in Chapter 3. The CORT methods are:

- **Method 1.** All of the lines of code that are missing from the program are provided as options.

- **Method 2.** All of the lines of code that are missing from the program, together with some extra lines of code that are not needed to complete the program, are provided. These extra lines act as "distracters".

- **Method 3.** Some of the lines of code that are missing from the program might be provided, however some other missing lines must be keyed-in by the learner.

To ensure reliability in the coding of student behaviours, each of the problems was coded by the researcher and an experienced colleague. Consistency was checked by comparing the coding schemas and results. A consistency of over 90% was achieved indicating high levels of reliability in this approach.

Appendix 8 contains: the detailed descriptions of the problems; the part-complete solutions and missing lines; and the problem solutions.

Problem 2

Problem Description

This was the first problem attempted by the students and was very simple. It was very similar to problem 1 which had been solved by the tutor for the students at the beginning of the computer laboratory as a way of demonstrating the CORT system. Because of this similarity, it was thought that using CORT method 1 would make the solution too simple, and therefore method 2 was used. There were 3 missing lines from the part-complete solution and 6 lines were given in the left-hand window, 3 being distracter lines. The missing lines were from three separate yet simple procedures.

Problem Solution

Students B and C brought the necessary lines across to the correct positions in the part-complete solution on their first attempt. They both carefully studied the part complete solution and the lines in the left-hand window before doing this. Because the problem was relatively trivial, they did not test the solution until all three lines had been placed into position. For these reasons their cognitive strategy and scaffolding levels were identified as 5 and 3 respectively.

Student A quickly brought the code into the part-complete solution and generated one simple syntax error. He soon found and corrected the error when he attempted to execute the program in the CORT system, indicative of a type 4 cognitive strategy. CORT provided a high level of scaffolding indicative of type 3.

Although there were 3 event procedures in the right-hand window, each of which required one line from the left-hand window, student D moved 3 lines of code into the first event procedure which demonstrated a misunderstanding of a structural type. She recognised that her solution was wrong but was unsure how to correct the program and asked the tutor for help. She was unsure of event procedures although this problem was similar to problem 1 which the tutor had gone through with all the students. The CORT system had therefore provided low level structural support to the student as the incorrect output from the program indicated that an error was present. She also made the same syntax error as student A and when she ran the program she recognised the problem and replaced the line of code with the correct line from within CORT. She had been engaged with the system at a fairly low level which suggested a cognitive strategy of type 2. The system had provided her with some support, however it did not help overcome the structural difficulty which was characteristic of type 2 scaffolding.

Table 7.5 summarises the types of supports, the levels of cognitive strategy, and the scaffolding provided for the students who were observed attempting problem 2.

Table 7.5: Supports and Levels of Cognitive Strategy and Scaffolding for Problem 2

Student Identifier	Syntax Support	Semantic Support	Structural Support	Algorithmic Support	Cognitive Strategy	Scaffolding Provided
A	✓				4	3
B					5	3
C					5	3
D	✓		✓		2	2

Problem 3

Problem Description

This problem was the first problem that required the student to declare and use variables; carry out some simple arithmetic processing; and to output values to a Visual BASIC form which acts as a program's interface to a user. There was no input of values from text boxes on the form, values being assigned to variables directly in the program. Because several new concepts had been introduced, CORT method 1 was utilised with all the lines of code in the left hand window being required in the solution to the problem.

Problem Solution

Student B printed off the part complete solution and lines from the left hand window, studied the code very carefully, and then moved the lines from the left hand window directly into their correct positions. Testing then indicated that the solution was correct. CORT had scaffolded him at a high level, identified as type 3. He was very engaged with the system and it provided him with the necessary supports to solve the problem. His cognitive strategy was characteristic of type 5.

Students C and D had structural problems with respect to positioning of the "Dim" statements (statements that declare the variables to be used in the program). They both moved statements that were assigning data to variables ("Let" statements) to positions in the program that were before the "Dim" statements. This seemed to indicate that the students did not understand the purpose of the "Dim" statements. Indeed student D stated that the "Dim" statements did not seem to "do" anything and this suggests that the students lacked an understanding of the difference between declarative and procedural programming statements. The CORT system helped the students recognise the problem as the error messages that were generated in Visual BASIC, when the programs were tested, indicated that the variables in the data assignment statements were unknown. This helped the students reposition the "Dim" statements.

Student C also had a problem with respect to the statement that clears the output (the "Cls" statement) in the output area (a "picture" box) of a form. This statement should have been positioned before the output statement, however she had the statements the other way round. This resulted in the output from the program being immediately cleared and it therefore appeared that there was no output whatsoever from the program. She corrected it by testing within Visual BASIC. The cognitive strategy employed by student C showed levels of consideration of type 3 whereas student D showed a higher level of consideration identified to be type 4. CORT provided high levels of scaffolding support for both students C and D indicative of type 3.

Student A tested his program with 6 lines of code still being in the left-hand window. When asked the reason for this, he stated that his strategy was to bring lines of code that he understood into the solution thereby creating an incomplete solution. He then tested this incomplete solution in Visual BASIC to "see what happened" in the belief that error messages and / or output would help him work out where the lines that were still in the left-hand window should go. The statements that he had omitted were the 5 "Dim" statements and the "Cls" statement. This strategy worked for him as the error messages that were output made him realise the need for the "Dim" statements and that they were needed before the "Let" statements. He then brought those statements into the correct position in his solution. He had the same problem as student C with respect to the positioning of the "Cls". However, because he had tested the program without the "Cls" statement and observed "correct" output, he worked out what the purpose of the "Cls" statement was and moved it to its correct position. He showed some levels of consideration in his cognitive strategy characteristic of type 3. CORT provided the necessary scaffolding for him to be successful and it was indicative of type 3.

The errors associated with the incorrect positioning of the "Dim" and "Cls" statements came about because their semantics were not understood. This then led to structural errors in the programs. In all cases the testing of the programs in the CORT system alerted students to their errors and, by experimenting with the lines of code, the students gained an understanding of the purpose of the statements. Table 7.6 shows the types of supports, the levels of cognitive strategy, and the scaffolding provided for the students who were observed attempting problem 3.

Table 7.6: Supports and Levels of Cognitive Strategy and Scaffolding for Problem 3

Student Identifier	Syntax Support	Semantic Support	Structural Support	Algorithmic Support	Cognitive Strategy	Scaffolding Provided
A		✓	✓		5	3
B					5	3
C		✓	✓		3	3
D		✓	✓		4	3

Problem 4

Problem Description

This problem was similar to problem 3 as it required the student to declare and use variables; carry out some simple arithmetic processing; and to output values. Again, there was no requirement to input values from text boxes on the screen required as values were assigned to variables directly in the program. This problem did have an extra degree of difficulty as it had requirements within it such as:

```
Increase the variable balance by 4.5% of its value
```

Because the problem was similar in nature to problem 3, CORT method 2 was utilised with only some of the lines of code in the left hand window being required in the solution to the problem.

Problem Solution

As with problem 3, student B studied the requirements and part complete solution carefully together with the lines of code in the left hand window. He then moved across the necessary lines into their correct positions and tested the program. He demonstrated a high level of cognitive strategy and the CORT system had provided the necessary support to help him solve the problem. This took about 30 minutes. For these reasons, the cognitive strategy and scaffolding levels were coded 5 and 3 respectively.

Students A, C and D all chose the following incorrect line of code for the output of the contents of the variable **balance**:

```
picDisplay.Print "Final balance is $"; "balance"
```

This was a semantic error indicating a lack of understanding of the difference between a variable and a string literal. Through testing, they all recognised that the output from the program was incorrect and they then went back into CORT in order to choose the correct line of code.

Students A and C both had the same algorithmic error as they both chose an incorrect set of assignment ("Let") statements for their solutions and did so quickly with little thought. They did place the incorrect set of assignment statements into the correct position in the part complete solution. They both recognised that the program output was incorrect and then replaced the lines of code with the "correct" set after reconsideration of the set of lines in the left-hand window.

Student D had a structural error as she placed an assignment statement at the top of the program, outside of the event procedure. The CORT system alerted her to the error and she moved the line to the correct position. She did spend some time deliberating over which set of assignment statements should be used and asked the tutor about the meaning of statements such as:

```
balance = balance + balance * 0.0525
```

She then moved the correct assignment statements into position and her program was correct.

The scaffolding levels for students A and C were type 3 as the students solved the problem by just using CORT. Student D demonstrated level 2 for scaffolding as she required some help from the tutor, CORT not providing all the help that she required.

Student D demonstrated a high level of consideration for her cognitive strategy, characteristic of level 4, as she only had two minor errors and had carefully thought about the problem. Students A and C had had some difficulties in determining how to solve the algorithm, demonstrating some levels of consideration in their approach which was indicative of a cognitive strategy of type 3.

Table 7.7: Supports and Levels of Cognitive Strategy and Scaffolding for Problem 4

Student Identifier	Syntax Support	Semantic Support	Structural Support	Algorithmic Support	Cognitive Strategy	Scaffolding Provided
A		✓		✓	3	3
B					5	3
C		✓		✓	3	3
D		✓	✓		4	2

Problem 5

Problem Description

This was the first problem that required data input through text boxes that were on a Visual Basic form. Some simple arithmetic processing was also required together with data output to the form. CORT method 2 was utilised as the new concepts that were introduced were not thought by the researcher to be too cognitively demanding.

Problem Solution

Student C was absent from the computer laboratory in which this problem was attempted.

Student A was thoughtful in his approach to this problem, solved it relatively quickly, but did have some semantic difficulties.

He chose the incorrect set of data input statements, the correct statements making use of the "Val" function which converts string data, as input through a text box, into numeric data. The run time error messages that were output in Visual BASIC alerted him to the problem and he then chose the correct statements.

He also placed the "Cls" statement in the wrong position resulting in the clearing of the output. He had made the same error in problem 3 and so he quickly recognised the error and moved the line to its correct position.

CORT had provided a high level of scaffolding for him, indicative of type 3. He did show high levels of consideration in his cognitive strategy, with the exception of his choice of data input statements, characteristic of type 4.

Student B had the same difficulty with the "Cls" statement as student A and corrected it after checking the output. He appeared to rush this problem, resulting in choosing the incorrect output statements, the output being displayed on two lines instead of three. He experimented with the other possible lines of code and corrected the problem. The numeric result from his program was also incorrect indicating an algorithmic error. The CORT system supported him in removing the error as he experimented with the other lines until the output was correct.

CORT had provided a high level of scaffolding for student B, characteristic of type 3. His cognitive strategy showed some levels of consideration, less than student A, and indicative of type 3.

Student D did not use CORT in a particularly thoughtful way when she attempted this problem. She too chose incorrect input statements like student A and she also chose the incorrect output statements. She did fix these with CORT's help but by using a trial and error approach.

She also had problems with the names of objects that were on the Visual BASIC form and which were also in the programming code. She made use of the CORT editor to add data declaration ("Dim") statements for the object names. Error messages concerning this structural error were then output in Visual BASIC alerting her to the problem and this helped her recognise the difference between objects and variables. She then removed the superfluous statements.

The cognitive strategy that she employed showed a lack of thought in solving this problem. The strategy was unplanned and indicative of type 1. CORT however again provided strong support and the scaffolding level was characteristic of type 3.

Table 7.8: Supports and Levels of Cognitive Strategy and Scaffolding for Problem 5

Student Identifier	Syntax Support	Semantic Support	Structural Support	Algorithmic Support	Cognitive Strategy	Scaffolding Provided
A		✓			4	3
B		✓		✓	3	3
D		✓	✓		1	3

Problem 6

Problem Description

This problem was the first problem that required data input from a sequential text file. There were two records within the text file and to solve the problem it was necessary to: input the first record; carry out some simple processing; output the results; and then repeat the input – process – output for the second record. A loop was not required as loops had not yet been introduced.

As most students initially find file handling conceptually difficult, CORT method 1 was used.

Problem Solution

Only students A and B attempted this problem during the computer laboratory. Student C was absent and student D had spent all of the computer laboratory time on the previous problem.

Student B was again a very deliberate in his approach to the solving of this problem. He moved all the lines into place correctly and had just one difficulty which was with the line:

```
Print teamName; " has "; points; " points"
```

He thought that the line must be wrong because the name of the variable and string literal were the same, however testing in that the CORT system showed that it was indeed correct. He had demonstrated a higher level of cognitive strategy in his approach characteristic of type 5. CORT provided him with strong scaffolding of type 3.

Student A had a similar difficulty with the above line of code. He was less deliberate in his approach to solving this problem and had several errors along the way. He had had difficulties with "Dim" statements in problem 3 and they also caused him difficulties in this problem. He placed a corresponding "Dim" statement before every line of code that used the variable within that "Dim" statement and used the CORT editor to create extra "Dim" statements. This resulted in an attempt to declare program variables more than once within the program. Error messages were output when the program was run in Visual BASIC and he then deleted these extra "Dim" statements.

He also had difficulties with the input - process - output structuring of the program. He firstly had the output statements before the input statements which he corrected after he viewed the output from Visual BASIC. He then had the two input statements together, followed by the two processing statements, and finally the two output statements. This resulted in the values within the input variables being overwritten by those from the second record before processing had taken place. The two outputs were identical and after some experimentation and retesting, the program worked correctly.

Student A had demonstrated only a low level of consideration that suggested a cognitive strategy of type 2. Again, CORT had provided the necessary scaffolding indicative of type 3.

Table 7.9: Supports and Levels of Cognitive Strategy and Scaffolding for Problem 6

Student Identifier	Syntax Support	Semantic Support	Structural Support	Algorithmic Support	Cognitive Strategy	Scaffolding Provided
A		✓	✓		2	3
B		✓			5	3

Problem 7

Problem Description

This problem required input via text boxes; processing of the data; and outputting of results to a form. Its solution required the use of: integer arithmetic operators, that had been introduced during the lecture; and of a relatively large number of assignment statements. CORT method 2 was used as it was thought that the solution might be too straightforward with students expending little mental processing, should CORT method 1 be used.

Problem Solution

This problem was attempted in week 5 and in addition to observing students A and B, observations of students E and F were made in place of C and D.

Integer operators had only been covered briefly in that week's lecture and all of the students had semantic difficulties with the lines of code that included them. Two examples of the statements required were:

```
Let numberOf100DollarNotes = wage \ 100
Let leftOver = wage Mod 100
```

The integer division operator "\" is the equivalent to "DIV" in many other programming languages and "Mod" is used to determine the remainder in an integer division.

Student B read the relevant section of the textbook to gain a more thorough understanding of the operators whereas the other three students attempted to determine the operators' meanings by experimentation with the CORT system.

All of the students found it demanding to determine the order of the thirteen assignments statements that were required for the algorithm that determined the breakdown of a monetary payment into $100, $50, $20 dollar notes etc. Students B was very strategic in his approach to the problem as he began by bringing just two of the lines of code into the right-hand window and then testing the code to view the output. He then gradually introduced more lines of code, tested the code, and then amended it as necessary until the output was correct.

Students A and F had a similar approach to that of student B, however they moved lines into the right-hand window with little deliberation and then tested the code to "see what happened". They both eventually got the correct answer but took longer than student B.

Student E had difficulties as she had begun by bringing the following lines of code into the right-hand window:

```
Let numberOf100DollarNotes = wage \ 100
Let numberOf50DollarNotes = leftOver \ 50
```

In the above, the value in the variable **leftOver** was zero, however she did not know how to use the Visual BASIC "debug" system to trace through the code and recognise this fact. The researcher had to intervene and help her in this aspect of the CORT system. She then corrected these initial lines, but then had difficulties ordering the lines of code correctly and this appeared to reveal a lack of understanding of the underlying conceptual or notional machine. CORT had not provided support for the algorithmic difficulties that she had.

For this problem, student B had demonstrated the highest level of cognitive strategy characteristic of type 5. Students A and F showed a lower level of cognitive strategy indicative of type 3. Student E's approach was unplanned and random and her cognitive strategy was identified as type 1. CORT had provided strong type 3 scaffolding for students A, B and F. Student E required help from the tutor which suggested that her scaffolding was type 2.

Table 7.10: Supports and Levels of Cognitive Strategy and Scaffolding for Problem 7

Student Identifier	Syntax Support	Semantic Support	Structural Support	Algorithmic Support	Cognitive Strategy	Scaffolding Provided

		✓		✓	3	3
A		✓		✓	3	3
B		✓		✓	5	3
E		✓		✓	2	2
F		✓		✓	3	3

Problem 8

Problem Description

This problem again required input via text boxes; processing of the data; and outputting of results to a form. Its solution required the use of some simple string processing that had been introduced in the lecture. Because it was thought that the cognitive load would not be too great, CORT method 3 was used such that there were extra lines in the left-hand window and it being necessary for the students to key-in 1 line using the CORT editor.

Problem Solution

Only students B and F attempted this problem in the laboratory as the other two students had spent all of their time on the previous problem.

Both students had difficulties with the syntax and semantics of the line of code that had to be keyed-in. The previous two lines in the solution were:

```
Let firstPart = Left(telNumber, 2)
Let middlePart = Mid(telNumber, 4, 4)
```

and the line that had to be keyed-in was:

```
Let lastPart = Right(telNumber, 4)
```

Student B had an extra parameter in the statement as he had matched the syntax of the "Mid" function rather than the "Left" function. The Visual BASIC editor alerted him to the problem and he was able to correct it. Student F keyed in:

```
Let lastPart = Last(telNumber, 4, 4)
```

She had chosen to use a non-existent function "Last" as she had thought that the last few characters of **telNumber** were required. She too had an extra parameter in the code. The CORT system did not help her determine that the function "Left" was required and she had to find this information from the textbook.

Although the students had received syntax error messages for the above, their errors stemmed from their lack of understanding of the semantics of the various string handling statements.

Student F also chose incorrect lines of code such that a telephone number, which should have been stored as a string, was stored as an integer. The CORT system output an arithmetic overflow error which was only of limited use in helping her recognise the actual problem with her code. She did replace 2 lines of code that were causing problems with the correct lines as they were the only alternatives. The program then worked correctly and her semantic error was solved.

Student B had shown a high level of consideration and some evidence of strategy in his approach and this was indicative   of type 4. Student F demonstrated some consideration in her approach to the problem suggesting a cognitive strategy of 3. CORT provided strong type 3 support for student B, however it had not helped student F identify the correct string function required and her scaffolding demonstrated type 2 characteristics.

Table 7.11: Supports and Levels of Cognitive Strategy and Scaffolding for Problem 8

Student Identifier	Syntax Support	Semantic Support	Structural Support	Algorithmic Support	Cognitive Strategy	Scaffolding Provided
B	✓				4	3
F	✓	✓			3	2

Problem 9

Problem Description

This problem again required input via text boxes; processing of the data; and outputting to a form. The numeric output had to be done three times with different numbers of decimal places and this had to be achieved by "calling" three different general procedures. CORT method 2 was utilised and each correct "call" statement had two associated distracter lines. It was hoped that the choosing of incorrect statements, for example with the wrong number of parameters, would help students gain an understanding of the underlying mechanisms that take place.

Problem Solution

The researcher was absent in week 6 when problems 9 and 10 were attempted. However, student E was also absent in week 6 and she decided to undertake the work that she had missed and to attempt problems 9 and 10 in week 7. Hence student E was the only student observed for problems 9 and 10.

The new concept of calling general procedures caused this student some conceptual difficulties and, probably because of her lack of understanding of the underlying mechanism, she used CORT in a rather haphazard way when she attempted to solve this problem.

There were several structural difficulties including:

- Having "Call" statements within the actual procedure that was to be called. For example:

```
Private Sub OutputToTwoPlaces(balance As Single)
     Call OutputToTwoPlaces(accountBalance)
End Sub
```

She indicated that she had placed the "Call" statement in this position because the names "OutputToTwoPlaces" matched.

- Placing "Call" statements to output results within the correct procedure but before the necessary processing had been done.

- Placing "call" statements outside of all procedures, for example just after "End Sub".

- Choosing an incorrect "Call" statement. For example, she incorrectly chose:

```
Call OutputToTwoPlaces
```

when she should have chosen:

```
Call OutputToTwoPlaces(accountBalance)
```

- Having the output "Print" statements within the main procedure rather than the general procedures that were being "Called".

The CORT system provided some limited help for the student with some of the above difficulties. Some of the error messages provided by Visual BASIC helped her. For example:

"Only comments may appear after End Sub ..."

However other error messages were less helpful. For example, when an incorrect "Call" statement was chosen, Visual BASIC gave an error message of:

"Compile Error, argument not optional"

and the student did not understand what this meant.

With the benefit of hindsight, this problem would have been better to use CORT method 1 such that there were no distracter lines. The CORT system did enable the student to eventually solve this problem but the researcher suspects that she still had not grasped the underlying mechanisms that were taking place during program execution. Her cognitive strategy demonstrated only a low level of consideration of type 2. CORT provided her with moderate type 2 scaffolding.

Table 7.12: Supports and Levels of Cognitive Strategy and Scaffolding for Problem 9

Student Identifier	Syntax Support	Semantic Support	Structural Support	Algorithmic Support	Cognitive Strategy	Scaffolding Provided
E			✓		2	2

Problem 10

Problem Description

This problem again required input via text boxes; processing of the data; and outputting to a form. The processing required the use of two user-defined functions. Because only a small number of lines were required to complete the solution, it was decided to use CORT method 2.

Problem Solution

As with problem 9, only student E was observed attempting this problem. User defined functions have some similarity to general procedures, which had been used within problem 9, however the way in which they are "called" is different. She again had structural difficulties which demonstrated a lack of understanding of the underlying mechanism. Because of this, her approach was similar to that of problem 9. Her mistakes included:

- Placing the output statements in the functions instead of the main procedure.

- Placing the statement to clear the output, "Cls", straight after the output statement. This had caused problems for other students who had been observed when attempting problems 3 and 5.

- Placing the assignment statements that carried out the processing in the main procedure instead of the functions.

- Placing the assignment statements, that carried out the processing, outside of the main procedure and the function definitions.

As with problem 9, the above positioning of statements, followed by testing in the Visual BASIC environment, eventually resulted in student E creating a correct solution. Some of the error messages that were output were helpful, such as:

"variable not defined for the variable miles"

"Only comments may appear after End Sub ..."

Also, the viewing of incorrect output, and the subsequent tracing of her partial programs helped her gain understanding and correct the code.

Her cognitive strategy for this problem was observed to be greater than for problem 9 with some levels of consideration but she still moved some lines in a random manner. Her approach was characteristic of type 3. CORT did provide her with all the necessary scaffolding to solve the problem and was identified as type 3.

Table 7.13: Supports and Levels of Cognitive Strategy and Scaffolding for Problem 10

Student Identifier	Syntax Support	Semantic Support	Structural Support	Algorithmic Support	Cognitive Strategy	Scaffolding Provided
E		✓	✓		3	3

Problem 11

Problem Description

This problem again required input via text boxes; processing of the data; and outputting to a form. The processing required the use of the selection control structure in the form of "If" statements. The cognitive load was kept relatively low by only having one main procedure in the program, calls to general procedure and functions not being required. As students initially often find the selection control structure difficult, CORT method 1 was used.

Problem Solution

Students A, B and F were observed attempting this problem, student F having arrived 35 minutes late for the one hour laboratory.

Student F was careful and deliberate in her approach to solving this problem and she moved the necessary lines into position without error. This was indicative of type 5 cognitive strategy. CORT   provided her with the necessary supports and the scaffolding was therefore identified as type 3.

Students A and B both had difficulties with the necessary logic. The problem required the input of a number that represented a number of hours that an employee had worked during a week. The aim of the program was then to determine the employee wage amount, the rates being different for up to 35 hours; over 35 hours and up to 45 hours; and over 45 hours. Both students manipulated the statements in the logical "If" statements, testing and tracing their programs at various points in Visual BASIC. They both finally obtained the correct solution however had done so without careful initial thought but by a controlled trial and testing method. The fact that they did get the correct solution suggests that in this instance, the CORT system had provided good scaffolding for the determination of the algorithm.

Student B stated that the words "End If" that appeared in "If" statements caused him confusion. An example would be:

```
If hoursWorked > 45 Then
      [processing ...]
End If
```

The "End If" line was one of the required lines that was in the left-hand window. He indicated that he thought that there should be a condition after it, as conditions normally followed the word "If". This was a semantic problem that CORT overcame as the line of code had to be used in the algorithm and so he knew that it must have been correct.

Both students A and B had demonstrated some levels of consideration in their thinking which suggested a type 3 cognitive strategy. CORT had provided them with the necessary type 3 scaffolding.

Table 7.14: Supports and Levels of Cognitive Strategy and Scaffolding for Problem 11

Student Identifier	Syntax Support	Semantic Support	Structural Support	Algorithmic Support	Cognitive Strategy	Scaffolding Provided
A				✓	3	3
B		✓		✓	3	3
F					5	3

Problem Description

This problem required input via text boxes; processing of the data; and outputting of results to a form. It had three event procedures and a user defined function. The aim of the program was to input the weight of a letter and then to calculate the cost of postage to the United States. The solution required the use of the "Select Case" control structure to determine the postage cost and this control structure had been introduced in that week's lecture.

Because the "Select Case" statement had a number of lines of code that were very similar, it was decided to use CORT method 3 for this problem. The students were informed that there were missing lines from the "Select Case" statement, however all of the lines in the left-hand window had to be used.

Problem Solution

Only student B was observed attempting this problem as students A and F had spent all of the laboratory time on the previous problem and, as stated earlier, student E had attempted the problems that she had missed when she was absent from the previous week's laboratory session.

Student B had two main difficulties with the program. The first one was algorithmic, the main procedure having an "If" statement that validated the input data. He had the logic incorrect as the function to determine the postage cost was only being "called" when the data was invalid, rather than the other way around. He corrected this logic after tracing the code in Visual BASIC, however he indicated that he had thought that the "normal" processing for valid data should have had to go in the "If" part and the processing for "invalid" data in the "Else" part, and yet this program had the logic the other way around. This seemed to reveal semantic misunderstanding of the "If" statement that was clarified by the CORT system.

The second difficulty that he had was with the syntax of the "Select Case" statement. The lines of code that had to be keyed in were:

```
Case 0 To 20
    Let PostageCost = 1.4
```

He started by guessing the syntax for the statement and received error messages from Visual BASIC. The CORT system did not help him with the syntax and he had to go to the textbook resource to find the details. He then completed the program.

He was observed to have employed a high level of consideration and some strategy in his approach which was characteristic of type 4 cognitive strategy. CORT provided him with some help but not with the syntax of the "Select Case" statement and this suggested type 2 scaffolding.

Table 7.15: Supports and Levels of Cognitive Strategy and Scaffolding for Problem 12

Student Identifier	Syntax Support	Semantic Support	Structural Support	Algorithmic Support	Cognitive Strategy	Scaffolding Provided
B				✓	4	2

Problem 13

Problem Description

This was the first problem that required the use of a repetition control structure in the form of a "While" loop. The solution required: the input and validation of a number; and the processing and output of a multiplication table within the loop. It had a main event procedure and a general procedure in which the processing and output took place. There were three other procedures in the program, each of which was very simple and which required just one line of code. Also, this was the first problem in which the students had to add a button object to the Visual BASIC interface, the complete interfaces having been provided in the previous problems. It was thought that the cognitive load on the students would be relatively high in this problem and so it was decided to us CORT method 1.

Problem Solution

Student A was absent from the laboratory session and so only students B, E and F were observed.

All three students had difficulties understanding a new function, "IsNumeric", that had been introduced. The CORT system did not help them and they had to either ask the tutor or find out information about the function from the textbook. Students E and F placed some lines of code outside of procedures and the error messages from Visual BASIC alerted them to the mistake.

The requirement to add a button object to the Visual BASIC form only caused student E a problem. Although such a process might not be considered programming in its truest sense, the ability to add such objects and change their properties is now part of software development. The CORT system provides no help concerning how to do this and, because CORT had included complete interfaces for all of the problems prior to this one, it might be considered that the scaffolding had been too great in this area for previous problems.

As expected, all three students had difficulty with the loop that was needed in the solution. The final structure of the loop was to be as follows:

```
Let C = 1
Do While C <= 12
      picDisplay.Print C; " x "; TableNum; " = "; C * TableNum
      Let C = C + 1
Loop
```

and the two statements that had to be moved from the left-hand window into the loop were the third and fourth in the above, the other three lines already being in the right-hand window.

Students B and E both initially had the statement that increments the counter, "Let C = C + 1", before the start of the loop. The testing in Visual BASIC resulted in an endless loop. Tracing of the code in Visual BASIC helped both overcome this difficulty. However, student B not only moved "Let C = C + 1" into the loop, but also "Let C = 1" resulting in another endless loop. Again tracing helped him correct this problem, however he then had the two statements that were correctly within the loop, the wrong way around resulting in incorrect output. Again, the trace mechanism helped him correct the problem.

It appears that for all three students, the CORT system helped them arrive at the correct loop structure for this problem. Also, along the way the students made a variety of mistakes that most likely helped their understanding of how the underlying loop structure works. At one point in the problem solving process, student B stated that he thought the beginning of the loop was at the statement "Let C = 1". When he had completed the problem, he indicated that he now had a deeper understanding and knew that the loop started at the "Do While" statement.

Student B also had an algorithmic error in connection with a nested "If" statement that was used in the validation of the data input. The following shows the structure of the statements that were initially in the right-hand window and it was only necessary for students to bring across two statements, each of which was an output error message:

```
If [condition 1] Then
       [processing]
       If [condition 2] Then
              [processing]
       Else

       End If
Else

End If
```

Student B brought across the line of code that would output the error message corresponding to [condition 1] to the position after the first "Else" and the line of code that would output the error message corresponding to [condition 2] to the position after the second "Else". He therefore had the error messages the wrong way round and when asked about their positions he stated that he thought that their order should be the same as the order of the conditions. Again, by using the tracing mechanism within the CORT system he was able to correct the problem.

The observations of the students suggested that student F approached the problem solution in the most strategic manner, had only made one small semantic error, and had used CORT in a careful and deliberate way to solve the algorithm involving the loop. This indicated a cognitive strategy of type 5. Student E demonstrated some consideration in her approach but was less careful in her testing. Her cognitive strategy was characteristic of type 4. Student B also showed consideration, had some strategy, but also made use of trial and error in various parts of the solution. This was indicative of type 4 cognitive strategy. The scaffolding level provided by CORT was high for both students B and F and was identified as type 3. It was identified as type 2 for student E because of CORT's lack of support for adding a button object to a form.

Table 7.16: Supports and Levels of Cognitive Strategy and Scaffolding for Problem 13

Student Identifier	Syntax Support	Semantic Support	Structural Support	Algorithmic Support	Cognitive Strategy	Scaffolding Provided
B		✓		✓	3	3
E		✓	✓	✓	4	2
F		✓	✓	✓	5	3

Problem Description

This problem also required the use of a "While" loop with data being input from a sequential text file. The first record in the file had to be input before the loop, and all of the other records had to be input within the loop, the processing of each record being straight forward. The output statement was to be after the loop had finished.

As the "While" statement had been used in the previous problem using CORT method 1, it was decided that CORT method 3 should be used. Hence, not all of the lines of code from the left-hand window were required and one line of code had to be keyed-in.

Problem Solution

Only student B was observed attempting this problem. Student A was absent and students E and F had arrived late for the laboratory session and spent the available time on the previous problem.

The CORT system provided Student B with structural support and support to determine the required algorithm. It also helped him recognise a syntax problem but it did not help him correct it. The structural difficulty concerned the choice of data input statement that was needed to obtain the first record. This record contained a person's name followed by their bank balance, and two data input statements were provided in the left-hand window, one of which was a distracter. The statements were:

```
Input #1, personName, initialBalance
Input #1, initialBalance, personName
```

He did not study the structure of the data in detail and chose the wrong "input" statement. However he recognised this when he ran the program and looked at the structure of the data in the file, something that he had not done earlier.

He also had difficulties with the algorithm which was supposed to use the above "Input" statement before a loop which was to input and process a series of transactions that were in the data file. Initially he placed the above "Input" statement within the loop causing the program to crash with an error message of "input past end of file". This forced him to then use Visual BASIC to trace through the code and to examine the contents of the key variables, thereby alerting him to the problem. He corrected the position of the "Input" statement.

The output statement had to be keyed-in and he had some difficulties with the necessary syntax even though he had viewed many lines of code with that syntax in previous problems. This seemed to indicate that although he could view and understand the syntax of such a line of code, he could not reproduce easily it. He went back and viewed the code of the previous problem in order to find the required syntax and then keyed-in the line correctly.

Student B had shown a high level of consideration in his approach with some evidence of strategy. This was characteristic of a type 4 cognitive strategy. CORT provided level 2 type scaffolding as it did not help him with all of the necessary syntax.

Table 7.17: Supports and Levels of Cognitive Strategy and Scaffolding for Problem 14

Student Identifier	Syntax Support	Semantic Support	Structural Support	Algorithmic Support	Cognitive Strategy	Scaffolding Provided
B	✓		✓	✓	4	2

Problem 15

Problem Description

This was an array processing problem, arrays having been introduced during that week's lecture. The requirements of the program were to load a one-dimensional numeric array of eight numbers from a text file; and output the array's contents such that:

- The first column contained the original eight numbers;

- The second column contained the eight numbers in reverse order; and

- The third column contained the sum of the corresponding numbers in columns 1 and 2.

Although array processing is difficult for most students, CORT method 3 was used with the cognitive load being kept relatively low by requiring only one line of code to be keyed-in and by only having two distracter lines in the left-hand window. The processing required was split between two procedures: an event procedure that executed at the start of the program (Form_Load); and an event procedure that executed when a button was clicked.

Problem Solution

Two different students, G and H, were observed in the laboratory in which this problem was attempted. Student B was also observed and student A was absent.

This problem contained a loop in both of the main procedures and this caused the students some difficulties. Student H brought most of the lines of code into the first procedure in the part-complete solution and he stated the reason for doing this was that he liked to try and solve the procedures in the order in which they appeared in the right-hand window. Student G used a similar method whereas Student B was observed to carefully read the problem statement, scroll deliberately through part-complete solution, and then move lines into the second of the main procedures. He indicated that he had started with this procedure as the problem indicated that the first requirement of the program was to load data into the arrays and this was the procedure that carried out this processing. He also however placed lines into this procedure that should have been in the other procedure.

Having lines of code in the "wrong" procedure usually caused error messages that indicated that variables had not been declared. This helped the students realise that they had made a mistake.

All three students had the structural error of placing the array declaration in a procedure rather than at the top of the program, at the "form level", such that the array would be available to all the procedures. The error messages caused the students to experiment and place the data declaration statement into other procedures, however there was always an error message output and they all finally realised that the statement should have been at the top of the program.

The loading of the array with data required a "While" loop and all three students brought across lines from the left-hand window as follows, the loop structure being incorrect:

```
Loop
Do While [condition]
```

The error message from Visual BASIC caused them all to transpose the statements. They also had some difficulties with the algorithm to load the data into the array. These difficulties were similar to those experienced by student B in problem 13 and included: having the loop counter initialisation statement within the loop causing an endless loop; and having the statement to increment the loop counter outside of the loop. Student B quickly corrected his code and this was probably because of his experiences with problem 13. Students G and H used the Visual BASIC debug and trace mechanism to help them and took longer to correct their programs.

Students G and H had difficulties of a semantic nature with the code to input data from the text file into an array element. The correct line was:

```
Input #1, fNumbers(index)
```

where fNumbers is the array name and index is a number coresponding to the index value. The following distracter was also in the left-hand window:

```
Input #1, index(fNumbers)
```

During their code manipulation and testing, they both chose the distracter line at some point which indicated that they did not understand the underlying meaning of the statement. The error message from Visual BASIC informed them that the distracter was incorrect and seemed to make them think more deeply about the meaning of the correct line. They did however ask their tutor for help about this.

Students B and H also tried to make use of the statement:

```
Input #1, fNumbers(index)
```

in the wrong context. The problem required the data in the array to be output in the output area of the Visual BASIC form. This should have been done with a Visual BASIC "Print" statement, however the students used the "Input" statement. On questioning, they stated that in order to output the required data, they wanted to "input data from the array" . This semantic misunderstanding was not easy for them to correct independently as the Visual BASIC error message of "bad file number" was very obscure and came about as a result of the incorrect line of code being in the wrong procedure.

The statement to output the data from the array caused syntactical difficulties for student H. The "Print" statement had to be keyed-in and although CORT alerted him to the syntax problem that he had, it did not help him correct it. He found the required syntax from the textbook.

Overall, student B had approached the problem solution in quite a considered way and it was indicative of type 4 cognitive strategy. Students G and H were less thoughtful but did show some consideration in their approach, and consequently their cognitive strategy was identified to be type 3. The scaffolding was high and identified to be level 3 for student B. CORT provided support for students G and H in several areas but not with respect to their semantic difficulty concerning the programming code to input data into an array element. Their scaffolding was characteristic of type 2.

Table 7.18: Supports and Levels of Cognitive Strategy and Scaffolding for Problem 15

Student Identifier	Syntax Support	Semantic Support	Structural Support	Algorithmic Support	Cognitive Strategy	Scaffolding Provided
B		✓	✓	✓	4	3
G		✓	✓	✓	3	2
H	✓	✓	✓	✓	3	2

Problem 16

Problem Description

This was again a problem that utilised arrays. There were two main event procedures in the program which did the following:

- When a button was clicked, a value would be obtained from a text box and placed in the next location in an array, an error message being output if the array was full.

- When a second button was clicked, the average of the numbers entered would be output to a form.

It was thought to be a relatively difficult problem, and so CORT method 1 was used.

Problem Solution

Students G and H did not have time to attempt this problem in the laboratory, student A was absent, and only student B was observed.

Although student B approached the problem solution in quite a considered way, he had one main difficulty with the algorithm for obtaining and placing the numeric values into the array. A loop was not needed in the procedure as the repetition was caused by a user continuously keying in a value and then clicking on the button on the form. However he brought the loop statement, that should have been placed in the procedure to determine the average of the numbers, into the procedure to place values into the array. He then got bogged down for a while and experimented with some other lines. The CORT system did eventually help him overcome the error as the loop variable was flagged as not being defined. He did need some limited help from his tutor. However this student's experience did suggest that CORT could be improved by associating sets of missing lines of code and distracters with certain procedures in the part-complete solution.

After he had overcome the above error, he had little difficulty finishing the problem correctly. Because he had approached the problem with some consideration his cognitive strategy was identified to be type 3. He was not fully supported by CORT in this problem, help having been required from his tutor, and the scaffolding was therefore identified as type 2.

Table 7.19: Supports and Levels of Cognitive Strategy and Scaffolding for Problem 16

Student Identifier	Syntax Support	Semantic Support	Structural Support	Algorithmic Support	Cognitive Strategy	Scaffolding Provided
B				✓	3	2

Problem 17

Problem Description

This was a difficult problem as it involved the loading of data from a text file into two parallel one-dimensional arrays, the use of a bubble sort on the data, and the use of a sequential search of the arrays. In order to reduce the cognitive load on the students, lines of code were removed from just two of the six procedures that made up the solution. The purpose of these two procedures was to sort the arrays and to search for an item in the arrays. Also, the lines that were removed and their associated distracter lines, were grouped in the left-hand window of CORT with textual information that informed the students which procedure they "belonged" to. Because of this cognitive load reduction, CORT method 2 was used.

Problem Solution

Students A, B, G and H attempted this problem.

Student A studied similar programming code in the textbook for sorting and searching algorithms. He then moved lines of code into the part-complete solution using the code in the textbook as a template to help him, and the program worked correctly when tested. During this process he asked the researcher what the meaning of the following statement was:

```
Let n = n + 1
```

This seemed to indicate a semantic misunderstanding and that he still had difficulties with the underlying conceptual machine and may well have solved this problem with little understanding of how the algorithms worked.

Student B attempted the "Sort" procedure first. He said that knowing which group of lines in the left-hand window were associated with the sort procedure helped him greatly and he only made one error during the building of the algorithm. The error was in the swapping of the adjacent contents of two array elements and the tracing and testing within the CORT system helped him overcome this. He indicated that having made this mistake helped him understand this mechanism.

Students G and H spent all of their laboratory time working on the search algorithm and they, together with student B, had some similar difficulties with this. The correct algorithm was:

```
Let n = 0
Let foundFlag = "no"
Do While foundFlag = "no" And n < fNumberOfNames
      Let n = n + 1
      If searchName = UCase(fNames(n)) Then
            Let foundFlag = "yes"
      End If
Loop
```

and the students had to move the second and fourth lines into the above from the left-hand window. They all tested the part-complete code without the line:

```
Let n = n + 1
```

and this gave a "subscript out of range" error. They all then realised that the variable "n" had to have a value greater than zero and they moved the above line to just after:

```
Let n = 0
```

which seemed to indicate that they were attempting to solve the immediate error without thinking of the bigger picture of the algorithm. The resultant algorithm was an endless loop and tracing the code in Visual BASIC alerted them to this, enabling them to correct the error. Along the way, student B also brought the distracter line of:

```
Let n = n + 2
```

into the loop and again the CORT system helped him overcome this error. He then used the CORT editor to change the line to "Let n = n + 1" although it was a CORT method 2 type problem. The student stated that although the moving of the distracter line into the loop had been a mistake, it had helped his understanding.

The three students all indicated that they were unsure of the semantics of the assignment statements relating to the use of "foundFlag" and this did not surprise the researcher as the concept of flags is generally a difficult one for novices. Students B and H both initially chose the distracter line of:

```
Let foundFlag = "yes"
```

rather than the correct line of

```
Let foundFlag = "no"
```

The resulting program trace revealed to them that the loop did not execute and they then corrected the code. They both indicated that they believed that they now had a better understanding of the concept of flags.

Student A had used a very careful, deliberate and strategic approach to this problem indicating a cognitive strategy of 5. The other three students, B, G and H, had showed some level of consideration in their approach indicative of type 3. CORT did provide all the necessary support for all of the students to solve the problem and was characteristic of level 3 scaffolding.

Table 7.20: Supports and Levels of Cognitive Strategy and Scaffolding for Problem 17

Student Identifier	Syntax Support	Semantic Support	Structural Support	Algorithmic Support	Cognitive Strategy	Scaffolding Provided
A					5	3
B				✓	3	3
G				✓	3	3
H				✓	3	3

Problem 18

Problem Description

This was a text file processing problem in which:

- Student test results could be added via a Visual BASIC form to a sequential text file;

- The file could be displayed;

- The file could be processed to produce two new text files with information on those students who obtained low and high marks; and

- The two new text files could have their data displayed.

There were five procedures in the part-complete solution and there were two groups of lines of code in the left-hand window that were associated with two of the procedures. Distracter lines were included in these groups. There was also information in CORT as to which group of lines belonged to which procedure.

It was necessary for all the lines of code to be keyed-in for the procedure that produced the file of students who obtained low marks. Although CORT method 3 was being used with what was a relatively difficult problem, this was thought to be appropriate as:

- The procedures in which the missing lines belonged had been indicated.

- The lines that had to be keyed-in were of the same structure as the procedure that produced the file of students who obtained high marks.

Problem Solution

Student G was absent and students A, B and H were observed attempting this problem.

Students A and H had similar syntax errors when they brought across two lines of code that were supposed to clear two textboxes and yet were syntactically incorrect. The error message that was output was rather obscure and it was only after the students had moved the lines into various positions in the part-complete solution, and the error messages did not disappear, that they recognised the syntax errors. The CORT system had only provided limited scaffolding in this area.

All of the students had semantic difficulties with the lines of code that were required to open the files at various points in the program. Each line of code that was needed to open a file had two associated distracter lines in the left-hand window. This was because sequential files can be opened in three different modes: for Input; for Output; and for Append.

All of the students believed that opening a file for input meant that it was then possible to input data into that file, and vice versa when a file was opened for output. This is opposite to the actual meanings of the statements. Because of this misunderstanding, the students brought the wrong file open statements into the part-complete solution and this resulted in a variety of error messages being output by Visual BASIC. The students did eventually correct the programs to include the correct file open statements. This was done by a process of trying the different file open statements in the solution and testing the code to see the result. Student B did this very carefully and deliberately, however students A and H did not put as much thought into this.

Student H had a semantic and structural difficulty. The semantic problem concerned the input from the text boxes. He placed a file open statement before the "Let" statements which placed data from the text boxes on the form into variables. He reasoned that he was inputting data and so he should open a file. This was incorrect and the CORT support provided error messages when he attempted to run the program. The student's structural issue was placing the statement to output data to a sequential text file before the statement that opened that file. Again, an error message from Visual BASIC alerted him to the mistake.

In solving this problem, student B had employed some strategy in his approach with a high level of consideration and his cognitive strategy was identified to be 4. Student A had demonstrated some level of consideration however his approach to choosing the file handling statements had been less thoughtful and his cognitive strategy was characteristic of level 3. Student H had only employed a low level of consideration characteristic of type 2 which resulted in his syntactical, semantic and structural difficulties. CORT provided student B full type 3 scaffolding to help him solve the problem. The limited syntactical help provided to students A and H indicated that the scaffolding provided by CORT was only at level 2.

Table 7.21: Supports and Levels of Cognitive Strategy and Scaffolding for Problem 18

Student Identifier	Syntax Support	Semantic Support	Structural Support	Algorithmic Support	Cognitive Strategy	Scaffolding Provided
A	✓	✓			3	2
B		✓			4	3

H		✓		✓		✓			2		2

7.3   Analysis of Summary Data

Each problem that was attempted by students using the CORT system has been described, together with an analysis of the supports and scaffolding that the system provided and of the levels of cognitive strategy that students practised. The data has been summarised in a series of tables. This section presents those tables and discusses the trends that emerged from the data.

7.3.1 Analysis of Data by Student

Table 7.22 shows a summary of the learning support data for each of the eight students that were observed and includes the support types, levels of cognitive strategy and levels of scaffolding.

Table 7.22: Summary of Learning Supports, Levels of Cognitive Strategy and Levels of Scaffolding for Each Student

Stud. ID	No. of Problems Observed	Syntax		Semantic		Structural		Algorithmic		Level of Cognitive Strategy (max 5)		Level of Scaffolding (max 3)	
		No.	%	No.	%	No.	%	No.	%	Median	Average	Median	Average
A	9	2	15	6	46	2	15	3	23	3	3.6	3	2.9
B	15	2	10	8	38	2	10	9	43	4	4.0	3	2.8
C	3			2	50	1	25	1	25	3	3.7	3	3.0
D	4	1	13	3	38	4	50			3	2.8	2.5	2.5
E	4			3	43	3	43	1	14	2.5	2.8	2	2.3
F	4	1	14	3	43	1	14	2	29	4	4.0	3	2.8
G	2			1	25	1	25	2	50	3	3.0	2.5	2.5
H	3	2	25	2	25	2	25	2	25	3	2.7	2	2.3

Total No. of Support Instances	8		28		16		20	
Overall % Support	11		39		22		28	

				Median	Average	Median	Average
Averages				3.2	3.3	2.6	2.6

CORT scaffolded with an overall average of 2.6 (range 1 - 3) demonstrating that it provided considerable help for students. CORT supported a level of cognitive strategy of 3.3 (range 1 - 5). This revealed that students were generally engaged with CORT and that they nearly always applied some consideration in their approaches to the tasks that they attempted.

The overall levels of CORT's four support types were 11%, 39%, 22%, and 28% for syntax, semantics, structure and algorithms respectively. It was expected that CORT would provide a low level of support for syntax errors as methods 1 and 2 do not require students to key in lines of code. Because of this, the possibilities of students being confronted with syntax problems is relatively low for the CORT system. The majority of difficulties that the students had, and for which CORT provided support, were semantic. The probable reason for this is that most students attempted problems within CORT, made little use of the textbook, and made use of CORT to scaffold them with respect to any semantic difficulties that they were confronted with. If they had not used CORT to try and solve their problems then they would have been forced to use other resources, such as the textbook, in order to determine the meaning of various programming statements. By using the CORT system, students were usually able to determine the meaning and semantics of statements by experimentation and consideration of the feedback that the CORT system provided them with. The levels of success achieved by students through their use of CORT confirmed the support CORT provided.

CORT also provided high levels of support for structural and algorithmic difficulties that students encountered. This is an important finding as there are generally few supports for these two areas when students learn to program using traditional techniques.

7.3.2 Analysis of Data by Problem Number

A summary of the data tabulated by problem number is shown in Table 7.23.

Table 7.23: Summary of Learning Supports, Levels of Cognitive Strategy and Levels of Scaffolding for Each Problem

Problem No.	No. of Students	CORT Method	Syntax No.	%	Semantic No.	%	Structural No.	%	Algorithmic No.	%	Level of Cognitive Strategy (max 5) Median	Avrg.	Level of Scaffolding (max 3) Median	Avrg.
2	4	2	2	66.7			1	33.3			4.5	4.0	3	2.8
3	4	1			3	50.0	3	50.0			4.5	4.3	3	3.0
4	4	2			3	50.0	1	16.7	2	33.3	3.5	3.8	3	2.8
5	3	2			3	60.0	1	20.0	1	20.0	3	2.8	3	3.0
6	2	1			2	66.7	1	33.3			3.5	3.5	3	3.0
7	4	2					4	57.1	3	42.9	3	3.3	3	2.8
8	2	3	2	66.7	1	33.3					3.5	3.5	2.5	2.5
9	1	2					1	100.0			2	2.0	2	2.0
10	1	2			1	50.0	1	50.0			3	3.0	3	3.0
11	3	1			1	33.3			2	66.7	3	3.7	3	3.0
12	1	3							1	100.0	4	4.0	2	2.0
13	3	1			3	37.5	2	25.0	3	37.5	4	4.0	3	2.7
14	1	3	1	33.3			1	33.3	1	33.3	4	4.0	2	2.0
15	3	3	1	10.0	3	30.0	3	30.0	3	30.0	3	3.3	2	2.3
16	1	1							1	100.0	3	3.0	2	2.0
17	4	2							3	100.0	3	3.5	3	3.0
18	3	3	2	33.3	3	50.0	1	16.7			3	3.0	2	2.3

The table shows the support types and the levels of cognitive support and scaffolding for each of the seventeen problems that were attempted by the students during the research experiment. Two patterns clearly emerge from the data. The first concerns the instances of semantic support provided by the CORT system as shown in columns 6 and 7. In the first nine problems, problem numbers 2 - 10, there were seventeen instances of semantic support for the total of twenty-five student observations that took place. In the eight remaining problems, problem numbers 11 - 18, there were only seven instances of semantic support for the total of sixteen student observations that took place. These results indicate that most semantic help took place earlier in the course when students were attempting to acquire much of the necessary semantic knowledge of various programming statements. By the latter part of the course, most students had constructed much of this semantic knowledge and required less help from the system.

The second finding concerns the instances of algorithmic support provided by the CORT system. In the first nine problems, problem numbers 2 - 10, there were six instances of algorithmic support for the total of twenty-five student observations that took place. In the eight remaining problems, problem numbers 11 - 18, there were fourteen instances of algorithmic support for the total of sixteen student observations that took place. These results indicate that most algorithmic help took place in the latter part of the course as the problems became progressively more difficult.

These two findings suggest that the CORT system provided most support for semantic difficulties early in the course and most support for algorithmic difficulties in the latter part of the course. It could therefore be argued that the design of the 17 problems is fairly sound. The progressive increase in difficulty of the problems has ensured that most students have been supported early on in their learning of programming language semantics at a time when the algorithmic difficulties that they faced were relatively low. Later in the course there were more difficult CORT problems and students faced many more algorithmic difficulties. However they were well supported by CORT. It seems that students no longer had to be as concerned with semantic difficulties. The cognitive load had been kept low in the early part of the course by ensuring the problem solutions had relatively simple algorithms. As the course progressed, less semantic support was necessary and it had been possible to increase the level of difficulty of the algorithms that were required for solutions, whilst keeping the cognitive load steady and not overloading students.

Table 7.24 contains the same data as that of Table 7.23, however the rows have been sorted by the "CORT Method" column which is the third column. Some properties of the data that seem to emerge from this table included the relatively large number of syntax supports that CORT had provided in method 3 type problems.

Table 7.24: Summary of Learning Supports, Levels of Cognitive Strategy and Levels of Scaffolding for Each Problem – Sorted by CORT Method

Problem No.	No. of Students	CORT Method	Syntax No.	Syntax %	Semantic No.	Semantic %	Structural No.	Structural %	Algorithmic No.	Algorithmic %	Level of Cognitive Strategy (max 5) Median	Avrg	Level of Scaffolding (max 3) Median	Avrg
3	4	1			3	50.0	3	50.0			4.5	4.3	3	3.0
6	2	1			2	66.7	1	33.3			3.5	3.5	3	3.0
11	3	1			1	33.3			2	66.7	3	3.7	3	3.0
13	3	1			3	37.5	2	25.0	3	37.5	4	4.0	3	2.7
16	1	1							1	100.0	3	3.0	2	2.0
2	4	2	2	66.7			1	33.3			4.5	4.0	3	2.8
4	4	2			3	50.0	1	16.7	2	33.3	3.5	3.8	3	2.8
5	3	2			3	60.0	1	20.0	1	20.0	3	2.8	3	3.0
7	4	2					4	57.1	3	42.9	3	3.3	3	2.8
9	1	2					1	100.0			2	2.0	2	2.0
10	1	2			1	50.0	1	50.0			3	3.0	3	3.0
17	4	2							3	100.0	3	3.5	3	3.0
8	2	3	2	66.7	1	33.3					3.5	3.5	2.5	2.5
12	1	3							1	100.0	4	4.0	2	2.0
14	1	3	1	33.3			1	33.3	1	33.3	4	4.0	2	2.0
15	3	3	1	10.0	3	30.0	3	30.0	3	30.0	3	3.3	2	2.3
18	3	3	2	33.3	3	50.0	1	16.7			3	3.0	2	2.3

Because the number of student observations varied between the three CORT methods, the data from Table 7.24 has been summarised in Table 7.25 in order to extract more meaning from the data.

7.3.3 Analysis of Data by CORT Method

In Table 7.25, the ratios of support instances to the number of student observations have been determined for each support type within each CORT method. Also, the overall average of levels of cognitive support and of levels of scaffolding have been determined.

Table 7.25: Summary of Learning Supports, Levels of Cognitive Strategy and Levels of Scaffolding for Each CORT Method

Cort Method	No. of Student Observations	Ratio of support instances : No. Student Observations Syntax	Semantic	Structural	Algorithmic	Lvl. Cog. Support (average)	Lvl. Scaffolding (average)
1	13	0.00	0.69	0.46	0.46	3.7	2.7
2	21	0.10	0.52	0.24	0.43	3.2	2.8
3	15	0.40	0.47	0.33	0.33	3.6	2.2

The data reveals several interesting findings. Firstly, CORT has not supported syntax errors when CORT method 1 was used. This is not surprising as such errors cannot be made in

---

method 1 type problems. CORT does however provide good syntax support for method 3 type problems when students have to key in some lines of code. The data also reveals that there is less algorithmic support for the higher CORT methods, the ratios of support instances to the number of student observations being 0.46, 0.43, and 0.33 respectively for CORT methods 1, 2 and 3. This seems to indicate that it is easier for students to determine an algorithm to solve a problem when all the required lines are available and there are no distracter lines. It is most difficult for students to determine a required algorithm when they have to key in lines and then CORT provides less support for them.

The table also shows that the levels of cognitive support were fairly even and strong across all three CORT methods. However, that level of scaffolding provided by CORT was lowest for method 3 type problems. Again, this was probably to be expected as the lines of code together with distracter lines provide strong scaffolding in methods 1 and 2. However method 3 type problems do not provide students with all the necessary line of code.

7.4 Summary of the CORT System's Support for the Learning Process

This chapter has reported on the observations that were made of students as they engaged with the part-complete solution process through the CORT system during the semester in which the research experiment took place. The results demonstrated the following outcomes:

- The system provided strong scaffolding for student learning.

- Students engaged well with the system and generally used a thoughtful and considered cognitive strategy.

- The highest level of support was for student semantic difficulties although there was also strong support for algorithmic and structural difficulties.

- The system support for semantic difficulties was higher in the early stages of the course.

- The system support for algorithmic difficulties was higher in the latter stages of the course.

- Students mainly had syntax difficulties with method 3 type problems when they had to key in lines of code. The system did provide support, if only by indicating that a difficulty existed.

- The system provides better algorithmic support for method 1 and 2 type problems than with method 3 type problems.

- The level of scaffolding provided by the system was lowest for method 3 problems.

The data suggest that the part-complete methods used in the CORT system have a strong influence on the supports and scaffolding levels that are provided. It is probably not unexpected that students receive lower levels of scaffolding when they have to key in lines of code themselves to complete a solution rather than choose lines of code that have been provided to them. Care is therefore necessary in the design of a set of problems for an introductory programming course so that the scaffolding is reduced gradually in order to try and keep the cognitive load that students experience fairly constant.

Chapter 8
The Impact of the CORT System on Learning Outcomes

8.1 Introduction

This chapter provides a description of a quantitative inquiry which explored the impact of the part-complete solution method (PCSM) within the CORT system on students' learning outcomes and achievements. It concerns: the data that were collected for this research; the data analysis method used; and the detailed analysis of the data.

8.2 Data Collected for this Research Question

Chapter 5 discussed the research design and the data collection that was undertaken for this research project. The data that were used to explore this third research question were as follows:

- Data concerning gender, age, previous achievement level, computer literacy level, and previous programming experience, collected from the initial questionnaire .

- The average time that students took to complete the set of problems and the average amount of help that students required, obtained from the problem questionnaires that students filled out for each problem that they attempted.

- Data concerning student learning outcomes, obtained from a test that was taken during the last week of the semester, and from a final examination. The examination was in two parts, the first part tested the students' ability to read and comprehend existing programming code, and the second part tested the students' ability to generate code having been given a problem specification.

8.2.1 Recoding of Data

There was some limited recoding of data. The "previous achievement level" corresponded to student course averages, this data having been taken from student records. The levels were recorded as percentages. In order to ensure three equivalent sized groups, the data were recoded, the cut-off points being shown in Table 8.1.

Table 8.1: Student Previous Achievement Levels

Previous Achievement Level	Previous Course Average
Low	<= 53%
Medium	> 53% and <68%
High	>= 68%

8.3   The Data Analysis Method

The data analysis tool, SPSS (Morgan & Griego, 1998) was used to help with the statistical analysis of the data. SPSS is a well known statistical package that is widely used in quantitative research.

The data were analysed in this research to determine if there were any significant differences in learning outcomes between the CORT and non-CORT students, and also whether students from these two student groups differed significantly in the times that they took to complete problems and in the amount of help that they required. The student group (CORT or non-CORT) was an independent variable in the study and further analysis was also undertaken to determine if other independent variables, such as gender, significantly interacted with student group with respect to learning outcomes, and time and help required to complete problems.

The six dependent variables used in the analysis were:

- Exam Part A (reading and comprehension of existing programming code) which was taken by students at the end of the course;

- Exam Part B (generation of programming code to solve a problem) which was taken by students at the end of the course;

- Exam Total (Exam Part A + Exam Part B);

- Week 15 Programming Completion Test which was taken by students near the end of the course;

- Average time taken per problem for the set of problems that the students undertook during the semester; and

- Average help required per problem for the set of problems that the students undertook during the semester.

The main independent variable was student group. Within student group, data were collected across various groups or independent variables: previous achievement level, age, computer literacy level, previous programming experience, and gender. These variables have been previously shown as influences on programming achievement (e.g., van Merrienboer, 1990b) and were identified in this study to aid in the analysis.

An initial set of analyses was undertaken to explore the effect that the independent variable, student group, had on each of the six dependent variables. This set of analyses could be classified as basic difference tests (Morgan & Griego, 1998) in which t-tests or one-way ANOVA tests are used for the data analysis. Such tests are used to determine if there is a significant difference between the means of the dependent variable for the groups within the independent variable. As the student group was comprised of two possible values, CORT or non-CORT, t-tests could be used for the six analyses. One-way ANOVA tests are used when the independent variable has three or more possible values.

The second set of analyses concerned the significance of the interaction of student group with each of the five other independent variables, with respect to the value of each dependent variable. For example, "Did gender and student group interact significantly with respect to student performance in exam part A (reading and understanding programming code)?". As there were five other independent variables and six dependent variables, thirty such analyses were carried out. Each of the analyses was categorised as a complex difference question, such questions involving more than one independent variable (Morgan & Griego, 1998). A factorial ANOVA associational statistic is appropriate under such situations, and more specifically a two-way ANOVA was utilised as each question involved two independent variables.

8.4   The Data Analysis

8.4.1 Programming Achievement between Groups
Four t-tests were carried out to determine if there were any significant differences between CORT and non-CORT students for each of the four dependent variables which concerned programming achievement: Exam Part A; Exam Part B; Exam Total; and Week 15 Programming Completion Test. The first test is described in some detail in order that the reader might gain an understanding of the way in which the statistics are interpreted.

8.4.1.1 Differences in Exam Part A Achievement among CORT and Non-CORT Students

Exam Part A was a test of the students' ability to read, trace and understand programming code. CORT supports the "Reading" method of learning programming (van Merrienboer & Krammer, 1987) and this analysis was important to determine if the CORT group achieved higher marks than their non-CORT compatriots in a test of such knowledge. The maximum mark was 20. The t-test was carried out using SPSS and the group statistics that were output are shown in Table 8.2.

Table 8.2: Group Statistics for Student Group and Exam Part A

	Group (CORT / Non-CORT)	N	Mean	Std. Deviation	Std. Error Mean
Exam Part A	CORT	24	10.58	4.149	.847
	Non-CORT	25	10.88	3.655	.731

The table shows that 24 CORT students and 25 non-CORT students took the exam and that their mean marks were 10.58 and 10.88 respectively. The standard deviations of 4.15 and 3.66 suggested a similar spread of marks between the groups.

Table 8.3 shows the results of the t-test for Exam Part A.

Table 8.3: T-Test: Student Group and Exam Part A

		Levene's Test for Equality of Variances		t-test for Equality of Means						
									95% Confidence Interval of the Difference	
		F	Sig.	t	df	Sig. (2-tailed)	Mean Difference	Std. Error Difference	Lower	Upper
Exam Part A	Equal variances assumed	.364	.549	-.266	47	.791	-.30	1.116	-2.541	1.948
	Equal variances not assumed			-.265	45.720	.792	-.30	1.119	-2.549	1.956

This table indicates the results for two statistical tests. The first is the Levene test, that tests the assumption that the variances of the two groups, CORT and non-CORT, are equal. If Levene's F value is **not** statistically significant, then equal variances are assumed. In this particular case, the significance is 0.549 and, as this is greater than 0.05 ($p > 0.05$), equal variances are assumed. Because of this, the "Equal variances assumed" outcome is utilised in analysing the t-test.

In this instance $t = -0.27$, with 47 degrees of freedom. The significance is 0.791. The result of the t-test

$$t(47) = -0.27, p > 0.05$$

revealed a non-significant difference between CORT and non-CORT students in their ability to read, trace and understand programming code.

8.4.1.2 Differences in Exam Part B Achievement among CORT and Non-CORT Students

Exam Part B, was a test of the students' ability to generate programming code in response to a problem statement. Generation of programming code is a much more difficult task than reading code (Linn & Dalbey, 1985) and CORT does not directly support it. In the weekly computer laboratories, non-CORT students had been required to generate all of their programs whilst the CORT students only had to complete part-complete solutions. The non-CORT students might therefore have had a learning advantage with respect to code generation.

The maximum possible mark for Exam Part B was 20 and Table 8.4 shows that there were 24 CORT students and 25 non-CORT students who took the exam and that their mean marks were 11.63 and 11.36 respectively. The standard deviations of 3.54 and 3.28 were again quite similar showing a consistent spread.

Table 8.4: Group Statistics for Student Group and Exam Part B

	Group (CORT / Non-CORT)	N	Mean	Std. Deviation	Std. Error Mean
Exam Part B	CORT	24	11.63	3.536	.722
	Non-CORT	25	11.36	3.277	.655

Table 8.5 shows the results of the t-test for Exam Part B.

Table 8.5: T-Test: Student Group and Exam Part B

		Levene's Test for Equality of Variances		t-test for Equality of Means					95% Confidence Interval of the Difference	
		F	Sig.	t	df	Sig. (2-tailed)	Mean Difference	Std. Error Difference	Lower	Upper
Exam Part B	Equal variances assumed	.005	.941	.272	47	.787	.27	.973	-1.693	2.223
	Equal variances not assumed			.272	46.360	.787	.27	.975	-1.697	2.227

Levene's F value was not significant, and equal variances could be assumed. The result of the t-test

$$t(47) = 0.27, p > 0.05$$

revealed a non-significant difference between CORT and non-CORT students in their ability to generate programming code in response to a problem statement.

This finding indicates CORT had provided strong support for program generation and the CORT students' achievement levels were as good as those of the non-CORT students.

8.4.1.3 Differences in Final Exam Achievement among CORT and Non-CORT Students

Exam Total, was the sum of parts A and B of the exam. It therefore tested both the students' ability to read and understand programming code and to generate programming code in response to a problem statement. Although analyses of the differences between the CORT and non-CORT groups were undertaken for the two separate parts of the exam, an analysis was carried out to determine if there were differences in overall programming ability.

Table 8.6 shows that the mean marks achieved for CORT and non-CORT were 22.21 and 22.28 respectively. The maximum possible mark was 40. The standard deviations were 5.95 and 6.00 respectively.

Table 8.6: Group Statistics for Student Group and Exam Total

	Group (CORT / Non-CORT)	N	Mean	Std. Deviation	Std. Error Mean
Exam Total	CORT	24	22.21	5.949	1.214
	Non-CORT	25	22.28	6.004	1.201

Table 8.7 shows the results of the t-test for Exam Total.

Table 8.7: T-Test: Student Group and Exam Total

		Levene's Test for Equality of Variances		t-test for Equality of Means						95% Confidence Interval of the Difference	
		F	Sig.	t	df	Sig. (2-tailed)	Mean Difference	Std. Error Difference		Lower	Upper
Exam Total	Equal variances assumed	.000	.984	-.042	47	.967	-.07	1.708		-3.508	3.364
	Equal variances not assumed			-.042	46.950	.967	-.07	1.708		-3.507	3.364

Levene's F value was not significant and equal variances could be assumed. The result of the t-test

$$t(47) = -0.042, p > 0.05$$

revealed a non-significant difference between CORT and non-CORT students ability to read, trace, understand programming code and to generate programming code in response to a problem statement. Given that no significant difference was found between the two groups in the constituent parts of the test, this result was not unexpected.

8.4.1.4 Differences in Week 15 Programming Completion Test Achievement among CORT and Non-CORT Students

A Completion Test was given in Week 15 which was the last week of the semester. The test was designed to test students' ability to complete part-complete programs when given a set of possible lines of code that could be utilised. The CORT group had used the completion method throughout the semester when attempting their set of problems, whereas the non-CORT group had generated all of their programs "from scratch". Because of this, it was thought that CORT students might have an advantage on such a "completion" test.

Table 8.8 indicates that only 25 students were present for the test, 11 CORT and 14 non-CORT. The means for the two groups were 57.55% and 50.50% respectively. The standard deviations for the two groups differed slightly at 21.59 and 24.57 respectively showing a greater spread of marks for the non-CORT group.

Table 8.8: Group Statistics for Student Group and Week 15 Programming Completion Test

	Group (CORT / Non-CORT)	N	Mean	Std. Deviation	Std. Error Mean
Week 15 Programming Completion Test	CORT	11	57.5455	21.58872	6.50924
	Non-CORT	14	50.5000	24.56937	6.56644

Table 8.9 shows the results of the t-test for the Week 15 Programming Completion Test.

Table 8.9: T-Test: Student Group and Week 15 Programming Completion Test

		Levene's Test for Equality of Variances		t-test for Equality of Means						
									95% Confidence Interval of the Difference	
		F	Sig.	t	df	Sig. (2-tailed)	Mean Difference	Std. Error Difference	Lower	Upper
Week 15 Test	Equal variances assumed	.290	.595	.750	23	.461	7.0455	9.39601	-12.39168	26.48259
	Equal variances not assumed			.762	22.659	.454	7.0455	9.24599	-12.09729	26.18820

Levene's F value was not significant and equal variances could be assumed. The result of the t-test

$t(23) = 0.75$, $p > 0.05$

revealed a non-significant difference between CORT and non-CORT students in their performance in a programming completion test.

The fact that the difference between the two groups was not significant was unexpected. Because of CORT's direct support for program completion it had been thought that the CORT group might perform significantly better than the non-CORT group. Despite a difference in the observed means of 7, the means were found not to be significantly different. This may have been caused by several factors such as small groups or a lack of sensitivity in the test instrument.

8.4.1.5 Summary of Programming Achievement between Groups
The four tests that were carried out revealed that there was not a significant difference in learning achievement between the CORT and non-CORT student groups. However the CORT students appeared to spend less time than the non-CORT students on the programming tasks and this may have limited the opportunities for the use of CORT to provide a learning advantage. Also, CORT may have only provided advantages to certain sub-groups of students. Both these possibilities are explored in later sections of this chapter.

8.4.2 Programming Achievement Differences among Sub-Groups
Analyses were also carried out to determine if there were any significant interactions between student group, CORT and non-CORT, and each of the other five independent variables or sub-groups: previous achievement level, age, computer literacy level, previous programming experience, and gender with respect to student achievement. Two-way ANOVA statistics were produced for each of the four dependent variables associated with student achievement: Exam Part A, Exam Part B, Exam Total, and Week 15 Programming Completion Test. The first tests are described in some detail in order that the reader might gain an understanding of the way in which the statistics are interpreted.

8.4.2.1 Previous Achievement Level
The CORT system has been designed to reduce cognitive load and provide scaffolding and learning supports for students. These two aspects have been associated with improved programming performance (e.g., Sweller, 1988) and analyses were undertaken of the interaction between the students' previous achievement, which was obtained from their

course averages, and the student group (CORT or non-CORT), with respect to their student achievement in the final exam and Week 15 Programming Completion Test.

Interaction between Group and Previous Achievement Level for Exam Part A

The level of interaction between student group and previous achievement level was determined for Exam Part A, the students' ability to read and understand programming code.

Table 8.10 shows the numbers associated with the student group and previous achievement level. It indicates that 49 students took the exam and that there were 15, 21 and 13 students with corresponding previous achievement levels of "low", "medium", and "high".

Table 8.10: Student Group and Previous Achievement Level: Basic Statistics

		Value Label	N
Group (CORT	1	CORT	24
/ Non-CORT)	2	Non-CORT	25
Previous	1	Low	15
achievement	2	Medium	21
level	3	High	13

Table 8.11 shows the descriptive statistics for this analysis. The data shows that for both CORT and non-CORT students, the marks were higher for those with greater levels of previous achievement. The standard deviations show a relatively larger spread of marks for the CORT, low previous achievers.

Table 8.11: Descriptive Statistics for Group, Previous Achievement and Exam Part A

Dependent Variable: Exam Part A

Group	Prev. Achievement	Mean	Std. Deviation	N
CORT	Low	9.50	5.732	8
	Medium	10.00	2.449	9
	High	12.57	3.599	7
	Total	10.58	4.149	24
Non-CORT	Low	9.14	4.140	7
	Medium	10.50	3.205	12
	High	13.67	2.658	6
	Total	10.88	3.655	25
Total	Low	9.33	4.880	15
	Medium	10.29	2.849	21
	High	13.08	3.121	13
	Total	10.73	3.866	49

The results of the two-way ANOVA test that was undertaken to explore results in Exam Part A across achievement is shown in Table 8.12.

Table 8.12: Two-way ANOVA for Group, Previous Achievement and Exam Part A

Dependent Variable: Exam Part A

Source	Type III Sum of Squares	df	Mean Square	F	Sig.	Partial Eta Squared
Corrected Model	110.646ª	5	22.129	1.568	.190	.154
Intercept	5538.389	1	5538.389	392.402	.000	.901
GROUP	1.986	1	1.986	.141	.709	.003
ACHIEVEM	108.128	2	54.064	3.830	.029	.151
GROUP * ACHIEVEM	3.753	2	1.876	.133	.876	.006
Error	606.905	43	14.114			
Total	6364.000	49				
Corrected Total	717.551	48				

a. R Squared = .154 (Adjusted R Squared = .056)

The row "ACHIEVEM" reveals that, irrespective of student group, students with higher previous achievement levels scored significantly higher in Exam Part A. The result is:

$F(2,43) = 3.83$, $P < 0.05$

The relevant data concerning the level of interaction between student group and previous achievement level with respect to Exam part A is in the row "GROUP * ACHIEVEM. The result of the two-way ANOVA test:

$F(2,43) = 0.133$, $p > 0.05$

reveals a non-significant interaction between CORT and non-CORT students in Exam Part A. This means that although the figures in Table 8.11 show that low achievers scored higher than non-CORT low achievers, and non-CORT medium and high achievers scored higher than their CORT counterparts, these differences are not significant.

Interaction between Group and Previous Achievement Level for Exam Part B

The level of interaction between student group and previous achievement level was determined for Exam Part B, the students' ability to generate programming code in response to a problem statement. As in the previous analysis, it was thought that weaker CORT students might perform better than weaker non-CORT students. The descriptive statistics are shown in Table 8.13.

Table 8.13: Descriptive Statistics for Group, Previous Achievement and Exam Part B

Dependent Variable: Exam Part B				
Group	Prev. Achievement	Mean	Std. Deviation	N
CORT	Low	12.63	3.739	8
	Medium	9.67	3.202	9
	High	13.00	2.944	7
	Total	11.62	3.536	24
Non-CORT	Low	10.86	3.848	7
	Medium	11.00	2.412	12
	High	12.67	4.274	6
	Total	11.36	3.277	25
Total	Low	11.80	3.764	15
	Medium	10.43	2.785	21
	High	12.85	3.460	13
	Total	11.49	3.373	49

The results of the two-way ANOVA test that was undertaken to explore results in Exam Part B across achievement is shown in Table 8.14.

Table 8.14: Two-way ANOVA for Group, Previous Achievement and Exam Part B

Dependent Variable: Exam Part B

Source	Type III Sum of Squares	df	Mean Square	F	Sig.	Partial Eta Squared
Corrected Model	70.179[a]	5	14.036	1.268	.295	.128
Intercept	6315.160	1	6315.160	570.409	.000	.930
GROUP	.764	1	.764	.069	.794	.002
ACHIEVEM	51.635	2	25.817	2.332	.109	.098
GROUP * ACHIEVEM	21.114	2	10.557	.954	.393	.042
Error	476.065	43	11.071			
Total	7015.000	49				
Corrected Total	546.245	48				

a. R Squared = .128 (Adjusted R Squared = .027)

Unlike the previous ANOVA test for Exam Part A, there was no significant result that indicated that students, irrespective of group, with higher previous achievement levels did better in Exam Part B. The result is:

$F(2,43)=2.332, p>0.05$

The results of the interaction between group and previous achievement

$F(2,43)=0.954, p>0.05$

reveals a non-significant interaction between group and previous achievement level in Exam Part B which is their ability to generate programming code in response to a problem statement.

Interaction between Group and Previous Achievement Level for Exam Total

Exam Total was the sum of parts A and B of the exam and it tested both the students' ability to read and understand programming code and to generate programming code in response to a problem statement. As in the previous analyses, it was thought that weaker CORT students might perform better than weaker non-CORT students.

Table 8.15 shows the descriptive statistics for this analysis. The trend in the figures is similar to those for Exam Part B, students with higher levels of previous achievement performing better in the exam with the exception of low and medium previous achievers in the CORT group.

Table 8.15: Descriptive Statistics for Group, Previous Achievement and Exam Total

Dependent Variable: Exam Total

Group	Prev. Achievement	Mean	Std. Deviation	N
CORT	Low	22.13	7.259	8
	Medium	19.67	3.571	9
	High	25.57	5.855	7
	Total	22.21	5.949	24
Non-CORT	Low	20.00	6.758	7
	Medium	21.58	4.833	12
	High	26.33	6.218	6
	Total	22.28	6.004	25
Total	Low	21.13	6.865	15
	Medium	20.76	4.346	21
	High	25.92	5.780	13
	Total	22.24	5.914	49

The results of the two-way ANOVA test that was undertaken to explore results in Exam Total across achievement is shown in Table 8.16.

Table 8.16: Two-way ANOVA for Group, Previous Achievement and Exam Total

Dependent Variable: Exam Total

Source	Type III Sum of Squares	df	Mean Square	F	Sig.	Partial Eta Squared
Corrected Model	278.222ª	5	55.644	1.708	.153	.166
Intercept	23710.821	1	23710.821	727.825	.000	.944
GROUP	.397	1	.397	.012	.913	.000
ACHIEVEM	252.297	2	126.149	3.872	.028	.153
GROUP * ACHIEVEM	36.038	2	18.019	.553	.579	.025
Error	1400.839	43	32.578			
Total	25926.000	49				
Corrected Total	1679.061	48				

a. R Squared = .166 (Adjusted R Squared = .069)

The results of the interaction between group and previous achievement:

$F(2,43)=0.553, p>0.05$

reveals a non-significant interaction between CORT and non-CORT students in Exam Total which is their ability to read, trace, understand programming code and to generate programming code in response to a problem statement.

Interaction between Group and Previous Achievement Level for Week 15 Programming Completion Test

The Week 15 Programming Completion Test directly tested the students' ability to complete part-complete programs. Again it was thought that weaker CORT students may perform better on this test than their non-CORT counterparts because of the learner supports that CORT had provided.

Table 8.16 shows the descriptive statistics for this analysis. Only 25 students took the test, 11 being from the CORT group and 14 being from the non-CORT group. The statistics indicate that for all three categories of achievement, the CORT students performed better than the non-CORT students. The mean marks were 46.33% and 42.00% for the CORT and non-CORT low previous achievers respectively. The spread of marks for the two groups was large at 23.71 and 39.60 respectively.

Table 8.16: Descriptive Statistics for Group, Previous Achievement and Week 15 Programming Completion Test

Dependent Variable: Week 15 Programming Completion Test

Group	Prev. Achievement	Mean	Std. Deviation	N
CORT	Low	46.3333	23.71357	3
	Medium	51.0000	13.52775	3
	High	68.2000	22.89541	5
	Total	57.5455	21.58872	11
Non-CORT	Low	42.0000	39.59798	2
	Medium	48.0000	22.31591	8
	High	59.7500	27.42718	4
	Total	50.5000	24.56937	14
Total	Low	44.6000	26.05379	5
	Medium	48.8182	19.67647	11
	High	64.4444	23.74927	9
	Total	53.6000	23.10664	25

The results of the two-way ANOVA test that was undertaken to explore results in the Week 15 Programming Completion Test across achievement are shown in Table 8.17.

Table 8.17: Two-way ANOVA for Group, Previous Achievement and Week 15 Programming Completion Test

Dependent Variable: Week 15 Programming Completion Test

Source	Type III Sum of Squares	df	Mean Square	F	Sig.	Partial Eta Squared
Corrected Model	1915.783a	5	383.157	.668	.652	.150
Intercept	57073.826	1	57073.826	99.503	.000	.840
GROUP	143.032	1	143.032	.249	.623	.013
ACHIEVEM	1525.096	2	762.548	1.329	.288	.123
GROUP * ACHIEVEM	34.593	2	17.296	.030	.970	.003
Error	10898.217	19	573.590			
Total	84638.000	25				
Corrected Total	12814.000	24				

a. R Squared = .150 (Adjusted R Squared = -.074)

The results of the interaction between group and previous achievement:

F(2,19)=0.030, p>0.05

reveals a non-significant interaction between the performance of CORT and non-CORT students in the Week 15 Programming Completion Test.

Discussion Concerning CORT and Students' Previous Achievement Levels

CORT was designed to provide supports and scaffolds for students who are learning to program. Previous research (e.g., Chansilp & Oliver, 2002, 2004) found no advantage in overall programming performance when using a technology enabled system, but significant advantages for low achievers. It was intended that CORT would particularly benefit the less able student and in the case of this research, such a student was one who had a relatively low previous achievement. However, the four ANOVA tests revealed that there was no significant interaction between the student group and student previous achievement levels with respect to student programming achievement tests. In all four tests, the descriptive statistics indicated that the CORT low achievers' marks were higher than their non-CORT counterparts. These differences were not large and the non-significant results might be due to the small number of students involved. The student numbers were 8 and 7 for the CORT and Non-CORT low achievers for Exam Parts A, B and for Exam Total. The student numbers were just 3 and 2 respectively for the Week 15 Programming Completion Test.

8.4.2.2 Student Age

Anecdotal evidence suggests that more mature students often find learning to program more difficult than younger students. They may for example have less basic computer literacy knowledge and also be more anxious about programming. They are more likely to get frustrated when they cannot generate a working program to solve a problem. It was thought that mature students might benefit from CORT's learning supports. Younger students were defined as being 20 and under, whereas mature students were defined as being over 20.

Four ANOVA tests were again undertaken to examine the interaction between student group and student age with respect to achievement. The numbers within the different categories are shown in Table 8.18 for Exam Part A, B and Exam Total, and in Table 8.19 for the Week 15 Programming Completion Test. The student numbers were relatively evenly distributed for the final exam. This was not the situation for the Programming Completion Test with only two students being in the young CORT category.

Table 8.18: Descriptive Statistics for Group, Age and Exam A, B and Total

Group	Age	N
CORT	20 or under	12
	21 or over	12
	Total	24
Non-CORT	20 or under	9
	21 or over	16
	Total	25
Total	20 or under	21
	21 or over	28
	Total	49

Table 8.19: Descriptive Statistics for Group, Age and Week 15 Programming Completion Test

Group	Age	N
CORT	20 or under	2
	21 or over	9
	Total	11
Non-CORT	20 or under	6
	21 or over	8
	Total	14
Total	20 or under	8
	21 or over	17
	Total	25

The results of the four, two-way ANOVA tests used to determine the significance of the interaction between student group and student age for student achievement are shown in Table 8.20.

Table 8.20: Two-Way ANOVA Tests for Group, Age and Level of Achievement

Achievement Measure	ANOVA Result	Significant?
Exam Part A	$F_{(1,45)} = 5.807$, $p<0.05$	✓
Exam Part B	$F_{(1,45)}=0.014$, $p>0.05$	
Exam Total	$F_{(1,45)}=2.456$, $p>0.05$	
Week 15 Programming Completion Test	$F_{(1,21)}=0.392$, $p>0.05$	

The only significant interaction between student group and age was for Exam Part A which tested a students' ability to read and understand programming code. Table 8.21 shows the descriptive statistics for this analysis. It indicates that the mean mark for Exam Part A was 9.00 and 12.22 for the CORT and non-CORT younger students respectively. The spread of marks was greater for the CORT students. However the mean mark was 12.17 and 10.13

respectively for the CORT and non-CORT mature students. Their marks were consistently spread.

Table 8.21: Descriptive Statistics for Group, Age and Exam Part A

Dependent Variable: Exam Part A

Group	Age	Mean	Std. Deviation	N
CORT	20 or under	9.00	3.766	12
	21 or over	12.17	4.041	12
	Total	10.58	4.149	24
Non-CORT	20 or under	12.22	1.856	9
	21 or over	10.13	4.225	16
	Total	10.88	3.655	25
Total	20 or under	10.38	3.442	21
	21 or over	11.00	4.199	28
	Total	10.73	3.866	49

The ANOVA result is shown graphically in the profile plots of Figure 8.1.

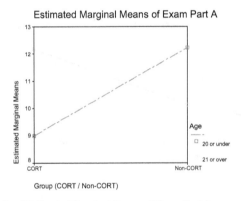

Estimated Marginal Means of Exam Part A

Figure 8.1: Profile Plots of Estimated Marginal Means of Exam Part A

This significant result shows that mature students who used CORT performed better than those who did not use CORT for Exam Part A. This part of the exam tested a student's ability to carefully read and trace programming code and those who achieve at higher levels would most probably have a well developed mental model of the way in which programs execute. It is unclear if CORT helped mature students develop such mental models or if they already had appropriate models. In the latter case, it could be suggested that mental models are better developed by not using CORT as students tend to experiment more during the generation of programs "from scratch". This would explain why younger students who did not use CORT achieved better than their CORT counterparts.

The question arises why the other three ANOVA tests did not show a significant interaction between student group and age. Firstly, Exam Part B tests the generation of code "from scratch" and CORT does not provide direct support for this. Secondly, the differences between the two groups' Exam Part A results must not have been so significant to cause a significant difference between the Exam totals. Finally, although the Week 15 Programming Completion Test also directly tested the reading of programming code like Exam Part A, the numbers who undertook the test were small and this may have influenced the outcome of the ANOVA test.

8.4.2.3 Computer Literacy Level

Students who learn programming often have poorly developed mental models of the conceptual machine and also have misconceptions of various language constructs in programming (Bayman & Mayer, 1983). For example, they might have difficulty in: knowing where data comes from when input; how data is stored in memory; and the mechanism of assignment statements. Generally, people with higher levels of computer literacy have better developed mental models of the mechanisms of computers.

CORT provides learning supports and scaffolding to students however it is uncertain if it helps develop their mental models. Hence the question to be explored is whether students with lower levels of computer literacy perform better with or without CORT. Again, four ANOVA tests were undertaken to explore the interaction between student group and student computer literacy level for student achievement. The computer literacy level was specified as moderate or extensive. There were no students in the "limited" and "no computer literacy" categories.

The numbers within the different categories are shown in Table 8.22 for Exam Part A, B and Exam Total, and in Table 8.23 for the Week 15 Programming Completion Test. Both tables show that there were more students with "moderate" literacy than with "extensive" literacy. There were only two students with extensive computer literacy in the non-CORT group for the Week 15 Programming Completion Test.

Table 8.22: Descriptive Statistics for Group, Computer Literacy and Exam A, B and Total

Group (CORT / Non-CORT)	Computer Literacy Level	N
CORT	Moderate	9
	Extensive	12
	Total	21
Non-CORT	Moderate	18
	Extensive	7
	Total	25
Total	Moderate	27
	Extensive	19
	Total	46

Table 8.23: Descriptive Statistics for Group, Computer Literacy and Week 15 Programming Completion Test

Group (CORT / Non-CORT)	Computer Literacy Level	N
CORT	Moderate	3
	Extensive	5
	Total	8
Non-CORT	Moderate	12
	Extensive	2
	Total	14
Total	Moderate	15
	Extensive	7
	Total	22

The results of the four, two-way ANOVA tests used to determine the significance of the interaction between student group and student computer literacy for student achievement are shown in Table 8.24.

Table 8.24: Two-Way ANOVA Tests for Group, Computer Literacy and Level of Achievement

Achievement Measure	ANOVA Result	Significant?
Exam Part A	$F_{(1,42)}=0.042$, $p<0.05$	✓
Exam Part B	$F_{(1,42)}=0.062$, $p>0.05$	
Exam Total	$F_{(1,42)}=2.603$, $p>0.05$	
Week 15 Programming Completion Test	$F_{(1,18)}=0.082$, $p>0.05$	

The only significant interaction between student group and Computer Literacy was for Exam Part A which tested a students' ability to read and understand programming code. Table 8.25 shows the descriptive statistics for this analysis. It indicates that the mean mark for Exam Part A was 8.44 and 11.56 respectively for the CORT and non-CORT students who had moderate computer literacy. The mean marks were 11.33 and 9.14 respectively for the CORT and non-CORT students who had extensive computer literacy. The spread of marks was relatively even for all four combinations of group and literacy.

Table 8.25: Descriptive Statistics for Group, Computer Literacy and Exam Part A

Dependent Variable: Exam Part A

Group	Computer Literacy Level	Mean	Std. Deviation	N
CORT	Moderate	8.44	3.972	9
	Extensive	11.33	3.846	12
	Total	10.10	4.073	21
Non-CORT	Moderate	11.56	3.666	18
	Extensive	9.14	3.237	7
	Total	10.88	3.655	25
Total	Moderate	10.52	3.984	27
	Extensive	10.53	3.702	19
	Total	10.52	3.828	46

This significant result suggests that students with moderate levels of computer literacy who did not use CORT have performed better on Exam Part A than those who did use CORT. The opposite is true for those students who had extensive computer literacy and this is shown graphically in the profile plot of Figure 8.2.

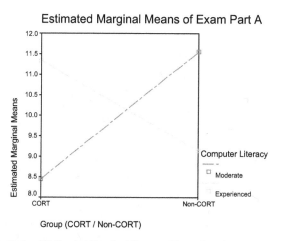

Figure 8.2: Profile Plots of Estimated Marginal Means of Exam Part A

Exam part A measures a student's ability to read, trace and understand programming code and this requires students to possess a sound mental model of a program's execution process. The results suggest that students with moderate levels of computer literacy have gained better mental models by learning in the "conventional" manner without the aid of CORT. A possible reason is that CORT reduces a student's capacity to experiment with code and to make mistakes, such activities perhaps being necessary in mental model construction.

Students with extensive computer literacy performed better with the aid of CORT. This could be because such students already had well developed mental models or were able to create such models relatively quickly. Then, the use of CORT provided them with the necessary learning supports to achieve at a high level.

A conclusion that might be drawn for this result is that students who have lower levels of computer literacy need to construct knowledge and relevant mental models about the conceptual machine before they use CORT to help them learn programming.

8.4.2.4 Previous Programming Experience

In an introductory programming unit like that in which this research has been carried out, it would usually be expected that students would have little previous programming experience. However some students may have gained limited familiarity with programming by, for example, the viewing and amendment of simple scripts on the Internet. Similarly to students who have extensive computer literacy, it would be expected that those students who have some previous programming knowledge may have better developed mental models than those with no previous knowledge. Students in the study were classified as having "none" or "limited" previous programming experience. In the original questionnaire that students completed at the beginning of the unit, there had been a category of "moderate" programming experience. However no students indicated that they were in this category.

The numbers within the different categories of programming experience are shown in Table 8.26 for Exam Part A, B and Exam Total, and in Table 8.27 for the Week 15 Programming Completion Test. The numbers were distributed fairly evenly for the exams, however this was not the case for the Week 15 Programming Completion Test where fewer students were present. In this test, there were 10 and 4 non-CORT students with no and limited previous programming experience respectively.

Table 8.26: Descriptive Statistics for Group, Previous Programming Experience and Exam A, B and Total

Group (CORT / Non-CORT)	Previous Programming Experience	N
CORT	None	11
	Limited	10
	Total	21
Non-CORT	None	14
	Limited	11
	Total	25

Total	None	25
	Limited	21
	Total	46

Table 8.27: Descriptive Statistics for Group, Previous Programming Experience and Week 15 Programming Completion Test

Group (CORT / Non-CORT)	Previous Programming Experience	N
CORT	None	4
	Limited	4
	Total	8
Non-CORT	None	10
	Limited	4
	Total	14
Total	None	14
	Limited	8
	Total	22

The results of the four, two-way ANOVA tests used to determine the significance of the interaction between student group and previous programming experience for student achievement are shown in Table 8.28.

Table 8.28: Two-Way ANOVA Tests for Group, Previous Programming Experience and Level of Achievement

Achievement Measure	ANOVA Result	Significant?
Exam Part A	$F_{(1,42)}=7.180$, $p<0.05$	✓
Exam Part B	$F_{(1,42)}=1.148$, $p>0.05$	
Exam Total	$F_{(1,42)}=5.774$, $p<0.05$	✓
Week 15 Programming Completion Test	$F_{(1,18)}=3.065$, $p>0.05$	

Two of the tests indicated that there were significant interactions between student group and previous programming experience for both Exam Part A and Exam Total. Tables 8.29 and 8.30 show the descriptive statistics for these analyses.

Table 8.29: Descriptive Statistics for Group, Previous Programming Experience and Exam Part A

Dependent Variable: Exam Part A

Group	Prev. Prog. Experience	Mean	Std. Deviation	N
CORT	None	8.55	4.204	11
	Limited	11.80	3.327	10
	Total	10.10	4.073	21
Non-CORT	None	12.00	3.138	14
	Limited	9.45	3.908	11
	Total	10.88	3.655	25
Total	None	10.48	3.970	25
	Limited	10.57	3.749	21
	Total	10.52	3.828	46

Table 8.30: Descriptive Statistics for Group, Previous Programming Experience and Exam Total

Dependent Variable: Exam Total

Group	Prev. Prog. Exp.	Mean	Std. Deviation	N
CORT	None	19.36	4.717	11
	Limited	23.30	5.519	10
	Total	21.24	5.375	21
Non-CORT	None	24.00	5.477	14
	Limited	20.09	6.172	11
	Total	22.28	6.004	25
Total	None	21.96	5.571	25
	Limited	21.62	5.954	21
	Total	21.80	5.687	46

These significant results are similar to those obtained for the student group and computer literacy. That is, non-CORT students without any previous programming experience performed better than CORT students without any previous programming experience in Exam Part A. The respective marks were 12.00 and 8.55. CORT students with limited previous programming experience performed better than their non-CORT counterparts, the marks being 11.80 and 9.45 respectively. This is shown graphically in the profile plot of Figure 8.3.

Estimated Marginal Means of Exam Part A

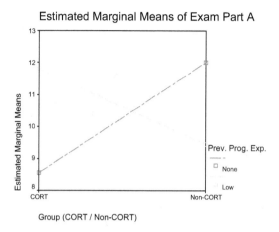

Group (CORT / Non-CORT)

Figure 8.3: Profile Plots of Estimated Marginal Means of Exam Part A

These significant differences were greater than for computer literacy, and this is why there was also a significant difference for Exam Total with respect to previous programming experience, even though no significant difference had emerged for Exam Part B.

The results are similar to those in computer literacy and suggest that students with no previous programming experience may need to construct knowledge and relevant mental models about the conceptual machine before they use CORT to help them learn programming. Those students who already have some programming knowledge appeared to achieve better with the aid of CORT as these students probably have better developed mental models and can then use CORT's learning supports to help them build relevant programming plans and schemata.

8.4.2.5 Gender

Research has shown that female students who have learnt to program using the completion method experienced less anxiety and lower drop-out rates than those learning using the more traditional "generation" method (van Merrienboer, 1990b). This suggests that females may be more comfortable using CORT as it directly supports the completion method and that this may impact on their performance.

As previously, four ANOVA tests were undertaken to explore the interaction between student group and gender for student achievement. The numbers within the different categories are shown in Table 8.31 for Exam Part A, B and Exam Total, and in Table 8.32 for the Week 15 Programming Completion Test.

Table 8.31: Descriptive Statistics for Group, Gender and Exam A, B and Total

Group (CORT / Non-CORT)	Gender	N
CORT	Male	18
	Female	6
	Total	24
Non-CORT	Male	14
	Female	11
	Total	25
Total	Male	32
	Female	17
	Total	49

Table 8.32: Descriptive Statistics for Group, Gender and Week 15 Programming Completion Test

Group (CORT / Non-CORT)	Gender	N
CORT	Male	9
	Female	2
	Total	11
Non-CORT	Male	6
	Female	8
	Total	14
Total	Male	15
	Female	10
	Total	25

The results of the four, two-way ANOVA tests used to determine the significance of the interaction between student group and gender for student achievement are shown in Table 8.33.

Table 8.33: Two-Way ANOVA Tests for Group, Gender and Level of Achievement

Achievement Measure	ANOVA Result	Significant?
Exam Part A	$F(1,45)=0.012$, $p>0.05$	
Exam Part B	$F(1,45)=0.953$, $p>0.05$	
Exam Total	$F(1,45)=0.404$, $p>0.05$	
Week 15 Programming Completion Test	$F(1,21)=0.022$, $p>0.05$	

The tests indicated that there was no significant difference between the males and females within the CORT and non-CORT groups. Female students in the CORT group may be more comfortable and less anxious than their non-CORT counterparts, however this has not been reflected in improved performance. An investigation into how CORT impacts on the affective domain of females could be an area of future investigation.

8.4.3 Time and Help Requirements between Groups

Two other important factors in programming outcomes and learning are the time taken by students to complete their weekly programming problems, and the amount of help that students required. A series of tests was used to explore whether the use of CORT revealed significant differences in these factors. It would be a strength of CORT if it could be shown to reduce time and / or help requirements.

8.4.3.1 Differences in Time Taken to Complete Programming Problems between CORT and Non-CORT Students

As part of their learning process, students were asked to estimate and record the time that they took to complete each programming problem. This was done as they attempted the computer laboratories during the semester. The data were recorded in their individual problem questionnaires. It has been suggested (van Merrienboer & De Croock, 1992) that students who have to generate code spend a lot of time searching for relevant worked examples. Because of this, it was thought that there could be a difference between the times taken by students to generate programs and the times taken to complete part-complete programs. The non-CORT group had to generate all their programs whereas the CORT group had to complete part-complete programs. The data collected enabled the testing of this proposition.

The "Average time taken per problem", was the average time that students took to complete each of the eighteen programming problems during the semester. Table 8.34 shows that data were collected for 21 CORT students and 23 non-CORT and that their mean average times were 25.1 and 33.4 minutes respectively. This indicates that the non-CORT group took an average of 8 minutes longer to complete each of their programming problems.

Table 8.34: Group Statistics for Student Group and Time Taken to Complete Problems

	Group (CORT / Non-CORT)	N	Mean	Std. Deviation	Std. Error Mean
Average time taken per problem	CORT	21	25.14	4.757	1.038
	Non-CORT	23	33.43	9.199	1.918

The data were then further analysed and Table 8.35 shows the results of the t-test for the students groups' times to complete programming problems.

Table 8.35: T-Test: Student Group and Average Time Taken per Problem

		Levene's Test for Equality of Variances		t-test for Equality of Means					95% Confidence Interval of the Difference	
		F	Sig.	t	df	Sig. (2-tailed)	Mean Difference	Std. Error Difference	Lower	Upper
Average time taken per problem	Equal variances assumed	4.393	.042	-3.701	42	.001	-8.29	2.240	-12.813	-3.771
	Equal variances not assumed			-3.802	33.603	.001	-8.29	2.181	-12.726	-3.858

In this case, Levene's F value **was** significant ($p<0.05$) and equal variances could **not** be assumed. The result of the t-test

$$t(33.6) = -3.80, p<0.05$$

revealed a significant difference between CORT and non-CORT students with respect to the average time taken per problem. The differences are shown graphically in the box plot of Figure 8.4. The box plot also gives a visual indication of the larger spread of times for the non-CORT group, the standard deviation being almost twice that of the CORT group. The boxes represent the middle 50% of cases, that is between the 25th and 75th percentiles. The horizontal line inside the box represents the median. The horizontal lines that are not within a box are known as whiskers and represent the expected range of times. The small circle represents an "outlier" or extreme value.

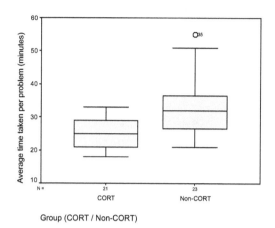

Figure 8.4: Box plot of "Average time taken per problem" for CORT / Non-CORT Students

The significant difference between the means of the two groups is perceived as very important especially when the previous analyses are taken into account. The previous analyses revealed no significant difference between the end-test performance of the CORT and non-CORT students. However the CORT students had taken only 76% of the time that the non-CORT students had taken. On average, the CORT students had each taken a total of 144 minutes less time to complete all of their problems during the class activities.

The results suggest that there may well have been significant differences in achievement between the two groups if the CORT students had spent as much time practising their programming skills as their non-CORT counterparts. Another conclusion that can be drawn is, that by using CORT, students can reduce the time required to achieve competence in programming.

8.4.3.2 Differences in Help Required to Complete Programming Problems among CORT and Non-CORT Students

Students were asked to estimate the amount of help that they required in the completion of each programming problem. Students could obtain help from other students, the tutor, or the textbook, and they recorded the data concerning this in their individual problem questionnaires.

It has been demonstrated in previous research that students who have to generate code from "scratch" to solve a problem will require more help and, for example, use textbooks and other resources to find programming code that has been used to solve a similar problem to the one that they are attempting (van Merrienboer & De Croock, 1992). The use of CORT could possibly reduce the reliance on help from a tutor and the need to search various resources when attempting to solve programming problems. This is because CORT provides learning supports via its part-complete solution approach.

The "Average help required per problem", was the average help that students required to complete each of the eighteen programming problems during the semester. The data were collected via the individual problem questionnaires that the students completed for each problem that they attempted. The help values were coded in the range 1 to 4. The codes corresponded to: no help; little help; moderate help; and extensive help respectively. Students estimated the help needed for each of the 18 problems and these values were then averaged. Table 8.36 shows that data were collected from 21 CORT students and 23 non-CORT students. The mean average help required was found to be 2.25 and 2.70 respectively on the 1 to 4 scale.

Table 8.36: Group Statistics for Student Group and Help Required to Complete Problems

	Group (CORT / Non-CORT)	N	Mean	Std. Deviation	Std. Error Mean
Average help required per problem	CORT	21	2.2524	.41427	.09040
	Non-CORT	23	2.7043	.53127	.11078

The data were then further analysed and Table 8.37 shows results of the t-test for the student groups' help requirements to complete programming problems.

Table 8.37: T-Test: Student Group and Average Help Required per Problem

		Levene's Test for Equality of Variances		t-test for Equality of Means						95% Confidence Interval of the Difference	
		F	Sig.	t	df	Sig. (2-tailed)	Mean Difference	Std. Error Difference	Lower	Upper
Average help required per problem	Equal variances assumed	1.131	.294	-3.125	42	.003	-.4520	.14461	-.74381	-.16012
	Equal variances not assumed			-3.161	41.038	.003	-.4520	.14298	-.74072	-.16321

Levene's F value was found to be not significant in this case and equal variances were not assumed. The result of the t-test

$t(42) = -3.13, p < 0.05$

revealed a significant difference between CORT and non-CORT students with respect to the average amount of help required per problem. The differences are shown graphically in the box plot of Figure 8.5. This indicates a greater spread of help requirements for the non-CORT group.

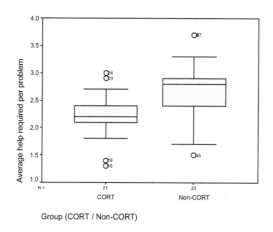

Group (CORT / Non-CORT)

Figure 8.5: Box plot of "Average help required per problem " for CORT / Non-CORT Students

The ratio scale of 1 to 4 that the students had used to estimate the help that they had required corresponded to none, little, moderate, and extensive. The box plot of Figure 8.5 reveals that most CORT students needed little help whereas the majority of non-CORT students required moderate help. Students also indicated the type of help that they needed for each problem. They obtained most help from their textbooks however a substantial amount was also obtained from their tutor. This finding has implications for the ability for students to learn programming independently. Often students have difficulties learning programming when they reach points, when solving a problem, that they cannot go beyond until they have had some help from a tutor (e.g., Garner, 2002). The fact that CORT students required significantly less help could be attributed to the high level of support that it provides. One implication of this would be that students using CORT would be able to learn programming more independently than non-CORT students and this would be especially beneficial for distance learning students.

The results reveal that CORT students sought less help than non-CORT students in their programming tasks. This suggests CORT could be a useful tool for supporting students needing to study programming independently or remotely.

8.4.4 Time and Help Requirements' Differences among sub-groups

The earlier t-tests had revealed that CORT students took significantly less time and required significantly less help than non-CORT students to complete the programming problems that they had been assigned. It was considered a possibility that within the CORT group, certain students, such as those with higher levels of computer literacy or some previous programming experience, might complete their tasks significantly faster and / or with less help, than those with for example, lower levels of computer literacy or without any programming experience.

Analyses were therefore carried out to determine if there were any significant interactions between student group and each of the other five independent variables: previous achievement level, age, computer literacy level, previous programming experience, and gender with respect to the time and help requirements of students. Tables 8.38 and 8.39 show the results of the two-way ANOVA tests that were undertaken.

Table 8.38: Statistical Tests for Student Group and Other Variables for Average Time Taken to Complete Problems

ANOVA Test	ANOVA Result	Significant?
Group + Previous achievement level	$F_{(2,38)}=0.151$, $p>0.05$	
Group + Age	$F_{(1,40)}=0.580$, $p>0.05$	
Group + Computer literacy level	$F_{(1,37)}=1.877$, $p>0.05$	
Group + Previous programming experience	$F_{(1,37)}=0.046$, $p>0.05$	
Group + Gender	$F_{(1,40)}=0.022$, $p>0.05$	

Table 8.39: Statistical Tests for Student Group and Other Variables for Average help Required to Complete Problems

ANOVA Test	ANOVA Result	Significant?
Group + Previous achievement level	$F_{(2,38)}=0.013$, $p>0.05$	
Group + Age	$F_{(1,40)}=0.101$, $p>0.05$	
Group + Computer literacy level	$F_{(1,37)}=0.252$, $p>0.05$	
Group + Previous programming experience	$F_{(1,37)}=0.001$, $p>0.05$	
Group + Gender	$F_{(1,40)}=0.473$, $p>0.05$	

The results indicate that the five independent variables that were tested did not significantly interact with the student group for both the time taken and the help required to complete the assigned programming problems.

8.4.5 Summary of the Impact of the PCSM within the CORT System on Learning Achievement

The results of the data analyses provide mixed outcomes concerning the impact of the PCSM within CORT on student learning. No significant difference was found in the relative achievement of students in the CORT and non-CORT groups in tests of programming achievement, while the results showed significant advantages for the CORT students in terms of time saving and levels of tutor help required. The results suggest that the system can help students to complete programming tasks more quickly and can provide higher levels of support, both factors providing advantage for novice programmers.

Although there was no significant difference between the CORT and non-CORT students in any of the achievement measures, differences did emerge between certain student sub-groups with respect to Exam Part A and these are summarised in Table 8.40.

Table 8.40: Significant Achievement Levels amongst Students for Exam Part A

		Higher Achievement		Lower Achievement	
		CORT	Non-CORT	CORT	Non-CORT
Age	Younger		✓	✓	
	Mature	✓			✓
Computer Literacy	Moderate		✓	✓	
	Extensive	✓			✓
Prev. Prog. Experience	None		✓	✓	
	Little	✓			✓

The table entries reveal a similar pattern amongst the categories. That is that the students who used the CORT system that achieved at a lower level were either younger, only moderately computer literate, or without any previous programming experience. Exam Part A was a measure of the students' ability to read and comprehend computer programs. The common factor among the categories may be that such students do not have a satisfactory and well defined mental model of the way in which computers execute programs and they therefore have greater difficulty comprehending code.

Research has shown that students with ill-developed mental models can be supported in the learning of programming by helping them visualise the execution process of the programs (e.g., Smith & Webb, 2000). The non-CORT students who learnt programming in a "conventional" manner had to spend a lot of time experimenting as they attempted to generate their programs. This may well have helped them develop appropriate mental models. However, students who used the CORT system were able to complete their programs relatively quickly and with less experimentation. This might not have helped students in their mental model development.

Those students who already had well developed mental models did benefit from using the CORT system. Students who were either mature, with high levels of computer literacy, or with some previous programming experience, performed better than their non-CORT counterparts.

The time that the CORT students required to complete all of the programming tasks was approximately three quarters of that of the non-CORT students. Significant differences in achievement may well have been demonstrated if the CORT students had spent the extra time that they had, practising further programming problems.

The CORT students were found to require little help when using the system whereas the non-CORT students required moderate help. Whilst this does not impact directly on achievement levels, it may affect the achievement levels of students who do not have easy access to sources of help. It is well known (e.g., Garner, 2002) that distance learning students of programming have difficulties when they reach a point in solving a programming problem, such that they cannot proceed further until they obtain help from a tutor. If such help is not readily available, or the time taken for a tutor to respond to a query is long, then student achievement may be reduced. The PCSM within CORT provides help and learning supports to students so that the extra help that students need is relatively low. Distance learning students may therefore benefit if they were to use the system in an introductory programming unit.

The fact that the system did not provide learning advantages was not an expected outcome of the study. It is possible that there could have been differences observed in achievement under different conditions. Factors that may have contributed include:

- A lack of sensitivity in the various exams and instruments to the learning supported by the system;

- Insufficient use of the system among the students for the treatment to make a difference; and

- Too small a sample size for differences to emerge.

Chapter 9
Summary and Conclusions

This chapter gives an overview of the research conducted; a summary of the findings; the limitations of the study; and recommendations for future research.

The study sought to explore a technology supported part-complete solution method (TSPCSM) for the learning of computer programming. The literature concerning student learning and particularly the teaching and learning of computer programming was reviewed and used to inform the development of a teaching and learning framework for programming that included learning resources, supports and activities. A technology supported tool, CORT, was then designed around the learning framework and developed to support the part-complete solution method and provide a suitable learning environment.

A quasi-experimental research design framework was utilised in the study which used both qualitative and quantitative research methods. A series of programming problems was developed for the CORT system and an experiment was undertaken with students who were studying introductory programming in a school of Management Information Systems at an Australian university. The data were analysed and they provided rich information concerning how students engaged with the CORT system; how the PCSM within CORT supported the learning process; and how the PCSM within CORT impacted upon their learning outcomes.

An overview of the study is shown in Table 9.1.

Table 9.1: Overview of the Study

Chapter	Title	Description
1	Introduction	Significance and purpose of the thesis.
2	The Teaching and Learning of programming	A review of the literature concerning the teaching and learning of computer programming, including: • The difficulties of learning to program including general problem solving skills; program design; language notation; the pragmatics of programming; and the cognitive load experienced by novice programmers; • The approaches to the teaching and learning of programming including the expert, spiral and reading approaches; • Approaches to teaching and learning that have been experimented with including the conceptual / notional machine; intelligent tutoring systems; experiential and situated approaches; programming plans; the use of part-complete solutions; and the cloze procedure; and • Tools used in the teaching and learning of programming including program visualisation tools; and algorithm design tools.
3	Student Learning and a Teaching and Learning Framework for programming	A review of the literature concerning student learning that considered: • Mental representation and how information is stored in memory; • Development of expertise and the differences between novices and experts in a domain of knowledge; • Mental processes and particularly information processing and knowledge construction; • Cognitive load theory and the three types of cognitive load that impact on learning: intrinsic, extraneous and germane; • Problem solving and the use of worked examples; • Scaffolding and problem solving; • Higher order thinking and its application to the learning of programming. The literature reviewed informed the development of a teaching and learning framework for the learning of programming.
4	Development of a Tool to Support the Part-Complete Solution Method (PCSM)	Using the teaching and learning framework developed in chapter 3, the tool (CORT) to support the PCSM was developed. An initial prototype was tested with students and the feedback informed the creation of a second version to be used in the full study.
5	Research Design	A research methodology was selected that made extensive use of qualitative techniques and that was complemented with quantitative techniques. The research questions were developed together with the detailed design and data collection methods. The methodology included the use of questionnaires, observation, interviews, and end tests. A data collection schedule was also finalised for the main study.
6	How Students Use CORT	The first research question was considered: "How students use CORT". Results from this usability study indicated that:: • The majority of students quickly became comfortable with the basic functionality of CORT; • Any difficulties that arose in the use of CORT were minimal and students quickly overcome them; • CORT had a small learning curve and the extraneous cognitive load imposed upon students by CORT's usability was minimal; • Potential changes to CORT were identified in order that the usability of CORT could be improved upon in a future version.

Chapter	Title	Description
7	How the CORT System supports the Learning Process	The second research question was considered: "How did the PCSM within CORT support the learning process?". Results indicated that: • The system provided strong scaffolding for student learning; and • Students engaged well with the system and generally used a thoughtful and considered cognitive strategy. The different types and levels of support that the system provided were also identified together with types of difficulties that students experienced when using the 3 different CORT methods.
8	The Impact of the CORT System on Learning Outcomes	The third research question was considered: "What impact did the use of the PCSM within CORT have on learning outcomes?". The data collected from end-tests were analysed and the results indicated that there was no significant difference in the relative achievement of students in CORT and non-CORT student groups. However, it was found that the CORT system helped students to complete programming tasks more quickly and also that it provided higher levels of support than that received by the non-CORT group. Differences also emerged between certain sub-groups of student with respect to their performance in "reading" and understanding existing programming code.
9	Summary and Conclusions	A summary of the thesis including: an overview of the research conducted; a summary of the findings; limitations of the study; and recommendations for further research.

9.1 Teaching and Learning Framework for Programming

The main purpose of the study was to test the **CO**de **R**estructuring **T**ool, CORT, that was developed to provide technology support for the part-complete solution method (PCSM) for learning programming as part of an encompassing teaching and learning framework.

The design of the framework was informed by research into the teaching and learning of programming and student learning in general:

• In problem solving it is necessary for learners to develop their cognitive schemata and mental models.

• To help build cognitive schemata, learners have to mentally process their mental representations or cognitive schemata.

• Constructivism suggests that the construction of knowledge by learners is dependent upon their existing schemata and therefore learning should be student centred with students being able to progress at their own pace.

- Cognitive load theory suggests that in problem solving domains, it is necessary to keep the extraneous cognitive load to a minimum as the domain itself has a very high intrinsic cognitive load. It is then possible to have some germane cognitive load imposed on learners to ensure that they actively engage with the material that they are studying.

- In the context of computer programming, one way of applying germane cognitive load is to utilise learning materials that require learners to complete solutions to part-complete programs that they have been given. Such part-complete programs can vary in their degree of completeness and such materials act as scaffolds to support student centred learning. This teaching and learning method is based upon the "Reading" method of learning programming which has the best "match" to cognitive load theory.

From the literature review, a framework of learning attributes that could provide support for learning in problem solving domains of knowledge such as programming was proposed. Elements of a technology supported PCSM environment to support those learning attributes were then identified and finally the teaching and learning framework for programming was designed to provide an overall environment for learning.

CORT was developed to provide the technology support for the PCSM. Its design was influenced by other computer programs that provide functionality permitting items to be easily moved between two parallel windows. An initial prototype was developed which was tested with a small group of students. The feedback that was received was then used to inform the development of a second version which was then used in the full experiment.

9.2 Research Design

Research methodologies were investigated and an overall process finalised for the study. The process was based on an epistemology of knowledge construction; a theoretical perspective of interpretivism-phenomenology; and a methodology of quasi-experimental action research with case studies.

Three research questions were posed to explore the use of CORT and the teaching and learning framework with students who were learning introductory programming:

1.   How did students use CORT?

2.   How did the PCSM within CORT support the learning process?

3.   What impact did the use of the PCSM within CORT have on learning outcomes?

Research instruments were developed together with a set of part-complete programming problems. Experimental and control groups were utilised in the experiment which took place over a 14 week semester at an Australian university. Data were collected via observation, interviews, questionnaires, document studies, and end-tests.

9.3 Research Results
The data collected were analysed for each of the 3 research questions.

9.3.1 Research Question 1
The first research question concerned how students used CORT. In order to determine how CORT influenced learning, it was necessary to determine if the way the CORT software was designed and developed hindered the students in any way.

The major data collection method that was used to explore this question was observation. Several students were observed over a 10 week period and 10 usability issues were identified. These issues were of 3 main types:

- Operation of the problem files;

- Manipulation of the lines of code; and

- Editing the lines of code.

The impediments these difficulties posed for learning tended to be minimal with students quickly overcoming difficulties through their experiences and continued use of CORT. Most of the difficulties disappeared early in the course. There were some minor interface issues with CORT however successful workarounds were found by all students.

It clearly emerged that CORT had a small learning curve and imposed a low extraneous cognitive load on students. This was seen to be an important finding as a necessary feature of the PCSM is to keep the extraneous cognitive load that students experience as low as possible. However, as with most initial versions of software, the usability of CORT could be improved and several potential changes emerged from the data analysis.

9.3.2 Research Question 2

The second research question sought to investigate how the PCSM within the CORT system supported the learning process. Data were mainly collected by the observation of students who were attempting CORT problems. Additional data were obtained from interviews and questionnaires and used to provide triangulation for certain aspects of the data analysis. Of particular interest in this research question were:

- The cognitive strategies that students used when attempting to solve problems with the CORT system;

- The types of support provided by CORT; and

- The scaffolding provided by CORT.

Five levels of cognitive strategy were identified ranging from unplanned and random through to a deliberate approach where a student would demonstrate a high level of planning and strategy. Four different support types were identified: syntax; semantic; structural; and algorithmic. Three levels of scaffolding provided by CORT were identified: provision of little help; provision of some help; and provision of a lot of help.

Students were observed attempting each of the 17 problems that had been developed for the experiment and the support types, cognitive strategy, and scaffolding provided were recorded. The data were then summarised and analysed in 3 different ways: by student observed; by CORT problem number; and by CORT method utilised.

The data analysis revealed that the CORT system scaffolded with an overall average of 2.6 (range 1 - 3) and supported a level of cognitive strategy of 3.3 (range 1 - 5). This demonstrated that system had provided considerable help for students and that students were generally engaged with the system during their learning. Also, the data revealed that most students applied some consideration in their approaches to the problems that they attempted. With respect to the 4 support types, the data indicated that the highest level of support was for semantic difficulties. However there were also high levels of support for structural and algorithmic difficulties.

When the data were analysed by problem number, it was found that most semantic help took place earlier in the course, when students were attempting to acquire much of the necessary semantic knowledge of various programming statements, and that most algorithmic help took place in the latter part of the course, when the problems became progressively more difficult. This result suggested that the design of the set of 17 problems was acceptable as students were able to obtain the semantic support that was necessary in the earlier part of the course, and then obtain algorithmic support as the CORT problems increased in their degree of difficulty.

Several interesting findings emerged when the data were analysed by CORT method. Each problem that students attempted utilised a particular CORT method, ranging from 1 to 3, which respectively: required all the lines of code from the left-hand window; required only some of the lines of code from the left-hand window; and required some or all of the lines of code from the left-hand window and some extra lines of code to be keyed in.

The data revealed that the levels of cognitive support were fairly even and strong across all three CORT methods, and that the level of scaffolding provided by the system was lowest for method 3 type problems. The latter was not surprising as high levels of scaffolding are provided for method 1 and 2 type problems in the form of the missing lines for a problem solution being available in the left-hand window of CORT. With method 3 type problems, such support is not available. The level of algorithmic support was particularly low for method 3 type problems. This result has implications for the CORT methods that should be used when students are being encouraged to develop their knowledge concerning some of the fundamental algorithms of programming.

9.3.3 Research Question 3

The third research question sought to investigate the impact that the use of the PCSM within CORT had on learning outcomes. Quantitative data were collected from end-tests that were undertaken by both the CORT and non-CORT groups. The results of the data analyses provided mixed outcomes concerning the impact of the CORT system on student learning. No significant difference was found in the relative achievement of students in the CORT and non-CORT groups in tests of programming achievement. However the data analyses concerning other factors did provide interesting results.

Data concerning the time taken to complete problems were analysed to determine how this factor was related to learning outcomes. The results indicated that the students who used CORT took significantly less time to complete the set of problems. Similar findings occurred in a previous study that compared 2 student groups that were learning algebraic problem solving (Sweller & Cooper, 1985). One group studied worked examples whilst the other was exposed to "conventional" instruction. End-tests were administered and it was found that learning was more efficient with respect to time, and yet no less effective, when the worked example method was used. Hence with respect to CORT, a conclusion that might be drawn is that if students who used the CORT system to learn programming were to spend as much time as students using a traditional teaching and learning method, then they may well achieve a higher level of expertise.

Data concerning the help that was required were also analysed to determine how this factor was related to learning outcomes. It was found that the students who used the CORT system required significantly less help than the non-CORT students. This suggests that the use of the system could be of benefit to distance learning students who have less access to their tutors and therefore require stronger supports from other learning resources.

The data were also analysed for sub-groups of students and some significant differences emerged concerning the ability to read and understand programming code. It was found that the students who used the CORT system who were less able to read and understand existing programming code compared to the equivalent non-CORT students were either younger, only moderately computer literate, or without any previous programming experience.

A possible explanation for this result is that these particular students may not have developed their mental models of the way in which computers execute programs to the same degree as the other students. These sub-groups of student most probably had ill-defined mental models of program execution when they started the programming course. It may be that generating programs from "scratch" helps these categories of student develop their mental models as they spend more time experimenting and debugging their code. With the CORT system, it has been shown that students reach correct solutions more quickly and this may mean that they have not had the opportunity to greatly improve their mental models of program execution.

However contrasting results emerged between the sub-groups as it was found that students who used the CORT system that were either mature, with high levels of computer literacy, or with some previous programming experience, performed better than their non-CORT counterparts. These students may already had well developed mental models of program execution when they started the course and the results suggest that the PCSM within CORT has provided strong support to such students. A number of questions emerged and are suggested in a later section as possible areas for further study.

9.4 Limitations of the Study

"Limitations are those conditions beyond the control of the researcher that may place restrictions on the conclusions of the study and their application to other situations" (Best & Khan, 1998, p.37). Some of the limitations that were identified in this study include:

- Sample size;

- Representativeness of the sample;

- Possible Observer Bias; and

- Sensitivity of the end-tests.

9.4.1 Sample Size

A possible limitation of the study is the number of subjects that were involved in the research. According to Charles (1988) a sample should comprise at leat 30 subjects. Although the total number of students in the study was 49, some of the numbers in the sub-groups were below 30. A greater sample size may have provided a level of data to demonstrate the achievement gains being sought. However Burns (1994, p.73) makes the point that "although for a given design an increase in sample size increases accuracy, it will not eliminate or reduce any bias in the selection procedure". Hence the sample size is less important than representativeness of a sample.

9.4.2 Representativeness of the sample

"Selection bias" is bias that occurs when "intact" classes are used as experimental and control groups. An example is: "Because of scheduling arrangements, an English class meeting during the fourth period may consist of particularly able students who are scheduled at that period because they are also enrolled in an advanced mathematics class" (Best and Kahn, 1998, p.166).

In this study, there were 4 computer laboratories and 1 lecture. Anecdotal evidence suggests that the more organised students enrol into units of study as soon as unit enrolment is opened, and that those students select computer laboratory times as close to the lecture time as possible. This may have occurred in this research thereby introducing selection bias.

Because of this possibility of bias, a quasi-experimental design framework was used in the study. Such designs are often used in Education and in such a design, it has been suggested that: "without some evidence of the equivalence of the groups in intelligence, maturity, readiness and other factors at the beginning of the experimental period, conclusions should be cautiously interpreted" Best and Kahn (1998, p.176).

9.4.3 Observer Bias

"When researchers are sole observers, they unconsciously tend to see what they expect to see and to overlook those incidents that do not fit their theory. Their own values, feelings, and attitudes, based upon past experience, may distort their observations" (Best and Kahn, 1998, p.295). In this study, the researcher designed and built CORT, and also acted as the participant-observer. Whilst every care was taken both in the design and implementation of the research project through the use of multiple data sources and exploratory processes, the subjectivity that comes from human activity and personal belief systems cannot be totally removed from a research process like this.

9.4.4 Sensitivity of the End-Tests

Programming is a complex and multi-faceted discipline and learning outcomes can be measured in many ways. The outcomes of learning programming will be manifest in a variety of ways including programming knowledge, skills and attitudes. In this study, achievement was measured using an end-of-semester pen and paper examination of 2 hours and 30 minutes duration. Whilst it provides a useful means for comparing achievement across a class group, it could not be considered the best method of determining the actual scope and extent of the learning that has taken place. The lack of sensitivity in the instrument to all aspects of programming learning may have limited its ability to accurately reveal learning outcomes, especially some of those influenced by the CORT system. A more sensitive instrument may have yielded different results for some students.

9.5 Recommendations for Future Research

The research conducted in this study confirmed the possibility of utilising a technology supported part-complete solution method, in the form of the CORT system, with students in introductory programming classes. The study investigated only one major aspect of learning outcome, i.e. student achievement in tests. Other outcomes that seem worthy of investigation are:

- The impact of the use of the CORT system on the time needed to learn;

- The type of part-complete CORT problem that is best able to support learning; and

- The impact of the development of students' mental models prior to the use of the CORT system.

Other possible future research might include:

- The use of the CORT system with remote learners;

- The impact of the CORT system on motivation and the affective domains of students.

9.5.1 Impact of the CORT system on the Time Needed to Learn

The study revealed that the CORT students achieved at the same level as the non-CORT students. However the CORT students took significantly less time on their tasks and problems. It was suggested that if the CORT students had spent the same amount of time solving part-complete programming problems with CORT as the non-CORT students spent solving programming problems in a "conventional" manner, then the CORT students may have achieved at a higher level. A possible future research question is:

Is there a significant difference in programming achievement between CORT and non-CORT students who have spent equal amounts of time learning introductory programming?

9.5.2 CORT Problem Type and the Support of Learning

Three CORT methods were used in the study and the amount of support and scaffolding afforded by the methods varied. It would be useful to determine which CORT method is preferable for different problem types. Also, the effect of adjusting the following within methods would be of interest:

- The number of lines removed from a programming solution;

- The number of distracter lines used in method 2 problems; and

- The number of lines that need to be keyed-in for method 3 type problems.

The research could be undertaken by using 2 CORT student groups and varying the methods and adjusting the missing lines. The groups would undertake the same set of programming problems in an experiment and possible experiments are shown in Table 9.2.

Table 9.2: Future Experiments into the Impact of CORT Methods

	CORT Group A	CORT Group B
Experiment 1	Uses Method 1	Uses Method 2
Experiment 2	Uses Method 1	Uses Method 3
Experiment 3	Uses Method 2	Uses Method 3
Experiment 4	Uses Method 1	Uses Method 1. More lines are removed from the solutions compared to Group A
Experiment 5	Uses Method 2	Uses Method 2 The same lines of code are removed from the solutions compared to Group A, however more distracter lines are included
Experiment 6	Uses Method 3	Uses Method 3, however more lines are removed from the solutions compared to Group A

For example, a possible future research question for Experiment 1 might be:

Is there a significant difference in programming achievement between a CORT group using Method 1 type part-complete problems and a CORT group using Method 2 type part-complete problems in an introductory programming course?

9.5.3 Development of Mental Models of Program Execution

Results from the study indicated that younger students, and students that were moderately computer literate or without any previous programming experience, did not perform as well using the CORT system as the equivalent non-CORT students. It was suggested that these students might not have well developed mental models of program execution. This proposition could be formally tested by having two CORT groups, one of which was initially exposed to learning resources and tasks that would be aimed at helping them develop their mental models of program execution. Then, both groups could undertake the same set of part-complete programming tasks using CORT and finally learning outcomes could be measured to determine if there were any differences. A possible future research question is:

Is there a significant difference in programming achievement between: a CORT group that has initially been given tasks to encourage the development of the

students' mental models of program execution; and a second CORT control
group, in introductory programming?

9.5.4 Use of the CORT System with Remote Learners

Results from the research indicated that the students who used the CORT system required less help than non-CORT students. This suggests that remote students, who have less access to tutor support and feedback than on-campus students may benefit from the CORT system. This could be tested by dividing a class of remote learners who were learning programming into two groups, one of which used the CORT system whilst the other used a conventional teaching and learning method. Data concerning the amount of help that the students requested from their tutors could then be collected and analysed. A possible research question is:

Is there a significant difference in the amount of help required between CORT
and non-CORT students who are learning introductory programming and are
remote learners?

9.5.5 Impact of the CORT System on Motivation and Affective Domains

Two of the main aims of the PCSM within CORT are to reduce the overall cognitive load that students experience when learning to program and to encourage higher order thinking. Reducing the cognitive load may have the effect of reducing the repeated and unresolved failures that impede progress and of lowering the motivation of students to continue with programming (Linn and Dalbey, 1985). The encouragement of higher order thinking can focus attention, minimise anxiety, and maintain motivation (Jones et al, 1987). Further research into the impact that the use of the CORT system may have on student motivation and on the affective domain of students would appear to be of interest. A possible research question is:

How does the use of the CORT system impact the motivation and the affective
domain of students who are learning to program?

9.6 Conclusions

This study set out to explore the efficacy and utility of the use of a technology supported part-complete solution method (TSPCSM) for the learning of introductory computer programming. A teaching and learning framework that encompassed the PCSM was developed and the CORT system was built to provide the technological support. The aim was to keep the cognitive load that students experienced during their learning of programming lower than that experienced in conventional instruction. This was done by keeping the extrinsic cognitive load low. However the set of part-complete programming tasks that students undertook was designed so that students were put under germane cognitive load thereby encouraging them to apply higher order thinking.

Results from the study indicated that the CORT system had a small learning curve and imposed a low cognitive load on students. The system provided high levels of cognitive support across all 3 CORT methods; strong scaffolding for learning; and students engaged well with the system, generally using a thoughtful and considered strategy. Although no differences in learning outcomes were found between the CORT group and the non-CORT control group, two key findings were that the students who used the CORT system required significantly less time and less help than the control group. This suggests that: differences in learning outcomes between CORT and non-CORT students might occur if equal amounts of time were spent attempting programming problems; and students using the CORT system may be able to work more autonomously than non-CORT students. Both of these suggestions could be the subject of further research. Also, the students who benefited most from the system appeared to have well developed mental models of program execution and it would seem that any instructional design should try and ensure the construction of such mental models before a PCSM is used.

The study found the CORT system to be supportive of learning and, while it did not demonstrate achievement gains, it did demonstrate efficiency of learning. More research is clearly needed to further explore the best ways to implement part-complete solutions so that learning advantages can be gained.

Finally, the aim of this study was to make a change to the method of teaching and learning of programming and to test that change in order to determine if it has potential for future practice. To this end, it has hopefully been successful and contributed to knowledge in this important discipline.

References

Anderson, J. R. (1983). *The architecture of cognition.* Cambridge, MA: Harvard University Press.

Anderson, J. R., Corbett, A. T., Koedinger, K. & Pelletier, R. (1995). Cognitive tutors: Lessons learned. *The Journal of Learning Sciences, 4,* 167-207.

Anderson, J. R., Farrell, R. & Sauers, R. (1984). Learning to program in LISP. *Cognitive Science, 8,* 87-129.

Anderson, J. R., Fincham, J. M. & Douglass, S. (1997). The role of examples and rules in the acquisition of a cognitive skill. *Journal of Experimental Psychology: Learning, Memory and Cognition, 23,* 932-945.

Anderson, J. R., Simon, H. A. & Reder, L. M. (2000). Applications and misapplications of cognitive psychology to mathematics education. *Texas Educational Review, Summer 2000.*

Athey, S. & Quick, D. (1997). *Using the experiential learning model with graduate students in a first programming class.* Paper presented at the Information Resources Management Association international conference 1997.

Atkinson, R., Renkl, A. & Merrill, M. (2003). Transitioning from studying examples to solving problems: Effects of self-explanation prompts and fading worked-out steps. *Journal of Educational Psychology, 95*(4), 774-783.

Atkinson, R. L. & Shiffrin, R. M. (1968). Human memory: A proposed system and its control processes. In J. T. Spence (Ed.), *The psychology of learning and motivation: Advances in research and theory* (Vol. 2). N.Y.: Academic.

Aviram, O. (1993). Appearance and reality in a stressful educational setting: Practices inhibiting school effectiveness in an Israeli boarding school. *Qualitative Studies in Education, 6*(1), 33-48.

Baddeley, A. (1992). Working memory. *Science, 255,* 556-559.

Baecker, R., DiGiano, C. & Marcus, A. (1997). Software visualization for debugging. *Association for Computing Machinery: Communications of the ACM, 40*(4), 44-54.

Barg, M., Fekete, A., Greening, T., Hollands, O., Kay, J., Kingston, J. H. & Crawford, K. (2000). Problem-based learning for foundation computer science courses. *Computer Science Education, 10*(2), 109-128.

Barr, A., Beard, M. & Atkinson, R. C. (1976). The computer as a tutorial laboratory: The Stanford BIP project. *International Journal of Man-Machine Studies, 8,* 567-596.

Bartlett, F. C. (1932). *Remembering.* Cambridge: Cambridge University Press.

Bayman, P. & Mayer, R. E. (1983). A diagnosis of beginning programmers' misconceptions of basic programming statements. *Communications of the ACM, 26*(9), 677-679.

Bayman, P. & Mayer, R. E. (1988). Using conceptual models to teach basic computer programming. *Journal of Educational Psychology, 80*(3), 291-298.

Ben-Ari, M. (2001). Constructivism in computer science education. *Journal of Computers in Mathematics & Science Teaching, 20*(1), 45-73.

Bergin, J., Stehlik, M., Roberts, J. & Pattis, R. (1996). *Karel++: A gentle introduction to the art of object-oriented programming.*: New York, Wiley.

Best, J. W. & Kahn, J. V. (1998). *Research in education* (8th ed.). Allyn and Bacon.

Bloom, B. S. (1956). *Taxonomy of educational objectives: Handbook 1. The cognitive domain.* N.Y.: David McKay.

Bogdan, R. & Biklen, S. (1992). *Qualitative research for education : An introduction to theory and methods* (3rd ed.). Boston: Allyn and Bacon.

Borg, W. R. & Gall, M. D. (1989). *Educational research : An introduction* (5th ed.). N. Y.: Longman.

Borg, W. R., Gall, J. P. & Gall, M. D. (1993). *Applying educational research : A practical guide* (3 ed.). N.Y.: Longman.

Bower, G. H. (1975). Cognitive psychology: An introduction. In W. K. Estes (Ed.), *Handbook of learning and cognitive processes: Introduction to concepts and issues* (Vol. 1). N.Y: Erlbaum.

Bransford, J. D. & Franks, J. J. (1971). The abstraction of linguistic ideas. *Cognitive Psychology, 2*, 331-350.

Bruce, C. & McMahon, C. (2002). *Contemporary developments in teaching and learning introductory programming: Towards a research proposal.* QUT. Retrieved 17 Feb 2005, from http://sky.fit.qut.edu.au/~bruce/pub/papers/T&L Report PB edited 3 Dec.pdf.

Bruce, C., Buckingham, L., Hynd, J., McMahon, C., Roggenkamp, M. & Stoodley, I. (2004). Ways of experiencing the act of learning to program: A phenomenographic study of introductory programming students at university. *Journal of Information Technology Education, 3*, 143-160.

Brusilovsky, P., Calabrese, E., Hvorecky, J., Kouchnirenko, A. & Miller, P. (1997). Mini-languages: A way to learn programming principles. *Education and Information Technologies*(2), 65-83.

Brusilovsky, P., Kouchnirenko, A., Miller, P. & Tomek, I. (1994). *Teaching programming to novices: A review of approaches and tools.* Paper presented at the Ed-Media 94, Vancouver, British Columbia, Canada.

Brusilovsky, P. & Spring, M. (2004). *Adaptive, engaging, and explanatory visualization in a C programming course.* Paper presented at the Ed-Media 2004, Lugano, Switzerland.

Burns, R. B. (1990). *Introduction to research methods in education.* Melbourne: Longman Cheshire.

Burns, R. B. (1994). *Introduction to research methods* (2nd ed.). Longman.

Carbone, A., Hurst, J., Mitchell, I. & Gunstone, D. (2000). *Principles for designing programming exercises to minimise poor learning behaviours in students.* Paper presented at the Fourth Australasian Computing Education Conference, Melbourne, Australia.

Carey, D. (1996). *Teaching algorithms and programming concepts using an object-oriented language.* Paper presented at the Australian Conference in Computer Education 96, Brisbane, Australia.

Carroll, W. (1994). Using worked examples as an instructional support in the algebra classroom. *Journal of Educational Computing Psychology, 86*, 360-367.

Chalk, P. (2002). *Community of practice: learning the craft of programming.* Paper presented at the LTSN-ICS One day conference on the teaching of programming.

Chandler, P. & Sweller, J. (1991). Cognitive load theory and the format of instruction. *Cognition and Instruction, 8*, 293-332.

Chandler, P. & Sweller, J. (1996). Cognitive load while learning to use a computer program. *Applied Cognitive Psychology, 10*, 151-170.

Chansilp, K. & Oliver, R. (2002). *Using multimedia to develop students' programming concepts.* Paper presented at the EDU-COM 2002, Khon-Kaen, Thailand.

Chansilp, K. & Oliver, R. (2004). *Students' responses to the use of a multimedia tool for learning computer programming.* Paper presented at the Ed-Media 2004, Lugano, Switzerland.

Charles, C. M. (1988). *Introduction to educational research.* N.Y.: Longman.

Chase, W. G. & Simon, H. A. (1973). The mind's eye in chess. In W. G. Chase (Ed.), *Visual Information Processing.* New York: Academic.

Chi, M. T. H., Glaser, R. & Rees, E. (1982). Expertise in problem solving. In R. Sternberg (Ed.), *Advances in the psychology of human intelligence.* Hillsdale, N.J.: Lawrence Erlbaum.

Clancy, M. J. & Linn, M. C. (1999). Patterns and pedagogy. *SIGCSE Bulletin, 31*(1), 33-42.

Clear, T. (1997). The nature of cognition and action. *ACM SIGCSE Bulletin, 29*(4), 25-29.

Cohen, L. & Manion, L. (1994). *Research methods in education* (4th ed.). N. Y.: Routhledge.

Cook, C., Bregar, W. & Foote, D. (1984). A preliminary investigation of the use of the cloze procedure as a measure of program understanding. *Information Processing & Management, 20*(1-2), 199-208.

Cordeiro, E. B. & Carspecken, P. F. (1993). How a minority of the minority succeed: a case study of twenty Hispanic achievers. *Qualitative Studies in Education, 6*(4), 277-290.

Craik, K. (1943). *The nature of explanation.* Cambridge: Cambridge University Press.

Crews, T. & Murphy, C. (2004). *Programming right from the start with Visual BASIC .NET.* Pearson.

Crews, T., Butterfield, J. & Blankenship, R. (2000a). *FLINT - A general purpose graphical CASE tool.* Paper presented at the ooictl-Business 2000 international conference, Shreveport, USA.

Crews, T., Butterfield, J. & Blankenship, R. (2000b). *The utility of flowcharts for novice programmers.* Paper presented at the ooictl-Business 2000 international conference, Shreveport, USA.

Crews, T., Butterfield, J. & Blankenship, R. (2002). *Right from the start: Leveling (then raising) the playing field.* Paper presented at the ISECON 2002, San Antonio.

Crews, T. & Ziegler, U. (1998). *The flowchart interpreter for introductory programming courses.* Paper presented at the 1998 Frontiers in Education Conference, Tempe, Arizona.

Crotty, M. (1998). *The foundations of social research: Meaning and perspective in the research process.* St. Leonards, NSW: Allen & Unwin.

De Kleer, J. & Brown, J. S. (1981). Mental models of physical mechanisms and their acquisition. In J. R. Anderson (Ed.), *Cognitive skill and their acquisition.* Hillsdale, N. J.: Erlbaum.

De Pauw, W. & Sevitsky, G. (1999). *Visualising reference patterns for solving memory leaks in Java.* Paper presented at the ECOOP 99, Lisbon, Portugal.

De Raadt, M., Watson, R. & Toleman, M. (2002). *Language trends in introductory programming courses*. Paper presented at the Informing Science 2002, University College Cork, Ireland.

Deek, F. & McHugh, J. (1998). *A review and analysis of tools for learning programming.* Paper presented at the Ed-Media 98, Freiburg, Germany.

Deek, F. P., McHugh, J. A. & Hiltz, S. R. (2000). Methodology and technology for learning programming. *The Journal of Systems & Information Technology, 4*(1), 25-37.

Dehoney, J. & Reeves, T. (1999). Instructional and social dimensions of class web pages. *Journal of Computing in Higher Education, 10*(2), 19-41.

Di Vesta, F. J. (1987). The cognitive movement and education. In J. A. Glover & R. Ronnings (Eds.), *Historical foundations of educational psychology* (pp. 203-233). N.Y.: Plenum Press.

Dreyfus, H. L. & Dreyfus, S. E. (1986). *Mind over machine.* N.Y.: Free Press.

du Boulay, B. (1986). Some difficulties in learning to program. *Journal of Educational Computing Research, 2*(1), 57-73.

du Boulay, B., O'Shea, T. & Monk, J. (1981). The black box inside the white box: Presenting computing concepts to novices. *International Journal of Man-Machine Studies, 14,* 237-249.

Duffy, T. M. & Cunningham, D. J. (1996). Constructivism: Implications for the design and delivery of instruction. In D. H. Jonassen (Ed.), *Handbook of research on educational communications and technology* (pp. 170-198). N.Y.: Macmillan.

Edward, N. (1997). *Development of a cost effective computer assisted learning (CAL) package to facilitate conceptual understanding.* Paper presented at the CAL97, University of Exeter, UK.

Ehrlich, K. & Soloway, E. (1984). An empirical investigation of the tacit plan knowledge in programming. In J. Thomas & M. L. Schneider (Eds.), *Human Factors in Computer Systems* (pp. 113-133). Norwood, N.J.: Ablex.

Eisner, E. W. (1979). Recent developments in educational research affecting art education. *Art Education, 32*, 12-15.

Eisner, E. W. (1991). *The enlightened eye: Qualitative inquiry and the enhancement of educational practice*. N.Y.: Macmillan.

Fincher, S. (1999). *What are we doing when we teach programming?* Paper presented at the 29th Annual Frontiers in Education Conference: Designing the future of science and engineering education, San Juan, Puerto Rico.

Fisher, J. C. (1993). A framework for describing developmental change among older adults. *Adult Education Quarterly, 43*(2), 76-89.

French, J. N. & Rhoder, C. (1992). *Teaching thinking skills: Theory and practice*. N.Y.: Garland Publishing.

Fowler, W. A. L. & Fowler, R. H. (1993). A hypertext approach to Computer Science education unifying programming principles. *Journal of Multimedia and Hypermedia, 2*(4), 433-441.

Garner, S. K. (2002). *COLORS for programming: A system to support the learning of programming*. Paper presented at the Informing Science 2002, University College Cork, Ireland.

Gerjets, P., Scheiter, K. & Catrambone, R. (2004). Designing instructional examples to reduce intrinsic cognitive load: Molar versus modular presentation of solution procedures. *Instructional Science, 32*, 33-58.

Gibbs, D. C. (2002). *An interactive introductory programming environment using a scripting language*. Paper presented at the Ed-Media 2002, Denver, Collarado.

Gilbert, R. F. & Forouzan, B. A. (1996). Comparison of student success in pascal and C language curriculums. *Special Interest Group Computer Science Education*, 252-255.

Glaser, R. (1984). Education and thinking: The role of knowledge. *American Psychologist*(39), 93-104.

Hagan, D. & Lowder, J. (1996). *Use of the World Wide Web in introductory computer programming*. Paper presented at the ASCILITE 96, Adelaide, South Australia.

Hall, W. E. & Zweben, S. H. (1986). The cloze procedure and software comprehensibility measurement. *IEEE Transactions on Software Engineering, May 1986*, 608-623.

Harvey, B. (1992). Apprentice computer programmers. *Australian Educational Computing, 5*(1), 11-13.

Hawryszkiewycz, I. T. (2001). *Systems analysis and design*: Prentice Hall.

Hyperdictionary. (2005). Retrieved 4 Feb 2005, from http://www.hyperdictionary.com/search.aspx?define=computer+programming.

Instructional Strategies Online (2001). *Cloze procedure*. Retrieved 11 Jan 2005, from http://www.saskschools.ca/curr_content/techclass/instr/strats/cloze/index.html.

Jenkins, T. (2002). *On the cruelty of really teaching programming*. Paper presented at the 2nd LTSN-ICS one day conference on the teaching of programming, University of Wolverhampton, UK.

Johnson, L. F. (1995). C in the first course considered harmful. *Association for Computing Machinery. Communications of the ACM, 38*(5), 99-102.

Johnson, W. L. & Soloway, E. (1985). PROUST: An automatic debugger for pascal programs. *Byte, 10*(4), 179-190.

Jonassen, D. H. (1991). Objectivism versus constructivism: Do we need a new philosophical paradigm? *Educational Technology Research and Development, 39*(3), 5-14.

Jonassen, D. H. (1994). Thinking technology: Towards a constructivist design model. *Educational Technology, April 1994*, 34-37.

Jonassen, D. H. (1995). *Constructivism: Implications for the design and delivery of instruction.*: N.Y.: Scholastic.

Jonassen, D. H. & Reeves, T. C. (1996). Learning with technology: Using computers as cognitive tools. In D. H. Jonassen (Ed.), *Handbook of research on educational communications and technology* (pp. 693-719). N.Y.: Macmillan.

Jones, B. F., Palinscar, A. S., Ogle, D. S. & Carr, E. G. (1987). *Strategic teaching and learning: Cognitive instruction in the content areas*. Alexandria, VA: Association for Supervision and Curriculum Development.

Kaijiri, K. (1998). *Program diagnosis system using the World Wide Web*. Retrieved 23 Oct 2003, from http://softeng-www.cs.shinshu-u.ac.jp/~kaijiri/MyHome/Resources/jckbse98-5.pdf.

Kalyuga, S., Chandler, P. & Sweller, J. (1998). Levels of expertise and instructional design. *Human Factors, 40*, 1-17.

Kennedy, R. (1996). *Why bother learning the language, just learn to program algorithmically*. Paper presented at the Australian Computers in Education Conference 96, Canberra, Australia.

Kerlinger, F. N. (1969). *Foundations of behavioral research*. N.Y.: Holt, Rinehart & Winston.

King, J., Feltham, J. & Nucifora, D. (1994). Novice programming in high schools: Teacher perceptions and new directions. *Australian Educational Computing,* (Sep 1994), 17-23.

Klare, G. R. (1974). Assessing readability. *Reading Research Quarterly*(10), 63-102.

Larkin, J. H. & Simon, H. A. (1987). Why a diagram is (sometimes) worth ten thousand words. *Cognitive Science, 11*, 65-99.

Laurillard, D. (1993). *Rethinking university teaching: A framework for the effective use of educational technology*. London Routledge.

Lave, J. (2004). *Situated Learning*. Retrieved 9 Sep 2004, from http://tip.psychology.org/lave.html.

Lave, J. & Wenger, E. (1990). *Situated learning: Legitimate peripheral participation*. Cambridge, UK: Cambridge University Press.

Levy, R., Ben-Ari, M. & Uronen, P. (2000). *An extended experiment with Jeliot 2000*. Paper presented at the Program Visualization Workshop, Porvoo, Finland.

Levy, R., Ben-Ari, M. & Uronen, P. (2003). The Jeliot 2000 program animation system. *Computers and Education, 40*(1), 1-15.

Lieberman, H. (1986). An example based environment for beginning programmers. *Instructional Science, 14*(3), 277-292.

Lincoln, Y. S. & Guba, E. G. (1985). *Naturalistic inquiry.* Beverly Hills, CA: Sage Publications.

Linn, M. C. (1992). How can hypermedia tools help teach programming? *Learning and Instruction, 2,* 119-139.

Linn, M. & Dalbey, J. (1985). Cognitive consequences of programming instruction. *Educational Psychologist, 20*(4), 191-206.

Lisack, S. K. (1998). *Helping students succeed in a first programming course: A way to correct background deficiencies.* Paper presented at the International Association for Computer Information Systems Conference, Cancun, Mexico.

Lowenthal, F. & Marcourt, C. (1998). Cognitive strategies observed during problem solving with LOGO. *Journal of Computer Assisted Learning, 14*(1), 130-139.

Marchionini, G. (1985). Teaching programming: A developmental approach. *The Computing Teacher, May,* 12-15.

Marcus, A. (1992). *Graphic design for electronic documents and user interfaces.* N.Y.: ACM Press.

Marcus, N., Cooper, M. & Sweller, J. (1996). Understand instructions. *Journal of Educational Psychology, 88,* 49-63.

Martinez, J. M. & Benko de Rotaeche, A. (1990). *Pedagogical, psychological and sociological aspects concerning the introduction of computer programming in a public secondary school in Venezuela.* Paper presented at the Fifth World Conference on Computers in Education, Sydney, Australia.

Mayer, R. E. (1975). Different problem-solving competencies established in learning computer programming with and without meaningful modes. *Journal of Educational Psychology, 67*(6), 725-734.

Mayer, R. E. (1981). The psychology of how novices learn computer programming. *Computing Surveys, 13*, 121-141.

Mayer, R. E. (1988). Introduction to research on teaching and learning computer programming. In R. E. Mayer (Ed.), *Teaching and learning computer programming: Multiple research perspective* (pp. 1-12). N.J.: Erlbaum.

McCracken, M., Almstrum, V., Diaz, D., Guzdial, M., Hagan, D., Kolikant, Y., Laxer, C., Thomas, L., Utting, I. & Wilusz, T. (2001). *A multi-national, multiinstitutional study of assessment of programming skills of first-year CS students.* Paper presented at the ITiCSE 2001, Canterbury, UK.

McLoughlin, C. (1997). *Investigating conditions for higher order thinking in telematics environments.* Unpublished PhD Thesis, Edith Cowan University, Perth.

McLoughlin, C. & Oliver, R. (1998). *Scaffolding higher order thinking in a telelearning environment.* Paper presented at the Ed-Media 98, Virginia.

Mercurio, J. A. (1979). Community involvement in cooperative decision making: Some lessons learned. *Educational Evaluation and Policy Analysis, 6*, 37-46.

Merriam, S. B. (1998). *Qualitative research and case study applications in education.* San Francisco: Jossey-Bass.

Merrill, M. D. (1992). Constructivism and instructional design. In T. Duffy & D. Jonassen (Eds.), *Constructivism and the technology of instruction: A conversation.* Hillsdale, N.J.: Erlbaum.

Miara, R. J., Musselman, J., Navarro, J. & Shneiderman, B. (1983). Program indentation and comprehensibility. *Communications of the ACM, 26*(10), 861-867.

Milbrandt, G. (1995). Using problem solving to teach a programming language. *Learning and Leading with Technology, 23*(2), 27-31.

Miles, M. B. & Huberman, A. M. (1994). *Qualitative data analysis: An expanded sourcebook* (2nd ed.). Thousand Oakes, CA.: SAGE Publications, Inc.

Miller, G. A. (1956). The magical number seven, plus or minus two: Some limits on our capacity to process information. *Psychological Review*(63), 81-97.

Milne, I. & Rowe, G. (2002). Difficulties in learning and teaching programming. *Education and Information Technologies, 7*(1), 55-66.

Milne, I. & Rowe, G. (2004). OGRE: Three-dimensional program visualization for novice programmers. *Education and Information Technologies, 9*(3), 219-237.

Minsky, M. (1975). A framework for representing knowledge. In P. H. Winston (Ed.), *The psychology of computer vision*. N.Y.: McGraw-Hill.

Morgan, G. & Griego, O. (1998). *Easy use and interpretation of SPSS for Windows*.

Morse, J. M. (1998). Designing funded qualitative research. In N. K. Denzin & Y. S. Lincoln (Eds.), *Strategies of qualitative inquiry*. Thousand Oaks, California: Sage Publications.

Mott, V. W. (1994). *The role of intuition in the reflective practice of adult education*. Paper presented at the Thirty-fifth annual adult education research conference, University of Tennessee, Knoxville.

National Science Foundation (1993). *User-friendly handbook for project evaluation*. Retrieved 21 May 2003, from http://www.ehr.nsf.gov/ehr/red/eval/handbook/handbook.htm.

National Science Foundation (1997). *User-friendly handbook for mixed method evaluations*. Retrieved 21 May 2003, from http://www.ehr.nsf.gov/ehr/rec/pubs/nsf97-153/pdf/mm_eval.pdf.

Neisser, U. (1976). *Cognition and reality*. San Francisco, CA: Freeman.

Nickerson, R. S., Perkins, D. N. & Smith, E. E. (1985). *The teaching of thinking skills*. N. J.: Lawrence Erlbaum.

Nikolova, I. & Collis, B. (1998). Flexible learning and design of instruction. *British Journal of Educational Technology, 29,* 59-72.

Norcio, A. F. (1980a). *Human memory processes for comprehending computer programs*. Paper presented at the Cybernetics and Society, Cambridge, Massachusetts.

Norcio, A. F. (1980b). *Comprehension aids for computer programs*. Paper presented at the American Psychological Association annual meeting, Montreal.

Norcio, A. F. (1981). *Chunking and understanding computer programs*. Paper presented at the Human-Machine Systems Symposium, Boston, USA.

Norcio, A. F. (1982). *Indentation, documentation and programmer comprehension*. Paper presented at the Human Factors in Computer Systems, Gaithersburg, Maryland.

Oliver, R. (1999). Exploring strategies for on-line teaching and learning. *Distance Education, 20*(2), 240-254.

Oliver, R. & Herrington, J. (2001). *Teaching and learning online.*: Centre for Research in Information Technology and Communications.

Ourusoff, N. (2003). *Using Jackson Structured Programming (JSP) and Jackson Workbench to teach program design*. Paper presented at the Informing Science 2003, Pori, Finland.

Paas, F. (1992). Training strategies for attaining transfer of problem-solving skill in statistics: A cognitive load approach. *Journal of Educational Psychology, 84*, 429-434.

Paas, F. & van Merrienboer, J. J. G. (1994). Variability of worked examples and transfer of geometrical problem-solving skills: A cognitive-load approach. *Journal of Educational Psychology, 86*, 122-133.

Paivio, A. (1974). Language and knowledge of the world. *Educational Researcher, 3*(9), 5-12.

Pattis, R. E. (1995). *A gentle introduction to the art of programming* (2nd ed.): New York, Wiley.

Patton, M. Q. (1990). *Qualitative evaluation and research methods* (2nd ed.). Newbury Park, CA.: Sage Publications.

Pea, R. D. (1986). Language independent conceptual bugs in novice programming. *Journal of Educational Computing Research*(2), 25-36.

Perkins, D. N., Hancock, C., Hobbs, R., Martin, F. & Simmons, R. (1986). Conditions of Learning in Novice Programmers. *Journal of Educational Computing Research, 2*(1), 37-56.

Perkins, D. N., Schwartz, S. & Simmons, R. (1988). Instructional strategies for the problems of novice programmers. In R. E. Mayer (Ed.), *Teaching and learning computer programming: Multiple research perspective* (pp. 153-178): Hillsdale, N.J.: Erlbaum.

Polya, G. (1957). *How to solve it: A new aspect of mathematical method* (2nd ed.). N.Y.: Doubleday.

Quilici, J. L. & Mayer, R. E. (1996). Role of examples in how students learn to categorize statistics word problems. *Journal of Educational Psychology, 88*, 144-161.

Rajan, T. (1992). Principles for the design of dynamic tracing environments for novice programmers. In M. Eisenstadt & M. Keane & T. Rajan (Eds.), *Novice programming environments: Explorations in human-computer interaction and artificial Intelligence*. London: Lawrence Erlbaum.

Ramadhan, H. A. (2000). Programming by discovery. *Journal of Computer Assisted Learning*(16), 83-93.

Redish, E. F. (1994). The implications of cognitive studies for teaching physics. *The American Journal of Physics, 62*(6), 796-803.

Reichardt, C. S. & Cook, T. D. (1979). Beyond qualitative versus quantitative methods. In T. D. Cook & C. S. Reichardt (Eds.), *Qualitative and quantitative methods in evaluation research*. Beverly Hills, CA: Sage.

Renkl, A., Atkinson, R., Maier, U. & Staley, R. (2002). From example study to problem solving: Smooth transitions help learning. *Journal of Experimental Education, 70*, 293-315.

Roehler, L. R. & Cantlon, D. J. (1996). *Scaffolding: A powerful tool in social constructivist classrooms*. Retrieved 15 Sep 2004, from http://www.educ.msu.edu/units/literacy/paperlr2.htm.

Ring, G. (1996). *Interface design considerations for educational multimedia*. Paper presented at the Third Interactive Multimedia Symposium, Perth, Western Australia.

Ring, G. & McMahon, M. (1997). *Web instruction: Searching for a theoretical basis*. Paper presented at the International Conference in Computers in Education 97, Kuching, Malaysia.

Robertson, L. (2003). *Simple Program Design*. Thomson.

Rodger, S. (2002). *Introducing computer science through animation and virtual worlds*. Paper presented at the 33rd SIGCSE Technical Symposium on Computer Science Education.

Rogalski, J. & Samurcay, R. (1993). Task analysis and cognitive model as a framework to analyse environments for learning programming. In E. Lemut, B. duBoulay & G. Dettori (Eds.), *Cognitive models and intelligent environments for learning programming*. Berlin: Springer-Verlag.

Rogers, C. R. (2004). *Experiential Learning*. Retrieved 22 Oct 2004, from http://tip.psychology.org/rogers.html.

Rogers, C. R. & Freiberg, H. J. (1994). *Freedom to learn*. Prentice Hall.

Roussev, B. (2003). *Teaching introduction to programming as part of the is component of the business*. Paper presented at the Informing Science 2003, Pori, Finland.

Rowe, H. (1993). *Learning with personal computers*. Victoria, Australia: Australian Council for Educational Research.

Rowe, G. & Thorburn, G. (1999). *Evaluation of VINCE - a tool for teaching introductory programming*. Paper presented at the 7th Annual Conference on the Teaching of Computing, University of Ulster, Northern Ireland.

Rowe, G. & Thorburn, G. (2000). VINCE - an on-line tool for teaching introductory programming. *British Journal of Education Technology, 31*(4), 359-370.

Schank, R. C. & Abelson, R. P. (1977). *Scripts, plans, goals and understanding*. Hillsdale, N.J.: Erlbaum.

Schneider, D. (2000). *An introduction to programming in Visual BASIC 6* (4th ed.). Prentice Hall.

Schneider, D. (2003). *An introduction to programming in Visual BASIC .NET* (5th ed.). Prentice Hall.

Schneider, W. & Shiffrin, R. (1977). Controlled and automatic human information processing: Detection, search and attention. *Psychological Review, 84*, 1-66.

Schneiderman, B. (1998). *Designing the user interface* (3rd ed.). Addison Wesley.

Schoenfeld, A. H. (1985). *Mathematical problem solving.* San Diego, CA: Academic Press.

Scholtz, J. & Wiedenbeck, S. (1992). The role of planning in learning a new programming language. *International Journal of Man-Machine Studies, 37*, 191-214.

Shackelford, R. (1998). *Introduction to computing and algorithms.* Addison-Wesley.

Shih, Y. F. & Alessi, S. M. (1994). Mental models and transfer of learning in computer programming. *Journal of Research on Computing in Education, 26*(2), 154-175.

Simon, H. & Gilmartin, K. (1973). A simulation of memory for chess positions. *Cognitive Psychology, 5*, 29-46.

Smith, P. A. & Webb, G. I. (1998). *Overview of a low-level program visualisation tool for novice C programmers.* Paper presented at the International Conference on Computers in Education 98, Beijing, China.

Smith, P. A. & Webb, G. I. (1999). *Evaluation of low-level program visualisation for teaching novice C programmers.* Paper presented at the International Conference on Computers in Education 99, Tokyo, Japan.

Smith, P. A. & Webb, G. I. (2000). The efficacy of a low-level program visualisation tool for teaching programming concepts to novice C programmers. *Journal of Educational Computing Research, 2*(2), 187-215.

Soloman, H. (2004). *Cognitive load theory.* Retrieved 4 Feb 2005, from http://tip.psychology.org/sweller.html.

Soloway, E. (1985). From problems to programs via plans: The content and structure of knowledge for introductory LISP programming. *Journal of Educational Computing Research, 1*, 157-172.

Soloway, E. (1986). Learning to program = Learning to construct mechanisms and explanations. *Communications of the ACM, 29*(9), 850-858.

Soloway, E., Spohrer, J. & Littman, D. (1988). E unum pluribus: Generating alternative designs. In R. E. Mayer (Ed.), *Teaching and learning computer programming: Multiple research perspective* (pp. 137-152): Hillsdale, NJ: Erlbaum.

Spiro, R. J., Jacobson, M. J. & Coulson, R. L. (1992). Cognitive flexibility, constructivism and hypertext: Random access instruction for advanced knowledge acquisition in ill-structured domains. In T. Duffy & D. Jonassen (Eds.), *Constructivism and the technology of instruction: A Conversation.* Hillsdale, N.J.: Erlbaum.

Staehr, L., Martin, M. & Byrne, G. (2001). *Computer attitudes and computing career perceptions of first year computing students.* Paper presented at the Informing Science 2001, Kracow University of Economics, Krakow, Poland.

Sweller, J. (1988). Cognitive load during problem solving: Effects on learning. *Cognitive Science, 12*, 257-285.

Sweller, J. (1994). Cognitive load theory, learning difficulty, and instructional design. *Learning and instruction, 4*, 295-312.

Sweller, J. (1999). *Instructional design in technical areas.* Australian Council for Educational Research.

Sweller, J. & Chandler, P. (1991). Evidence for cognitive load theory. *Cognition and Instruction, 8*, 351-362.

Sweller, J. & Cooper, G. A. (1985). The use of worked examples as a substitute for problem solving in learning algebra. *Cognition and Instruction, 2*(1), 59-89.

Sweller, J., van Merrienboer, J. J. G. & Paas, F. (1998). Cognitive architecture and instructional design. *Educational Psychology Review, 10*, 251-296.

StartVBdotnet.com. (2005). Retrieved 7 Feb 2005, from
http://www.startvbdotnet.com/dotnet/vb.aspx.

Tesch, R. (1990). *Qualitative research: Analysis types and software tools*. London: Falmer
Press.

Tindall-Ford, S., Chandler, P. & Sweller, J. (1997). When two sensory modes are better than
one. *Journal of Experimental Psychology: Applied, 3*, 257-287.

Tisdell, E. J. (1993). Interlocking systems of power, privilege, and oppression in adult higher
education classes. *Adult Education Quarterly, 43*(4), 203-226.

Thomas, M. & Zweben, S. H. (1986). *The effects of program-dependent and program-
independent deletions on software cloze tests*. Paper presented at the Empirical Studies
of Programmers, Washington, DC.

Tolhurst, D. (1993). Implications of the studies of experts and novices of computer
programming. *Australian Educational Computing, 8*(July 1993).

Tsai, S. E. (1992). *Development of schema knowledge in the classroom: Effects upon
problem representation and problem solution of programming*. Paper presented at the
Annual conference of the American Educational Association, San Francisco,
California, USA.

Tsay, J. (2004). *Visual BASIC .NET programming*. Prentice Hall.

van Merrienboer, J. J. G. (1990a). Instructional strategies for teaching computer
programming: Interactions with the cognitive style reflection-impulsivity. *Journal of
Research on Computing in Education, 23*(1), 45-53.

van Merrienboer, J. J. G. (1990b). Strategies for programming instruction in high school:
Program completion vs. program generation. *Journal of Educational Computing
Research, 6*(3), 265-285.

van Merrienboer, J. J. G. & De Croock, M. B. M. (1992). Strategies for computer-based
programming instruction: Program completion versus program generation. *Journal of
Educational Computing Research, 8*(3), 365-394.

van Merrienboer, J. J. G. & Dijkstra, S. (1997). The four-component instructional design model for training complex cognitive skills. In R. D. Tennyson & F. Schott (Eds.), *Instructional design: Theory and research (Vol. 1)*. Lawrence Erlbaum.

van Merrienboer, J. J. G. & Krammer, H. (1987). Instructional strategies and tactics for the design of introductory computer programming courses in high school. *Instructional Science, 16*(3), 251-285.

van Merrienboer, J. J. G., Krammer, H. P. M. & Maaswinkel, R. M. (1994). Automating the planning and construction of programming assignments for teaching introductory computer programming. In R. D. Tennyson (Ed.), *Automating instructional design, development, and delivery* (pp. 61-77). Springer Verlag.

van Merrienboer, J. J. G. & Paas, F. (1990). Automation and schema acquisition in learning elementary computer programming. *Computers in Human Behavior*(6), 273-289.

Vygotsky, L. (1978). *Mind in society: The development of higher psychological processes*. Cambridge, MA: Harvard University Press.

Ward, M. & Sweller, J. (1990). Structuring effective worked examples. *Cognition and Instruction, 7*, 1-39.

Webb, C. J. (1997). *The human processes in introductory computer programming*. Paper presented at the National Computer Studies Teachers' Conference, QUT, Queensland.

Werner, L., Hanks, B. & McDowell, C. (2004). *Female computer science students who pair program persist*. Retrieved 18 Jan, 2005, from http://www.cse.ucsc.edu/~charlie/pubs/jeric2004.pdf.

Whyte, W. F. (1989). Action research for the twenty-first century: Participation, reflection and practice. *American Behavioral Scientist, 32*(5).

Wild, M. & Quinn, C. (1997). Implications of educational theory for the design of instructional multimedia. *British Journal of Educational Technology, 29*(1), 73-82.

Wilson, R. J. & Rutherford, A. (1989). Mental models: Theory and application in human factors. *Human Factors, 31*(6), 617-634.

Winn, W. & Snyder, D. (1996). Cognitive perspectives in psychology. In D. H. Jonassen (Ed.), *Handbook of research on educational communications and technology* (pp. 112-142). N.Y.: Macmillan.

Winslow, L. (1996). Programming pedagogy - A psychological overview. *SIGCSE Bulletin, 28*(3).

Wood, D., Bruner, J. & Ross, G. (1976). The role of tutoring and problem solving. *Journal of Child Psychology and Psychiatry, 17*, 89-100.

WordReference.com. (2005). Retrieved 4 Feb 2005, from http://www.wordreference.com/definition/computer_programming.

Zhu, X. & Simon, H. A. (1987). Learning mathematics from examples and by doing. *Cognition and Instruction, 4*, 137-166.

Zuber-Skerritt, O. (1992). *Action research in higher education: Examples and reflections.* London: Kogan Page.

Appendix 1
Unit Outline: Software Development II

Description

This unit introduces students to the fundamental concepts which are needed to develop software. These concepts include problem solving techniques and tools, data and file structures and program development steps.

Objectives

- Demonstrate a knowledge of data types and structures;

- Explain what is meant by "event driven" programming;

- Draw Interface sketches of Windows Style Programs for problems of simple to medium complexity;

- Create "Object / Property / Settings tables for problems of simple to medium complexity;

- Use the features of an event driven programming environment;

- Implement solutions in an event driven programming language for problems of simple to medium complexity ; and

- Design test data to test programs.

Unit Content

There are **12 modules** in this unit.

Module Num.	Topic	Chapter (Schneid)
1	Introduction to Visual BASIC; Program Development Lifecycle; Programming Tools; Visual BASIC Objects and Events	1, 2, 3
2	Numbers and String; Input / Output and the design objects; Design methods for event driven programming	3
3	Input from sequential text files	3
4	Built-in numeric and string functions; Modularisation of programs and the use of general procedures	3, 4
5	General procedures and the use of parameters; User-defined functions and their use in programming **Informal feedback on work done to date (on assignment 1)**	4
6	The decision control structure including the **If** and **Select Case** statements.	5
7	The repetition control structure and the design of deterministic and non deterministic loops.	6
8	One dimensional array processing: creating / accessing; using **Hand-in assignment 1**	7
9	One dimensional array processing: searching and sorting	7

10	Sequential file processing including creating, searching for items, deleting items	8
11	Additional Controls and Objects	9
12	Review and Past Exam Paper **Hand-in assignment 2**	

Teaching And Learning Processes

Each week will include:

- A one hour lecture/seminar. This will introduce the major points of each topic and include discussions of a variety of programming problems.

- A two hour laboratory session in which solutions to problems will be implemented in the event-driven programming language Visual BASIC. **Details of these sessions will be placed on Blackboard.**

Assessment

| Assignment 1: **15%** | Assignment 2: **30%** | Final Exam: **55%** |

To be successful in the unit:

- a minimum mark of 50% must be gained on each of the three components of the assessment. **You must therefore pass the final exam.**

- the overall percentage mark must be 50% or more

A penalty of 5% per day of the total mark gained in an assignment is imposed for late submissions of assignments.

Resources

- Schneider, David I., (2000) *An Introduction to Programming Using Visual BASIC*, Prentice Hall. (Required)

Appendix 2
Student Consent Form: CORT Group

Software Development Research

Dear Software Development Student

This semester we are conducting some research that utilises a new software tool called CORT within the software development unit. The research will investigate the potential benefits that CORT offers to students' learning of computer programming and will explore strategies to maximise its learning potential. The research will include the following data collection methods:

- Observation
- Student interviews
- Student Questionnaires
- Personal journal completion
- Student exercises
- Student end tests

Participation in the research is voluntary and all results will be confidential and held securely. It will be mainly carried out in the "normal" computer laboratories that you attend. The interviews will require approximately 30 minutes of your personal time.

Participation in the research will not influence or effect your grades.

Any questions concerning the project can be directed to Stuart Garner of the School of MIS

- Tel: 9273 8267
- Email: s.garner@ecu.edu.au

If you have any concerns about the project or would like to talk to an independent person, you may contact Professor Ron Oliver (9370 6372).

--------✂---
....

Consent Form for Project: "Exploring the potential of using technology with a part-complete solution method in the learning of programming"

Name ....   Student Number
....

I have read the information above and any questions that I have asked have been answered to my satisfaction.

I agree to participate in this activity, realising that I may withdraw at any time.

I agree to the research data gathered from me for this study being published **providing my confidentiality is maintained.**

Participant signature: ....   Date:
....

Appendix 3
Student Consent Form: Non-CORT Group

Software Development Research

Dear Software Development Student

This semester we are conducting some research into the teaching and learning of computer programming. You are in one of the "control" groups and in this research we will be asking you to fill in a simple questionnaire.

Participation in the research is voluntary and all results will be confidential and held securely.

Participation in the research will not influence or effect your grades.

Any questions concerning the project can be directed to Stuart Garner of the School of MIS

- Tel: 9273 8267
- Email: s.garner@ecu.edu.au

If you have any concerns about the project or would like to talk to an independent person, you may contact Professor Ron Oliver (9370 6372).

Consent Form for Project: "Exploring the potential of using technology with a part-complete solution method in the learning of programming"

Name .... Student Number
....

I have read the information above and any questions that I have asked have been answered to my satisfaction.

I agree to participate in this activity.

I agree to the research data gathered from me for this study being published **providing my confidentiality is maintained.**

Participant signature: .... Date:
....

Appendix 4
Computing Knowledge and Experience Questionnaire

Please tick the appropriate box in response to the following questions. Please add comments if necessary.

1.　What is your Gender?

　　☐　Male
　　☐　Female

2.　Which of the following age ranges are you in?

　　☐　20 years or under
　　☐　21 years ➜ 30 years
　　☐　31 years ➜ 40 years
　　☐　41 years or over

3.　How would you rate your current computing expertise? (Tick one box only)

　　☐　**Limited:** you have not used computers very much at home, school or university.
　　☐　**Moderate:** eg. you use computers for email, Web browsing, word processing etc. You have a limited knowledge of Windows.
　　☐　**Extensive:** eg. you use computers for email, Web browsing, word processing, spreadsheeting, database (eg "Access"). You can change a program's preferences or options. You have a good knowledge of Windows with the ability to create folders, zip files, use the Control Panel etc

　　Comments:　　_____

　　　　　　　　　_____

4.　What is your previous computer programming experience? (Tick one box only)

　　☐　**None**
　　☐　**Limited:** eg. You have done a programming course at school, you have taught yourself to program, you have used and amended scripts for the Web.
　　☐　**Moderate:** eg. You have done a formal programming course, you have written some large computer programs.

　　Comments:　　_____

　　　　　　　　　_____

5.   What is your science and maths knowledge? (Tick one box only)

☐   **Limited**: eg. you have no passes in science and maths at TEE.
☐   **Moderate**: eg. you have at least one pass at TEE in a science subject such as physics or
      chemistry (not biology) and / or at least one pass in a TEE maths subject.
☐   **Extensive**: for example you consider yourself good at science and maths and have achieved
      high scores in two or more TEE science (do not include biology) and maths subjects

Comments: _____

             _____

Appendix 5
Individual Problem Questionnaires

Please click in the appropriate boxes below:

1. Approximately how long did it take to complete the problem?

☐ LESS THAN 15 MINUTES
☐ 16 TO 20 MINUTES
☐ 21 TO 25 MINUTES
☐ 26 TO 30 MINUTES
☐ 31 TO 35 MINUTES
☐ 36 TO 40 MINUTES
☐ 41 TO 45 MINUTES
☐ MORE THAN 45 MINUTES

2. What help / resources did you use in solving the problem? (can put a "x" in more than one box)

☐ NONE
☐ TUTOR
☐ FELLOW STUDENT
☐ SCHNEIDER TEXTBOOK
☐ OTHER: please type details here ➔

3. How much help did you use in solving the problem?

☐ NONE
☐ LITTLE
☐ MODERATE
☐ EXTENSIVE

4. What features of CORT did you use? (put a "x" in the appropriate boxes)

☐ VIEW PROBLEM DESCRIPTION
☐ VIEW PROBLEM INTERFACE
☐ CHANGED FONT IN PREFERENCES
☐ EXPAND - REDUCE LEFT-HAND WINDOW
☐ EXPAND - REDUCE RIGHT-HAND WINDOW
☐ INSERT BLANK LINE BEFORE
☐ INSERT BLANK LINE AFTER
☐ REMOVE BLANK LINE(S)
☐ CORT CODE EDITOR

Appendix 6
Software Development II: Program Completion Test

Example Only

These questions **1 to 8** require you to complete computer programs with lines of code that are given to you.

The following is an **example only** to show you how to write out your answers.

The Problem

The following program requests a whole number of inches and converts it to feet and inches. Note that 12 inches equals 1 foot. There are several lines missing from the program and possible lines of code are given to you. **You do not have to use all the possible lines** to complete the solution.

Possible lines of code

```
1. Let feet = inches \ 12
2. Let feet = inches Mod 12
3. Let inches = inches \ 12
4. Let inches = inches Mod 12
5. Let inches = Val(txtInches.Text)
```

Part-complete Program

```
      Option Explicit
      Private Sub cmdConvert_Click()
         Dim inches As Single, feet as Single

A.       picDisplay.Print "Number of feet = "; feet
B.       picDisplay.Print "Number of inches = "; inches
      End Sub
```

Write out the letters of the lines of the existing code and the numbers of the missing lines in the correct order.

Now suppose that you think that the code for the solution is:

```
Option Explicit
Private Sub cmdConvert_Click()
  Dim inches As Single, feet as Single

  Let inches = Val(txtInches.Text)
  Let feet = inches \ 12
  Let inches = inches Mod 12
  picDisplay.Print "Number of feet = "; feet
  picDisplay.Print "Number of inches = "; inches
End Sub
```

Then you would write down as your answer:

5, 1, 4, A, B

---

1. The following program inputs an initial bank balance from a textbox. It then calculates the new balance after one year assuming that the interest rate is 6%. There are several lines missing from the program and possible lines of code are given to you. You do not have to use all the possible lines to complete the solution.

Possible lines of code

```
1. Let balance = 0.06 * balance
2. Let balance = 6 * balance
3. Let balance = balance + 0.06 * balance
4. Let balance = balance + 6 * balance
5. Let finalBalance = balance + 0.06 * balance
6. Let finalBalance = balance + 6 * balance
7. Let balance = Val(txtBalance.Text)
```

Part-complete Program

```
     Option Explicit
     Private Sub cmdNewBalance_Click()
        Dim balance As Single

A.      picDisplay.Print "Final balance is $"; balance
        End Sub
```

Write out the letters of the lines of the existing code and the numbers of the missing lines in the correct order.

2. The following program inputs and processes data from a data (text) file. The file, called games.txt, contains the following data:

```
"Chelsea", 3, 4, 7
"Manchester United", 14,
     0, 0
```

The data indicates for example that the Chelsea won 3 games, lost 4 games, and drew 7 games. Points are awarded as follows: 3 points for a win, 1 point for a draw, 0 points for a loss. The program should process data from the file and output the total points for each team. There are several lines missing from the program and possible lines of code are given to you. You do not have to use all the possible lines to complete the solution.

Possible lines of code

```
1.   Input #1, teamName, gamesWon, gamesLost, gamesDrawn
2.   Let points = gamesWon * 3 + gamesDrawn + gamesLost
3.   Let points = gamesWon * 3 + gamesDrawn + gamesLost
4.   Let points = gamesWon * 3 + gamesDrawn
5.   Let points = gamesWon * 3 + gamesDrawn
6.   picDisplay.Print teamName; " has "; points; " points"
7.   picDisplay.Print teamName; " has "; points; " points"
```

Part-complete Program

```
     Option Explicit
     Private Sub cmdDisplayPoints_Click()
        Dim teamName As String
        Dim gamesWon As Integer, gamesLost As Integer
        Dim gamesDrawn As Integer
        Dim points As Integer

A.      Open "A:\games.txt" For Input As #1
B.      picDisplay.Cls
C.      Input #1, teamName, gamesWon, gamesLost, gamesDrawn
D.      Close #1
     End Sub
```

Write out the letters of the lines of the existing code and the numbers of the missing lines in the correct order.

3. The following program inputs, from a textbox, a date of birth. Assume that the input is always 8 characters in the format:

dd/mm/yy

For example, the 3rd November 2001 would be entered as:

03/11/01

The program should output, on separate lines, the three parts of the date. For example, the output for the above date that was entered would be:

Day: 03
Month: 11
Year: 01

There are several lines missing from the program and possible lines of code are given to you. You do not have to use all the possible lines to complete the solution.

Possible lines of code

```
1.  Let dayPart = Left(dateOfBirth, 2)
2.  Let dayPart = Mid(dateOfBirth, 2)
3.  Let dayPart = Right(dateOfBirth, 2)
4.  Let monthPart = Mid(dateOfBirth, 2, 4)
5.  Let monthPart = Mid(dateOfBirth, 4, 2)
6.  Let monthPart = Mid(dateOfBirth, 3, 2)
7.  Let monthPart = Mid(dateOfBirth, 2, 3)
8.  Let yearPart = Left(dateOfBirth, 2)
9.  Let yearPart = Mid(dateOfBirth, 2)
10. Let yearPart = Right(dateOfBirth, 2)
11. Let dateOfBirth = txtDateOfBirth.Text
12. Let dateOfBirth = Val(txtDateOfBirth.Text)
```

Part-complete Program

```
        Option Explicit
        Private Sub cmdOutputBirthDetails_Click()
            Dim dateOfBirth As String
            Dim dayPart As String
            Dim monthPart As String
            Dim yearPart As String

A.          picDisplay.Print "Date of birth details"
B.          picDisplay.Print
C.          picDisplay.Print "Day "; dayPart
D.          picDisplay.Print "Month "; monthPart
E.          picDisplay.Print "Year: "; yearPart
        End Sub
```

Write out the letters of the lines of the existing code and the numbers of the missing lines in the correct order.

4. The following program calculates and outputs the population densities of Hawaii and Alaska in America. There are several lines missing from **cmdDisplay_Click** in the program and possible lines of code are given to you. You do not have to use all the possible lines to complete the solution.

Possible lines of code (missing from cmdDisplay_Click)

```
1. Call CalculateDensity(1184000, "Hawaii", 6471)
2. Call CalculateDensity(607000, "Alaska", 591000)
3. Call CalculateDensity("Hawaii", 1184000, 6471)
4. Call CalculateDensity("Alaska", 607000, 591000)
5. Call CalculateDensity
6. Call CalculateDensity
7. Let density = CalculateDensity("Hawaii", 1184000, 6471)
8. Let density = CalculateDensity("Alaska", 607000, 591000)
```

Part-complete Program

```
      Option Explicit
      Private Sub cmdDisplay_Click()
A.       picDisplay.Cls
      End Sub

      Private Sub CalculateDensity(state As String, pop As Single,
         area As Single)
      Dim rawDensity As Single, density As Single
      Rem The density (number of people per square mile)
      Rem will be displayed rounded to a whole number
      Let rawDensity = pop / area
      Let density = Round(rawDensity)
      picDisplay.Print "The density of "; state; " is"; density;
      picDisplay.Print "people per square mile."
      End Sub
```

Write out the letters of the lines of the existing code and the numbers of the missing lines in the correct order.

5. The following program inputs from textboxes the income and expenses for a company. It displays the message "No profit or loss" if the income and expenses are equal. If they are not equal, it displays the profit or loss.

There are several lines missing from the program and possible lines of code are given to you. You do not have to use all the possible lines to complete the solution.

Possible lines of code

```
1.  Else
2.  End If
3.  Let profit = income - expenses
4.  Let loss = expenses - income
5.  If expenses < income Then
6.  picDisplay.Print "No profit or loss"
7.  picDisplay.Print "Profit is "; FormatCurrency(profit)
8.  picDisplay.Print "Loss is "; FormatCurrency(loss)
```

Part-complete Program

```
      Option Explicit
      Private Sub cmdShow_Click()
         Dim expenses As Single, income As Single
         Dim profit As Single, loss As Single

A.       Let expenses = Val(txtExpenses.Text)
B.       Let income = Val(txtIncome.Text)
C.       picDisplay.Cls
D.       If expenses = income Then
E.       Else
F.       End If
      End Sub
```

Write out the letters of the lines of the existing code and the numbers of the missing lines in the correct order.

6. The following program inputs from a textbox the balance in a company's bank account. Assuming that the account has 4% annual interest paid into it, the program should output how many years it will take for the balance to become more than $80000.

There are several lines missing from the program and possible lines of code are given to you. You do not have to use all the possible lines to complete the solution.

Possible lines of code

```
1.  Loop
2.  Do While balance < 80000
3.  Do While balance <= 80000
4.  Do While balance > 80000
5.  Do While balance >= 80000
6.  Let balance = balance + 0.04 * balance
7.  Let numYears = numYears + 1
8.  Let numYears = 0
```

Part-complete Program

```
    Option Explicit
    Private Sub cmdYears_Click()
        Dim balance As Single, numYears As Integer

A.      Let balance = Val(txtBalance.Text)
B.      picDisplay.Cls
C.      picDisplay.Print "In"; numYears; "years balance will be over
        $80000"
    End Sub
```

Write out the letters of the lines of the existing code and the numbers of the missing lines in the correct order.

7. The following program inputs 6 names contained in the file **names.txt** into an array. This is done in the **Form_Load** event procedure. Then, when a button is clicked, the program displays two columns, the first column containing the original 6 names and the second column contains the 6 names in reverse order. Example output would be:

Original Order	Reverse Order
Brenda	Sue
Mike	Chris
Heather	Tony
Tony	Heather
Chris	Mike
Sue	Brenda

There are several lines missing from the program and possible lines of code are given to you. You do not have to use all the possible lines to complete the solution.

Possible lines of code

```
The following are possible lines for cmdDisplayColumns_Click()
1.  picDisplay.Print fNames(index), fNames(6 - index)
2.  picDisplay.Print fNames(index), fNames(6 + index)
3.  picDisplay.Print fNames(index), fNames(7 - index)
4.  picDisplay.Print fNames(index), fNames(7 + index)
5.  picDisplay.Print fNames(index), fNames(index - 6)
6.  picDisplay.Print fNames(index), fNames(index + 6)
7.  picDisplay.Print fNames(index), fNames(index - 7)
8.  picDisplay.Print fNames(index), fNames(index + 7)
9.  Next index
10. Next fNames
11. For index = 1 To 6
12. For index = 1 To fNames

The following are possible lines for Form_Load()
13. Input #1, fNumbers(index)
14. Let index = index + 1
15. Let index = 1
16. Loop
17. Do While Not EOF(1)
18. Do While EOF(1)
```

Part-complete Program

```
        Option Explicit
        Dim fNames(1 To 6) As Single
        Private Sub cmdDisplayColumns_Click()
           Dim index As Integer

A.      picDisplay.Print "Original", "Reverse"
B.      picDisplay.Print "Order", "Order"
C.      picDisplay.Print
        End Sub

        Private Sub Form_Load()
           Dim index As Integer

D.      Open "A:\names.txt" For Input As #1
E.      Close #1
        End Sub
```

Write out the letters of the lines of the existing code and the numbers of the missing lines in the correct order.

8. Suppose the sequential text file, **customers.txt**, contains customer banking data. Example data is:

"Harrison T", 23679.56
"Mason P", 677.90
"Peters K", 899.77
"Roberts L", 23.12
etc

In the above, the first record indicates that **Harrison T** has **$23679.56** in their bank account.

The number of records in the file is unknown. The following program creates two new sequential text files called **fees.txt** and **nofees.txt**. It copies all records from **customers.txt** into **fees.txt** where the amount of money in the account is less than $1000 and it copies the rest of the records into **nofees.txt**.

There are several lines missing from the program and possible lines of code are given to you. You do not have to use all the possible lines to complete the solution.

Possible lines of code

```
1.  Open "A:\fees.txt" For Input #3
2.  Open "A:\fees.txt" For Output As #2
3.  Open "A:\nofees.txt" For Input As #3
4.  Open "A:\nofees.txt" For Output As #3
5.  If customerBalance < 1000 Then
6.  If customerBalance <= 1000 Then
7.  Else
8.  End If
9.  Input #1, customerName, customerBalance
10. Write #2, customerName, customerBalance
11. Write #3, customerName, customerBalance
12. Close #2
13. Close #3
```

Part-complete Program

```
      Option Explicit
      Private Sub cmdCreatefiles_Click()
         Dim customerName As String
         Dim customerBalance As Single

A.       Open "A:\customers.txt" For Input As #1
B.       Do While Not EOF(1)
C.       Loop
D.       Close #1
      End Sub
```

Write out the letters of the lines of the existing code and the numbers of the missing lines in the correct order.

Appendix 7
Software Development II: Examination

READING TIME:	5 minutes
WORKING TIME:	2 hours 30minutes
TOTAL TIME:	2 hours 35 minutes
ATTEMPT:	**All** questions in section A and **one** question from section B.

General Instructions:

1   Students are **not** permitted to write on the examination paper or in the answer booklet during reading time.

2   This is a closed book examination. Text books/reference books/notes are not permitted. Please write all your answers in the answer booklet.

Section A is worth 20 marks.
Section B is worth 20 marks.

Total Marks: 40

Section A - Answer all questions. Each question is worth 2 marks.

1. Which of the following expressions will yield the string "John Smith", where nom1 = "John Brown" and nom2 = "Janet Smith"?

    (A) Mid(nom1, 1, 4) & Mid(nom2, 7, 5)
    (B) Left(nom1, 4) & Right(nom2, 5)
    (C) Left(nom1, 5) & Right(nom2, 5)
    (D) None of the above.

2. What will be the output of the following program when the command button is clicked?

```
Private Sub cmdButton_Click()
  Dim var1 As Integer, var2 As Integer, var3 As Integer, num As Integer
  var1 = 2
  var2 = 4
  var3 = 6
  Call Add(num)
  picDisplay.Cls
  picDisplay.Print num
End Sub

Private Sub Add(num As Integer)
  Dim var1 As Integer, var2 As Integer, var3 As Integer
  num = var1 + var2 + var3
End Sub
```

    (A) 0
    (B) 12
    (C) 6
    (D) None of the above

3. Consider the following event procedure that calls a user-defined function named **Cube**, which returns the cube of a number.

```
Private Sub cmdButton_Click()
  Dim num As Single, result As Single
  num = Val(InputBox("Enter a number to cube:"))
  result = Cube(num)
  picDisplay.Print "The cube of"; num; "is"; result
End Sub
```

Which of the following is a correct Function definition for **Cube**?

```
1.  Private Function Cube(var As Single) As Single
       Cube = var ^ 3
    End Function

2.  Private Function Cube(num As Single) As Single
       Cube = num ^ 3
    End Function
```

(A)   1 only
(B)   2 only
(C)   Both 1 and 2
(D)   Neither 1 nor 2

4. What will be the output of the following program when the command button is clicked?

```
Private Sub cmdDisplay_Click()
  Dim num As Integer
  num = 10
  Call DisplayMult(num)
  num = 5
  Call DisplayMult(num)
  num = 2
  Call DisplayMult(num)
End Sub

Private Sub DisplayMult(num As Integer)
  If num <= 3 Then
      picOutput.Print 3 * num;
    Else
      If num > 7 Then
        picOutput.Print 7 * num;
      End If
  End If
End Sub
```

(A)   70 14
(B)   30 6 14
(C)   70 6
(D)   No output

5. What is wrong with the following Do While loop?

```
index = 1
Do While index <> 10
  picDisplay.Print "Hello"
  index = index + 2
Loop
```

(A) It should have been written with a Do Until loop.
(B) It is an infinite loop.
(C) The test variable should not be changed within the loop itself.
(D) nothing

6. What will be the output of the following program when the command button is clicked?

```
Private Sub cmdButton_Click()
  Dim sum as Single, num as Single
  Open "DATA.TXT" For Input As #1
  Do While Not EOF(1)
    Input #1, num
    sum = sum + num
  Loop
  Close #1
  picDisplay.Print "The sum of all data is "; sum
End Sub
```

Contents of DATA.TXT: 12, 9, 32

(A) 12, 9, 32
(B) 63
(C) a runtime error
(D) Nothing

7. What will be the output of the following program when the command button is clicked?

```
Private Sub cmdButton_Click()
  Dim vowel As String
  Open "DATA.TXT" For Input As #1
  Do While EOF(1)
    Input #1, vowel
    picDisplay.Print vowel;
  Loop
  Close #1
  picDisplay.Print ", and sometimes y"
End Sub
```

Contents of DATA.TXT: "a", "e", "i", "o", "u"

(A) , and sometimes y
(B) a, and sometimes y
(C) aeiou, and sometimes y
(D) aeiou

8. What is the output of the following program segment?

```
Dim numbers(1 To 4) As Single, h As Single, i As Integer, k As Integer
h = 0
Open "DATA.TXT" For Input As #1
For i = 1 To 4
  Input #1, numbers(i)
Next i
Close #1
For k = 1 to 4
  h = h + numbers(k)
Next k
picDisplay.Cls
picDisplay.Print h
```

Contents of DATA.TXT: 2, 4, 2, 3

(A) 11
(B) 2
(C) 7
(D) 4
(E) None of the above

9. What is wrong with the following program segment?

```
Dim nom As String, number As String
Open "PHONEDIR" For Input As #2
Input #2, nom, number
Do While Not EOF(2)
  If nom = "Jim" Then
      picDisplay.Print "Jim's number is"; number
  End If
  Input #2, nom, number
Loop
Close #2
```

(A) The file should have been opened as #1.
(B) If Jim's name and number are the last entries in the file, they will not be processed by the If statement.
(C) "number" should be a numeric variable.
(D) The Do While statement should read Do While EOF(2).
(E) There is nothing wrong with the program segment.

10. What is the problem (if any) with the following Select Case block which is intended to determine the price of a movie depending on the patron's age?

```
Private Sub cmdButton_Click()
  age = Val(InputBox("Enter your age:"))
  Select Case age
    Case Is >= 65        'Senior citizen
      price = 4.50
    Case Is >= 5         'Regular price
      price = 6.00
    Case Is >= 0         'Child (no charge with parents)
      price = 0
    Case Else
      picDisplay.Print "Entry error"
  End Select
End Sub
```

(A) Everyone will get in free at the child rate.
(B) The output will always be "Entry error."
(C) The Case Is statements have bad syntax.
(D) There is nothing wrong.

Section B - Answer ONE question only. This section is worth 20 marks.

Question 1

A file called **"marks.txt"** contains names and test marks for students. Names can appear more than once. A program is required that accepts a name as input, via a textbox, and outputs the average of the marks for that student and that student's highest mark.

The name entered should not be sensitive to the case of the letters. For example, if the text file contained the following and the name entered was "brenda", then an average of 40 would be output together with the highest mark of 63.

```
"Alf", 56
"Brenda", 63
"Gladys", 45
"BRENDA", 34
"Adnams", 44
"brenDA", 23
```

If the name does not appear in the file then a message "Name not in file" should be output.

Note that **an array is not required**.

For the above:

(a) Create a task / object / event (TOE) chart.
(b) Draw an interface sketch naming all objects.
(c) Write **detailed pseudo code or Visual BASIC code**, including details of variables and their types.
(d) Draw up a test table showing the input data, expected output and the reasons for each test. Make sure that the tests that you suggest would **thoroughly** test the program.

[20 marks]

Question 2

A program is required which keeps track of the time taken to run 100 metre races at an athletics meeting. There are three races and 15 runners. Each runner will run all three races. The program accepts each runner's name and run-times for the three races as input via textboxes. The names are placed in a one-dimensional array and the **average time** of each runner's three races is placed in another one-dimensional array.

The program should be able to output

- all the runner names and average times in a picture box

- the name of the runner with the lowest average time.

For the above:

(a)   Create a task / object / event (TOE) chart.
(b)   Draw an interface sketch naming all objects.
(c)   Write **detailed pseudo code or Visual BASIC code**, including details of variables and their types.
(d)   Draw up a test table showing the input data, expected output and the reasons for each test. Make sure that the tests that you suggest would **thoroughly** test the program.

[20 marks]

End of Exam

Appendix 8
CORT Problems

Problem 2 CORT Method 2 (some lines needed)

Problem Description

Make use of CORT to complete this program. The program should allow a user to type in their name in a textbox. There should be 3 command buttons. One should change the text to red, the second should make the text bold, and the third should underline the text.

Possible Lines of Code and Part-complete Solution

Possible Lines	Part Complete Solution
Let txtName.FontBold = True Let txtName.FontBold = False Let txtName.FontUnderline = True Let txtName.FontUnder = True Let txtName.ForeColor = vbRed Let txtName.ForeColor = Red	Private Sub cmdMakeBold_Click() End Sub Private Sub cmdMakeRed_Click() End Sub Private Sub cmdMakeUnderline_Click() End Sub

Correct Solution

```
Private Sub cmdMakeBold_Click()
  Let txtName.FontBold = True
End Sub

Private Sub cmdMakeRed_Click()
  Let txtName.ForeColor = vbRed
End Sub

Private Sub cmdMakeUnderline_Click()
  Let txtName.FontUnderline = True
End Sub
```

Problem Description

Make use of CORT to complete this program that should output the total cost of 3 items bought at a shop after a 25% discount

The program should do the following:

- Declare all variables in Dim statements.
- Assign the value 26.15 to the variable firstItem.
- Assign the value 29.95 to the variable secondItem..
- Assign the value 32.85 to the variable thirdItem..
- Add up the values and place the result in the variable totalCost.
- Calculate the discount and place this in the variable discountAmount.
- Calculate the final cost and place this in finalCost.
- Output the final cost

Possible Lines of Code and Part-complete Solution

Possible Lines	Part Complete Solution
picDisplay.Print "Final Cost is "; finalCost Let finalCost = totalCost - discountAmount Let discountAmount = 0.25 * totalCost Let totalCost = firstItem + secondItem + thirdItem Dim secondItem As Single Dim thirdItem As Single Let firstItem = 26.15 Let secondItem = 29.95 Let thirdItem = 32.85 picDisplay.Cls Dim totalCost As Single Dim discountAmount As Single Dim finalCost As Single	Option Explicit Private Sub cmdDisplayCost_Click() Dim firstItem As Single End Sub

Correct Solution

```
Option Explicit

Private Sub cmdDisplayCost_Click()
   Dim firstItem As Single
   Dim secondItem As Single
   Dim thirdItem As Single
   Dim totalCost As Single
   Dim discountAmount As Single
   Dim finalCost As Single

   Let firstItem = 26.15
   Let secondItem = 29.95
   Let thirdItem = 32.85
   Let totalCost = firstItem + secondItem + thirdItem
   Let discountAmount = 0.25 * totalCost
   Let finalCost = totalCost - discountAmount
```

```
picDisplay.Cls
picDisplay.Print "Final Cost is "; finalCost
End Sub
```

Problem 4: CORT Method 2 (some lines needed)

Make use of CORT to complete this program that should output the balance after three years for a an initial deposit of $500. The interest in the first 2 years in 4.5% per annum and the interest in the third year is 5.25%.

The program should do the following:

- Declare all variables in Dim statements.
- Assign the value 500 to the variable balance
- Increase the variable balance by 4.5% of its value.
- Increase the variable balance by 4.5% of its value.
- Increase the variable balance by 5.25% of its value.
- Output the final balance in a picture box

Possible Lines of Code and Part-complete Solution

Possible Lines	Part Complete Solution

picDisplay.Print "Final balance is $"; "balance"
picDisplay.Print "Final balance is $"; balance
balance = balance + balance * 0.045
balance = balance + balance * 0.045
balance = balance * 0.045
balance = 500
balance = balance + balance * 0.0525
balance = balance * 0.045
balance = balance * 0.0525
	Option Explicit
	
	Private Sub cmdNewBalance_Click()
	  Rem Calculate the new balance
	  Dim balance As Single
	
	End Sub

Correct Solution

```
Option Explicit

Private Sub cmdNewBalance_Click()
  Rem Calculate the new balance
  Dim balance As Single

  balance = 500
  balance = balance + balance * 0.045
  balance = balance + balance * 0.045
  balance = balance + balance * 0.0525

  picDisplay.Print "Final balance is $"; balance
End Sub
```

Problem 5: CORT Method 2 (some lines needed)

Problem Description

Make use of CORT to complete this program. The program should input a person's name, credit card type (Visa, Bankcard or Mastercard), outstanding balance, and annual interest rate (eg, 15%). The program should then calculate the monthly interest payment on that balance. The output should be something like:

> Monthly interest payment for John Howard
> is $53 for Visa card with an outstanding
> balance of $4240

Possible Lines of Code and Part-complete Solution

Possible Lines	Part Complete Solution
Let balance = Val(txtBalance.Text) Let balance = txtBalance.Text Let interestRate = Val(txtInterestRate.Text) Let interestRate = txtInterestRate.Text Rem Calculate the interest payment Let interestPayment = interestRate / 100 * balance / 12 Let interestPayment = interestRate / 100 * balance Let interestPayment = interestRate / 100 * balance * 12 picDisplay.Print "Monthly interest payment for "; personName picDisplay.Print "Monthly interest payment for "; personName; picDisplay.Print "Monthly interest payment for ", personName picDisplay.Print "is $"; interestPayment; " for "; CCtype; " card with an outstanding" picDisplay.Print "is $"; interestPayment; " for "; CCtype; " card with an outstanding"; picDisplay.Print "is $", interestPayment, " for ", CCtype, " card with an outstanding" picDisplay.Print "balance of $"; balance picDisplay.Print "balance of $"; balance; picDisplay.Print "balance of $", balance	Option Explicit Private Sub cmdMonthlyInterest_Click() Rem Calculate the monthly interest Dim personName As String, CCtype As String Dim balance As Single, interestRate As Single Dim interestPayment As Single Rem Place all the input data into variables Let personName = txtPersonName.Text Let CCtype = txtCardType.Text Rem output the result picDisplay.Cls End Sub

Correct Solution

```
Option Explicit

Private Sub cmdMonthlyInterest_Click()

Rem Calculate the monthly interest
Dim personName As String, CCtype As String
Dim balance As Single, interestRate As Single
Dim interestPayment As Single

Rem Place all the input data from the textboxes into variables
Let personName = txtPersonName.Text
Let CCtype = txtCardType.Text
Let balance = Val(txtBalance.Text)
Let interestRate = Val(txtInterestRate.Text)
```

```
Rem Calculate the interest payment
Let interestPayment = interestRate / 100 * balance / 12

Rem output the result
picDisplay.Cls
picDisplay.Print "Monthly interest payment for "; personName
picDisplay.Print "is $"; interestPayment; " for "; CCtype; " card with an outstanding"
picDisplay.Print "balance of $"; balance
End Sub
```

Problem 6: CORT Method 1 (all lines needed)

Problem Description

Make use of CORT to complete this program that inputs and processes data from a data (text) file. The file, called soccer.txt contains the following data:

> "Duncraig Dribblers", 10, 4, 2
> "Churchlands Layabouts", 4, 3, 7

The data indicates for example that the Duncraig Dribblers won 10 games, lost 4 games, and drew 2 games. Points are awarded as follows: 3 points for a win, 1 point for a draw, 0 points for a loss.

The program should input that data from the file and then output the total points for each team. Note that there is a deliberate mistake somewhere in the program.

Possible Lines of Code and Part-complete Solution

Possible Lines	Part Complete Solution

Close #1
picDisplay.Cls
Dim gamesDrawn As Integer
Dim points As Integer
Input #1, teamName, gamesWon, gamesLost, gamesDrawn
Input #1, teamName, gamesWon, gamesLost, gamesDrawn
picDisplay.Print teamName; " has "; paints; " points"
picDisplay.Print teamName; " has "; paints; " points"
points = gamesWon * 3 + gamesDrawn
points = gamesWon * 3 + gamesDrawn
	Option Explicit
	
	Private Sub cmdDisplayPoints_Click()
	  Rem This program displays the points obtained by 2
	  Rem soccer teams
	
	  Dim teamName As String
	  Dim gamesWon As Integer, gamesLost As Integer
	
	  Open "A:\00130\soccer.txt" For Input As #1
	
	End Sub

Correct Solution

```
Option Explicit

Private Sub cmdDisplayPoints_Click()
  Rem This program displays the points obtained by 2
  Rem soccer teams

  Dim teamName As String
```

```
Dim gamesWon As Integer, gamesLost As Integer
Dim gamesDrawn As Integer
Dim points As Integer

Open "A:\00130\soccer.txt" For Input As #1

picDisplay.Cls
Input #1, teamName, gamesWon, gamesLost, gamesDrawn
points = gamesWon * 3 + gamesDrawn
picDisplay.Print teamName; " has "; points; " points"
Input #1, teamName, gamesWon, gamesLost, gamesDrawn
points = gamesWon * 3 + gamesDrawn
picDisplay.Print teamName; " has "; points; " points"
Close #1
End Sub
```

Problem 7: CORT Method 2 (some lines needed)

Problem Description

A program is required that obtains, via a textbox, an amount of money that is to be paid as a wage to a worker. The amount is a whole number of dollars. The number of $100, $50, $20, $10, $5 notes and $2, $1 coins that should be given to the worker should be output in a picture box. For example, if the wage were $278 then the following would be output:

Number of $ 100 notes: 2
Number of $ 50 notes: 1
Number of $ 20 notes: 1
Number of $ 10 notes: 0
Number of $ 5 notes: 1
Number of $ 2 coins: 1
Number of $ 1 coins: 1

Possible Lines of Code and Part-complete Solution

Possible Lines	Part Complete Solution

Let numberOf1DollarCoins = leftOver
Let leftOver = wage Mod 100
Let numberOf100DollarNotes = wage \ 100
Let numberOf100DollarNotes = wage Mod 100
Let leftOver = leftOver Mod 50
Let numberOf50DollarNotes = leftOver \ 50
Let numberOf50DollarNotes = leftOver Mod 50
Let leftOver = leftOver Mod 20
Let numberOf20DollarNotes = leftOver \ 20
Let numberOf20DollarNotes = leftOver Mod 20
Let leftOver = leftOver Mod 10
Let numberOf10DollarNotes = leftOver \ 10
Let numberOf10DollarNotes = leftOver Mod 10
Let leftOver = leftOver Mod 5
Let numberOf5DollarNotes = leftOver \ 5
Let numberOf5DollarNotes = leftOver Mod 5
Let leftOver = leftOver Mod 2
Let numberOf2DollarCoins = leftOver \ 2
Let numberOf2DollarCoins = leftOver Mod 2
	'=================================
	============
	'This program obtains a wage from a user and outputs the
	'number and value of notes and coins that should be placed
	'in the pay packet
	'=================================
	============
	Option Explicit
	
	Private Sub cmdPayDetails_Click()
	  'Declare the variables required
	  Dim numberOf100DollarNotes As Integer
	  Dim numberOf50DollarNotes As Integer
	  Dim numberOf20DollarNotes As Integer
	  Dim numberOf10DollarNotes As Integer

Possible Lines	Part Complete Solution
	Dim numberOf5DollarNotes As Integer Dim numberOf2DollarCoins As Integer Dim numberOf1DollarCoins As Integer Dim wage As Integer, leftOver As Integer 'Obtain the wage Let wage = Val(txtWage.Text) 'Determine the number of notes and coins needed 'Output the results picDisplay.Cls picDisplay.Print "Wages Report" picDisplay.Print "================" picDisplay.Print "Number of $ 100 notes: "; numberOf100DollarNotes picDisplay.Print "Number of $ 50 notes: "; numberOf50DollarNotes picDisplay.Print "Number of $ 20 notes: "; numberOf20DollarNotes picDisplay.Print "Number of $ 10 notes: "; numberOf10DollarNotes picDisplay.Print "Number of $ 5 notes: "; numberOf5DollarNotes picDisplay.Print "Number of $ 2 coins: "; numberOf2DollarCoins picDisplay.Print "Number of $ 1 coins: "; numberOf1DollarCoins End Sub

Correct Solution

```
Option Explicit

Private Sub cmdPayDetails_Click()
 'Declare the variables required
 Dim numberOf100DollarNotes As Integer
 Dim numberOf50DollarNotes As Integer
 Dim numberOf20DollarNotes As Integer
 Dim numberOf10DollarNotes As Integer
 Dim numberOf5DollarNotes As Integer
 Dim numberOf2DollarCoins As Integer
 Dim numberOf1DollarCoins As Integer

 Dim wage As Integer, leftOver As Integer

 'Obtain the wage
 Let wage = Val(txtWage.Text)

 'Determine the number of notes and coins needed
 Let numberOf100DollarNotes = wage \ 100
 Let leftOver = wage Mod 100
 Let numberOf50DollarNotes = leftOver \ 50
 Let leftOver = leftOver Mod 50
 Let numberOf20DollarNotes = leftOver \ 20
 Let leftOver = leftOver Mod 20
 Let numberOf10DollarNotes = leftOver \ 10
 Let leftOver = leftOver Mod 10
 Let numberOf5DollarNotes = leftOver \ 5
 Let leftOver = leftOver Mod 5
 Let numberOf2DollarCoins = leftOver \ 2
 Let leftOver = leftOver Mod 2
 Let numberOf1DollarCoins = leftOver
```

```
                'Output the results
                picDisplay.Cls
                picDisplay.Print "Wages Report"
                picDisplay.Print "================"
                picDisplay.Print "Number of $ 100 notes: "; numberOf100DollarNotes
                picDisplay.Print "Number of $ 50 notes: "; numberOf50DollarNotes
                picDisplay.Print "Number of $ 20 notes: "; numberOf20DollarNotes
                picDisplay.Print "Number of $ 10 notes: "; numberOf10DollarNotes
                picDisplay.Print "Number of $ 5 notes: "; numberOf5DollarNotes
                picDisplay.Print "Number of $ 2 coins: "; numberOf2DollarCoins
                picDisplay.Print "Number of $ 1 coins: "; numberOf1DollarCoins
            End Sub
```

Problem 8: CORT Method 3 (some lines needed, one line to key-in)

Problem Description

A program is required that obtains, via a textbox, a telephone number. Examples of numbers that might be entered are:

    08 9275 5623
    09 7612 4296

The numbers are always of the same structure but may have leading or trailing spaces entered too. The program should output, on separate lines, the three parts of the number, Eg:

    STD Code: 08
    Exchange: 9275
    Number: 5623

Possible Lines of Code and Part-complete Solution

Possible Lines	Part Complete Solution

Dim telNumber As String
Dim telNumber As integer
Let telNumber = txtTelNumber.Text
Let telNumber = val(txtTelNumber.Text)
Let telNumber = Trim(telNumber)
Let txtTelNumber.Text = Trim(telNumber)
Let firstPart = Left(telNumber, 2)
Let firstPart = Left(telNumber, 4)
Let middlePart = Mid(telNumber, 4, 4)
Let middlePart = Mid(telNumber, 2, 4)
Let middlePart = Mid(telNumber, 4, 2)
	Option Explicit
	Private Sub cmdOutputNumber_Click()
	  Dim firstPart As String
	  Dim middlePart As String
	  Dim lastPart As String
	
	  'Obtain the telephone number
	
	  'Trim leading and trailing spaces
	
	  'Obtain first part
	
	  'Obtain middle part
	
	  'Obtain last part

Possible Lines	Part Complete Solution
	'Output the details picDisplay.Print "Telephone Number Details" picDisplay.Print picDisplay.Print "STD Code: "; firstPart picDisplay.Print "Exchange: "; middlePart picDisplay.Print "Number: "; lastPart End Sub

Correct Solution

```
Option Explicit
Private Sub cmdOutputNumber_Click()
   Dim telNumber As String
   Dim firstPart As String
   Dim middlePart As String
   Dim lastPart As String

   'Obtain the telephone number
   Let telNumber = txtTelNumber.Text

   'Trim leading and trailing spaces
   Let telNumber = Trim(telNumber)

   'Obtain first part
   Let firstPart = Left(telNumber, 2)

   'Obtain middle part
   Let middlePart = Mid(telNumber, 4, 4)

   'Obtain last part
   Let lastPart = Right(telNumber, 4)

   'Output the details
   picDisplay.Print "Telephone Number Details"
   picDisplay.Print
   picDisplay.Print "STD Code: "; firstPart
   picDisplay.Print "Exchange: "; middlePart
   picDisplay.Print "Number: "; lastPart
End Sub
```

Problem 9: CORT Method 2 (some lines needed)

Problem Description

A program is required that obtains an account balance and the values of two transactions. The program should output the new balance in a picture box in three ways:

1. To two decimal places
2. To three decimal paces
3. To four decimal places, right justified in a 15 space column.

Possible Lines of Code and Part-complete Solution

Possible Lines	Part Complete Solution

Call OutputToTwoPlaces(newBalance)
Call OutputToTwoPlaces(accountBalance)
Call OutputToTwoPlaces
Call OutputToThreePlaces(newBalance)
Call OutputToThreePlaces(accountBalance)
Call OutputToThreePlaces
Call OutputToFourPlaces(newBalance)
Call OutputToFourPlaces(accountBalance)
Call OutputToFourPlaces
picDisplay.Print FormatCurrency(balance, 2)
picDisplay.Print FormatCurrency(balance, 3)
End Sub
Private Sub OutputToFourPlaces(balance As Single)
picDisplay.Print Format(FormatCurrency(balance, 4),
"@@@@@@@@@@@@@@@")
picDisplay.Print Format(FormatCurrency(balance, 4),
"***************")
picDisplay.Print Format(FormatCurrency(balance, 4),
"==============")
	'==============================
	'This program determines a new balance after 2
	'transactions have been applied
	'==============================
	Option Explicit
	
	Private Sub cmdNewBalance_Click()
	  Dim valueOne As Single, valueTwo As Single
	  Dim accountBalance As Single, newBalance As
	Single
	
	  'Obtain the input
	  Let accountBalance =
	Val(txtAccountBalance.Text)
	  Let valueOne = Val(txtValueOne.Text)
	  Let valueTwo = Val(txtValueTwo.Text)
	
	  'Work out new balance
	  Let newBalance = accountBalance - valueOne -
	valueTwo
	
	  'Output the new balance
	  picDisplay.FontName = "courier new"
	  picDisplay.Cls
	  picDisplay.Print " 1"
	  picDisplay.Print "123456789012345"
	  picDisplay.Print
	
	End Sub
	
	Private Sub OutputToTwoPlaces(balance As
	Single)
	
	End Sub
	
	Private Sub OutputToThreePlaces(balance As
	Single)
	
	End Sub

Correct Solution

```
'==============================
'This program determines a new balance after 2
'transactions have been applied
'==============================
Option Explicit

Private Sub cmdNewBalance_Click()
  Dim valueOne As Single, valueTwo As Single
  Dim accountBalance As Single, newBalance As Single

  'Obtain the input
  Let accountBalance = Val(txtAccountBalance.Text)
  Let valueOne = Val(txtValueOne.Text)
  Let valueTwo = Val(txtValueTwo.Text)

  'Work out new balance
  Let newBalance = accountBalance - valueOne - valueTwo

  'Output the new balance
```

```
picDisplay.FontName = "courier new"
picDisplay.Cls
picDisplay.Print "        1"
picDisplay.Print "123456789012345"
picDisplay.Print
Call OutputToTwoPlaces(newBalance)
Call OutputToThreePlaces(newBalance)
Call OutputToFourPlaces(newBalance)
End Sub

Private Sub OutputToTwoPlaces(balance As Single)
  picDisplay.Print FormatCurrency(balance, 2)
End Sub

Private Sub OutputToThreePlaces(balance As Single)
  picDisplay.Print FormatCurrency(balance, 3)
End Sub

Private Sub OutputToFourPlaces(balance As Single)
  picDisplay.Print Format(FormatCurrency(balance, 4), "@@@@@@@@@@@@@@")
End Sub
```

Problem 10: CORT Method 2 (some lines needed)

Problem Description

A program is required that will convert nautical miles to kilometres. The conversion is different and depends on whether international nautical miles or UK/US nautical miles are being converted. Two user-defined function procedures should be used to carry out the required conversions. Note that:

> 1 nautical mile (international) = 1.852Km
> 1 nautical mile (UK/US) = 1.85318Km

A user should key-in the number of nautical miles within a text box, click on a relevant button, and the equivalent number of kilometres should be output in a picture box to 4 decimal places.

Possible Lines of Code and Part-complete Solution

Possible Lines	Part Complete Solution
picDisplay.Print numNauticalInternationalMiles; "International nautical miles converts to " picDisplay.Cls picDisplay.Print FormatNumber(numKilometres, 4); " Kilometres" picDisplay.Print numNauticalUKUSMiles; "UK / US nautical miles converts to " picDisplay.Print FormatNumber(numKilometres, 4); " Kilometres" Let numKilometres =	'============================== 'This program converts from Nautical miles to 'Kilometres '============================== Option Explicit Private Sub cmdConvertFromInternational_Click() Dim numNauticalInternationalMiles As Single Dim numKilometres As Single

Possible Lines	Part Complete Solution
IntMilesToKMs(numNauticalInternationalMiles) Let UKUSMilesToKMs = miles * 1.82 Let UKUSMilesToKMs = miles * 1.85318 Let IntMilesToKMs = miles * 1.852 Let IntMilesToKMs = miles * 1.85318	'Obtain the number of miles Let numNauticalInternationalMiles = Val(txtNauticalMiles.Text) 'Do the conversion using the function 'Output the result picDisplay.Cls End Sub Private Sub cmdConvertFromUKUS_Click() Dim numNauticalUKUSMiles As Single Dim numKilometres As Single 'Obtain the number of miles Let numNauticalUKUSMiles = Val(txtNauticalMiles.Text) 'Do the conversion using the function Let numKilometres = UKUSMilesToKMs(numNauticalUKUSMiles) 'Output the result End Sub Private Function IntMilesToKMs(miles As Single) As Single End Function Private Function UKUSMilesToKMs(miles As Single) As Single End Function

Correct Solution

```
'==============================
'This program converts from Nautical miles to
'Kilometres
'==============================
Option Explicit

Private Sub cmdConvertFromInternational_Click()
Dim numNauticalInternationalMiles As Single
Dim numKilometres As Single

'Obtain the number of miles
Let numNauticalInternationalMiles = Val(txtNauticalMiles.Text)

'Do the conversion using the function
Let numKilometres = IntMilesToKMs(numNauticalInternationalMiles)

'Output the result
picDisplay.Cls
picDisplay.Print numNauticalInternationalMiles; "International nautical miles converts to "
```

```
    picDisplay.Print FormatNumber(numKilometres, 4); " Kilometres"
End Sub

Private Sub cmdConvertFromUKUS_Click()
  Dim numNauticalUKUSMiles As Single
  Dim numKilometres As Single

  'Obtain the number of miles
  Let numNauticalUKUSMiles = Val(txtNauticalMiles.Text)

  'Do the conversion using the function
  Let numKilometres = UKUSMilesToKMs(numNauticalUKUSMiles)

  'Output the result
  picDisplay.Cls
  picDisplay.Print numNauticalUKUSMiles; "UK / US nautical miles converts to "
  picDisplay.Print FormatNumber(numKilometres, 4); " Kilometres"
End Sub

Private Function IntMilesToKMs(miles As Single) As Single
  Let IntMilesToKMs = miles * 1.852
End Function

Private Function UKUSMilesToKMs(miles As Single) As Single
  Let UKUSMilesToKMs = miles * 1.85318
End Function
```

Problem 11: CORT Method 2 (some lines needed)

Problem Description

A program is required that will calculate the weekly pay for a shop worker. The basic pay rate is $12 per hour. A worker receives this basic pay rate for the first 35 hours worked. The rate for the next ten hours (ie up to 45 hours) is "time and a half" which is $18 per hour. The rate for any hours worked above 45 hours for a week is "double time" which is $24 per hour.

The total hours worked for a week should be entered into a text box and the program should then output the amount of pay.

Possible Lines of Code and Part-complete Solution

Possible Lines	Part Complete Solution

Let weeklyPay = 35 * 12 + 10 * 18 + (hoursWorked - 45) * 24
Let weeklyPay = 35 * 12 + (hoursWorked - 35) * 18
Let weeklyPay = hoursWorked * 12
If hoursWorked > 35 Then
Else
End If
	'=============================
	'This program calculates weekly pay
	'=============================
	Option Explicit
	
	Private Sub cmdCalculatePay_Click()
	  Dim hoursWorked As Single
	  Dim weeklyPay As Single
	
	  'Obtain the number of hours
	  Let hoursWorked = Val(txtHoursWorked.Text)

Possible Lines	Part Complete Solution
	If hoursWorked > 45 Then
	Else
	End If
	'Output the pay picDisplay.Cls picDisplay.Print "Weekly pay is "; FormatCurrency(weeklyPay, 2) End Sub
	Private Function UKUSMilesToKMs(miles As Single) As Single
	End Function

Correct Solution

```
'=============================
'This program calculates weekly pay
'=============================
Option Explicit

Private Sub cmdCalculatePay_Click()
  Dim hoursWorked As Single
  Dim weeklyPay As Single

  'Obtain the number of hours
  Let hoursWorked = Val(txthoursWorked.Text)

  If hoursWorked > 45 Then
    Let weeklyPay = 35 * 12 + 10 * 18 + (hoursWorked - 45) * 24
  Else
    If hoursWorked > 35 Then
      Let weeklyPay = 35 * 12 + (hoursWorked - 35) * 18
    Else
      Let weeklyPay = hoursWorked * 12
    End If
  End If

  'Output the pay
  picDisplay.Cls
  picDisplay.Print "Weekly pay is "; FormatCurrency(weeklyPay, 2)
End Sub
```

Problem 12: CORT Method 3 (all lines needed, some lines to key-in)

Problem Description

Write a program which has a user defined function procedure to determine the cost of posting a letter, of "large letter size", from Australia to the USA by air mail. The function should accept the weight of the letter in grammes, and return the cost in dollars according to the

---

following table. Test the function by obtaining various letter weights from a textbox and then outputting the postage cost. Use a Select Case statement in the function.

Weight Step	Cost in dollars
Up to 20g	1.40
Over 20g up to 50g	1.50
Over 50g up to 125g	2.50
Over 125g up to 250g	4.70
Over 250g up to 500g	9.00

If the weight entered is greater than 500g then an error message should be output.

Possible Lines of Code and Part-complete Solution

Possible Lines	Part Complete Solution

picDisplay.Cls
MsgBox "Error in postage cost"
picDisplay.Print "Postage cost is: ";
FormatCurrency(costOfPostage)
Let costOfPostage = PostageCost(letterWeight)
	Option Explicit
	
	Private Sub cmdClearOutput_Click()
	
	End Sub
	
	Private Sub cmdGo_Click()
	  Rem Letter Costs
	
	  Dim letterWeight As Single, costOfPostage As Single
	
	  Rem Obtain input
	  Let letterWeight = Val(txtLetterWeight.Text)
	
	  If letterWeight <= 0 Or letterWeight > 500 Then
	
	  Else
	   'Calculate & output postage cost
	
	  End If
	End Sub
	
	Private Sub cmdQuit_Click()
	  End
	End Sub
	
	Private Function PostageCost(letterWeight As Single) As Single
	  'This function calculates postage cost.
	
	  Select Case letterWeight
	
	  End Select
	
	End Function

Correct Solution

```
Option Explicit

Private Sub cmdClearOutput_Click()
  picDisplay.Cls
End Sub

Private Sub cmdGo_Click()
  Rem Letter Costs

  Dim letterWeight As Single, costOfPostage As Single

  Rem Obtain input
  Let letterWeight = Val(txtLetterWeight.Text)

  If letterWeight <= 0 Or letterWeight > 500 Then
    MsgBox "Error in postage cost"
  Else
    'Calculate & output postage cost
    Let costOfPostage = PostageCost(letterWeight)
    picDisplay.Print "Postage cost is: "; FormatCurrency(costOfPostage)
  End If
End Sub

Private Sub cmdQuit_Click()
  End
End Sub

Private Function PostageCost(letterWeight As Single) As Single
  'This function calculates postage cost.

  Select Case letterWeight
    Case 0 To 20
      Let PostageCost = 1.4
    Case 21 To 50
      Let PostageCost = 1.5
    Case 51 To 125
      Let PostageCost = 2.5
    Case 126 To 250
      Let PostageCost = 4.7
    Case 251 To 500
      Let PostageCost = 9
  End Select

End Function
```

Problem 13: CORT Method 1 (all lines needed)

Problem Description

Write a program which accepts a number between 2 and 20 and then outputs the times table corresponding to that number. The number entered should be validated. Firstly check that a number has been entered (use the IsNumeric function) and then, if it is a number, check that the number is in the correct range.

When the program is run, the focus should initially be set to (ie: the cursor is within) the txtTableNum textbox. This can be done in the form activate event procedure.

A Do While loop should be used to output the table.

Possible Lines of Code and Part-complete Solution

Possible Lines	Part Complete Solution

MsgBox "Number is not in range"
MsgBox "A valid number was not entered"
End
Let C = C + 1
txtTableNum.Text = ""
txtTableNum.SetFocus
txtTableNum.SetFocus
picDisplay.Cls
picDisplay.Print C; " x "; TableNum; " = "; C * TableNum
	'=================================
	'This program outputs "times" tables
	'=================================
	Option Explicit
	
	Private Sub cmdClear_Click()
	 'Clear the picture box and the text box and place the cursor
	 'into the txtTableNum text box
	
	End Sub
	
	Private Sub cmdGo_Click()
	 'This is the main procedure
	
	 Dim TableNum As Integer
	
	 'Obtain and validate the Table number
	
	 If IsNumeric(txtTableNum.Text) Then 'Is it numeric?
	  Let TableNum = Val(txtTableNum.Text) 'Change to a number
	  If TableNum >= 2 And TableNum <= 20 Then 'Is it in range?
	   Call OutputTable(TableNum) 'Output the table
	  Else
	
	  End If
	 Else
	
	 End If
	End Sub
	
	Private Sub cmdQuit_Click()
	 'Quit the program
	
	End Sub
	
	Private Sub Form_Activate()
	 'Place the cursor in the text box
	
	End Sub
	
	Private Sub OutputTable(TableNum As Integer)
	 'output the times table
	
	 Dim C As Integer
	
	 Let C = 1
	 Do While C <= 12

Possible Lines	Part Complete Solution
	Loop
	End Sub

Correct Solution

```
'================================
'This program outputs "times" tables
'================================
Option Explicit

Private Sub cmdClear_Click()
  'Clear the picture box and the text box and place the cursor
  'into the txtTableNum text box
  picDisplay.Cls
  txtTableNum.Text = ""
  txtTableNum.SetFocus
End Sub

Private Sub cmdGo_Click()
  'This is the main procedure

  Dim TableNum As Integer

  'Obtain and validate the Table number

  If IsNumeric(txtTableNum.Text) Then 'Is it numeric?
    Let TableNum = Val(txtTableNum.Text) 'Change to a number
    If TableNum >= 2 And TableNum <= 20 Then 'Is it in range?
      Call OutputTable(TableNum) 'Output the table
    Else
      MsgBox "Number is not in range"
    End If
  Else
    MsgBox "A valid number was not entered"
  End If
End Sub

Private Sub cmdQuit_Click()
  'Quit the program
  End
End Sub

Private Sub Form_Activate()
  'Place the cursor in the text box
  txtTableNum.SetFocus
End Sub

Private Sub OutputTable(TableNum As Integer)
  'output the times table

  Dim C As Integer

  Let C = 1
  Do While C <= 12
    picDisplay.Print C; " x "; TableNum; " = "; C * TableNum
    Let C = C + 1
  Loop

End Sub
```

Problem 14: CORT Method 1 (all lines needed)

Problem Description

Write a program which obtains a person's name and initial bank balance from a text file. It should then obtain from the file a series of transaction values which are either positive (credits) or negative (debits). These should be added to the initial bank balance to give a final bank balance.

The program should output the person's name, initial bank balance and final bank balance, and the number of transactions processed. A text file exists called transactions.txt and contains the following:

```
"Gladys Mablethorpe", 1045.22
150.00
-940.00
-567.87
43.22
99.95
-67.32
```

In the above, Gladys Mablethorpe has an initial balance of $1045.22 and her transactions are: $150 deposited, $940 withdrawn etc.

The program has a textbox into which the full path and filename (transactions.txt) are entered. The initial value of the text property of this textbox has already been set.

Possible Lines of Code and Part-complete Solution

Possible Lines	Part Complete Solution

picDisplay.Cls
Dim numberOfTransactions As Integer
Open txtFileName.Text For Input As #1
Open transactions.txt For Input As #1
Input #1, personName, initialBalance
Input #1, initialBalance, personName
Input #1, transactionValue
Let finalBalance = initialBalance
Let initialBalance = finalBalance
Let finalBalance = finalBalance + transactionValue
Let finalBalance = finalBalance - transactionValue
Let numberOfTransactions = numberOfTransactions + 1
End
	Option Explicit
	
	Private Sub cmdQuit_Click()
	  'Quit the program
	
	End Sub
	
	Private Sub cmdClearOutput_Click()
	
	End Sub
	
	Private Sub cmdGo_Click()
	  Rem Bank Balance
	
	  Dim personName As String
	  Dim initialBalance As Currency, finalBalance As Currency
	  Dim transactionValue As Currency

Possible Lines	Part Complete Solution
	Rem Initialise the number of transactions Let numberOfTransactions = 0 Rem Get the name and old balance Rem Get all the transactions Do While Not EOF(1) Loop Close #1 Rem Output the details End Sub

Correct Solution

```
Option Explicit

Private Sub cmdQuit_Click()
  'Quit the program
  End
End Sub

Private Sub cmdClearOutput_Click()
  picDisplay.Cls
End Sub

Private Sub cmdGo_Click()
  Rem Bank Balance

  Dim personName As String
  Dim initialBalance As Currency, finalBalance As Currency
  Dim transactionValue As Currency
  Dim numberOfTransactions As Integer

  Open txtFileName.Text For Input As #1

  Rem Initialise the number of transactions
  Let numberOfTransactions = 0

  Rem Get the name and old balance
  Input #1, personName, initialBalance

  Let finalBalance = initialBalance

  Rem Get all the transactions
  Do While Not EOF(1)
    Input #1, transactionValue
    Let finalBalance = finalBalance + transactionValue
    Let numberOfTransactions = numberOfTransactions + 1
  Loop
  Close #1

  Rem Output the details
  picDisplay.Print "Banking Details: "; personName
  picDisplay.Print "Old balance: "; FormatCurrency(initialBalance)
  picDisplay.Print "New balance: "; FormatCurrency(finalBalance)
  picDisplay.Print "Number of transactions: "; numberOfTransactions
End Sub
```

Problem 15: CORT Method 3 (all lines needed, some lines to key-in)

Problem Description

Write a program which inputs 8 numbers contained in the file numbers.txt into an array. This should be done in the Form_Load event procedure.

Then, when a button is clicked, the program should display three columns, the first column containing the original 8 numbers, the second column containing the 8 numbers in reverse order, and the third column containing the sum of the corresponding numbers in columns 1 and 2.

Possible Lines of Code and Part-complete Solution

Possible Lines	Part Complete Solution
Dim fNumbers(1 To 8) As Single Do While Not EOF(1) Do While EOF(1) Loop Let index = index + 1 Input #1, fNumbers(index) Input #1, index(fNumbers) picDisplay.Print picDisplay.Print "Order", "Order" picDisplay.Print "Original", "Reverse", "Sum"	Option Explicit 'Declare the array at the form level Private Sub cmdDisplayColumns_Click() 'Display the 3 columns Dim index As Integer 'Output a heading For index = 1 To 8 Next index End Sub Private Sub cmdQuit_Click() 'Quit the program End End Sub Private Sub Form_Load() 'Load the array from the data file Dim index As Integer Open "A:\00230\numbers.txt" For Input As #1 Let index = 1 Close #1 End Sub

Correct Solution

```
Option Explicit

'Declare the array at the form level
Dim fNumbers(1 To 8) As Single

Private Sub cmdDisplayColumns_Click()
```

```
'Display the 3 columns
Dim index As Integer

'Output a heading
picDisplay.Print "Original", "Reverse", "Sum"
picDisplay.Print "Order", "Order"
picDisplay.Print

For index = 1 To 8
  picDisplay.Print fNumbers(index), fNumbers(9 - index), fNumbers(index) + fNumbers(9 - index)
Next index
End Sub

Private Sub cmdQuit_Click()
  'Quit the program
  End
End Sub

Private Sub Form_Load()
  'Load the array from the data file
  Dim index As Integer

  'Open "A:\00230\numbers.txt" For Input As #1
  Open App.Path & "\numbers.txt" For Input As #1
  Let index = 1

  Do While Not EOF(1)
    Input #1, fNumbers(index)
    Let index = index + 1
  Loop

  Close #1
End Sub
```

Problem 16: CORT Method 1 (all lines needed)

Problem Description

Write a program that places daily temperatures into an array. A temperature should be keyed-into a textbox and then placed in the next location in an array when a button is clicked. Hence, when the program is run, the first temperature entered will be placed into array location one, the second temperature into array location two etc.

There should be a second button on the form. When this button is clicked, the average temperature should be output. Note:

- The array should have 10 locations. Hence up to 10 temperatures can be entered.
- When placing a temperature in the array, check that the array is not full. If it is full, then output a message.
- Clear the textbox after the temperature has been placed into the array and place the cursor into the textbox.
- The array will need to be declared at the form level.
- The counter used to keep track of the number of temperatures entered also needs to be declared at the form level.

Possible Lines of Code and Part-complete Solution

Possible Lines	Part Complete Solution

Dim fTemperatures(1 To 10) As Single
Dim fNumberOfTemperatures As Single
Next C
For C = 1 To fNumberOfTemperatures
Let fNumberOfTemperatures = fNumberOfTemperatures + 1
Let fTemperatures(fNumberOfTemperatures) = Val(txttemperature.Text)
Let sumOfTemperatures = sumOfTemperatures + fTemperatures(C)
Let txttemperature.Text = ""
Let fNumberOfTemperatures = 0
txttemperature.SetFocus
MsgBox "Sorry, you already have 10 temperatures"
	Option Explicit
	
	Private Sub cmdAverage_Click()
	'Calculate the average temperature
	Dim C As Integer
	Dim sumOfTemperatures
	Dim averageTemperature As Single
	
	Let averageTemperature = sumOfTemperatures / fNumberOfTemperatures
	
	'Output the result
	picDisplay.Cls
	picDisplay.Print "Average temperature is "; averageTemperature; " Celsius"
	picDisplay.Print "Number of temperatures entered = "; fNumberOfTemperatures
	End Sub
	
	Private Sub cmdGettemperature_Click()
	'Place the temperature entered into the array unless the array is full
	If fNumberOfTemperatures < 10 Then
	
	Else
	
	End If
	End Sub
	
	Private Sub Form_Load()
	'Initialise the number of temperatures to zero
	End Sub

Correct Solution

```
Option Explicit

Dim fTemperatures(1 To 10) As Single
Dim fNumberOfTemperatures As Single

Private Sub cmdAverage_Click()
  'Calculate the average temperature
  Dim C As Integer
  Dim sumOfTemperatures
  Dim averageTemperature As Single

  For C = 1 To fNumberOfTemperatures
    Let sumOfTemperatures = sumOfTemperatures + fTemperatures(C)
  Next C

  Let averageTemperature = sumOfTemperatures / fNumberOfTemperatures

  'Output the result
  picDisplay.Cls
  picDisplay.Print "Average temperature is "; averageTemperature; " Celsius"
  picDisplay.Print "Number of temperatures entered = "; fNumberOfTemperatures
End Sub

Private Sub cmdGettemperature_Click()
  'Place the temperature entered into the array unless the array is full
```

```
If fNumberOfTemperatures < 10 Then
    Let fNumberOfTemperatures = fNumberOfTemperatures + 1
    Let fTemperatures(fNumberOfTemperatures) = Val(txttemperature.Text)
    Let txttemperature.Text = ""
    txttemperature.SetFocus
Else
    MsgBox "Sorry, you already have 10 temperatures"
End If
End Sub

Private Sub Form_Load()
    'Initialise the number of temperatures to zero
    Let fNumberOfTemperatures = 0
End Sub
```

Problem 17: CORT Method 2 (some lines needed)

Problem Description

Write a program which declares (using Dim statements) two parallel arrays of student names and their marks called fNames() and fMarks() at the form level. Note that the brackets after fNames and fMarks simply indicate that they are arrays and the "f" prefix indicates that the arrays are at the form level.

The arrays can hold up to 15 names and marks and these should be obtained from a text file called results.txt. This should be done in the Form Load event procedure. It is important that no more than 15 names and marks are placed in the arrays otherwise a "subscript out of range" message will be output. The names and marks are in no particular order.

The program should be able to do the following when appropriate buttons are clicked:

- Output the names and marks to a picture box.
- Sort the arrays into name order and redisplay the output.
- Sort the arrays into mark order and redisplay the output.
- Search the array of names for a name that has been entered into a textbox and output the corresponding mark or an error message if the name is not present.
- Lines of code are only missing from cmdSortOnMark_Click and cmdSearch_Click.
- The lines in the left-hand window have been separated such that the first set of lines is for the event procedure cmdSortOnMark_Click and the second set is for the event procedure cmdSearch_Click.

Possible Lines of Code and Part-complete Solution

Possible Lines	Part Complete Solution

```**```
```****Use the following in cmdSortOnMark_Click```
```**```
```For passNum = 1 To fNumberOfNames - 1```
```For i = 1 To fNumberOfNames - passNum```
	```Rem ====== Form Level Area ======```
	```Option Explicit```
	```Rem Declare Names array```
	```Dim fNames(1 To 15) As String```

Possible Lines	Part Complete Solution

If fMarks(i) > fMarks(i + 1) Then
If fMarks(i) < fMarks(i + 1) Then
End If
Next passNum
Next i
tempName = fNames(i)
fNames(i) = tempName
fNames(i) = fNames(i + 1)
fNames(i + 1) = tempName
tempMark = fMarks(i)
fMarks(i) = fMarks(i + 1)
fMarks(i + 1) = tempMark
****
****Use the following in cmdSearch_Click****
****
Let foundFlag = "no"
Let foundFlag = "yes"
Let n = n + 1
Let n = n + 2
picDisplay.Print "Name does not exist"
	Rem Declare Marks array
	Dim fMarks(1 To 15) As Single
	Rem Keep a track of the number of names
	Dim fNumberOfNames As Integer
	Rem ================================
	Private Sub cmdOutputAllDetails_Click()
	  Rem This outputs the contents of the 2 arrays
	  Call OutputDetails
	End Sub
	Rem ================================
	Private Sub cmdSearch_Click()
	  Dim searchName As String
	  Rem the subscript of the array
	  Dim n As Integer
	  Rem Flag to indicate if found
	  Dim foundFlag As String
	
	  Rem Obtain the search name
	  Let searchName = UCase(txtSearchName.Text)
	
	  picDisplay.Cls
	  Let n = 0
	
	  Do While foundFlag = "no" And n < fNumberOfNames
	    If searchName = UCase(fNames(n)) Then
	      Let foundFlag = "yes"
	    End If
	  Loop
	
	  If foundFlag = "yes" Then
	    picDisplay.Print "Mark is "; fMarks(n)
	  Else
	
	  End If
	
	End Sub
	Rem ================================
	Private Sub cmdSortOnMark_Click()
	  Rem This sorts the arrays into name order and then outputs the details
	
	  Dim passNum As Integer
	  Dim i As Integer
	  Dim tempName As String
	  Dim tempMark As Single
	
	  Rem Now display the details again
	  Call OutputDetails
	
	End Sub
	Rem ================================
	Private Sub cmdSortOnName_Click()
	  Rem This sorts the arrays into name order and then outputs the details
	
	  Dim passNum As Integer
	  Dim i As Integer
	  Dim tempName As String
	  Dim tempMark As Single
	
	  For passNum = 1 To fNumberOfNames - 1
	    For i = 1 To fNumberOfNames - passNum
	      If fNames(i) > fNames(i + 1) Then
	        Rem swap names

Possible Lines	Part Complete Solution
| | ```
        tempName = fNames(i)
        fNames(i) = fNames(i + 1)
        fNames(i + 1) = tempName
        Rem Swap marks
        tempMark = fMarks(i)
        fMarks(i) = fMarks(i + 1)
        fMarks(i + 1) = tempMark
      End If
    Next i
  Next passNum

  Rem Now display the details again
  Call OutputDetails
End Sub
Rem ==================================
Private Sub Form_Load()
  Rem Obtain the data from the file Tute9-
1Data.txt

  Open "A:\00250\results.txt" For Input As #1
  Let fNumberOfNames = 0

  Do While Not EOF(1) And fNumberOfNames <
15
    Let fNumberOfNames = fNumberOfNames + 1
    Input #1, fNames(fNumberOfNames),
fMarks(fNumberOfNames)
  Loop

  Close #1
End Sub
Rem ==================================
Private Sub OutputDetails()
  Rem This outputs the contents of the arrays
  Dim index As Integer

  picDisplay.Cls
  For index = 1 To fNumberOfNames
    picDisplay.Print fNames(index), fMarks(index)
  Next index
End Sub
Rem ==================================
``` |

Correct Solution

```
Option Explicit
Rem Declare Names array
Dim fNames(1 To 15) As String
Rem Declare Marks array
Dim fMarks(1 To 15) As Single
Rem Keep a track of the number of names
Dim fNumberOfNames As Integer

Private Sub cmdOutputAllDetails_Click()
  Rem This outputs the contents of the 2 arrays
  Call OutputDetails
End Sub

Private Sub cmdSearch_Click()
  Dim searchName As String
  Rem the subscript of the array
  Dim n As Integer
  Rem Flag to indicate if found
  Dim foundFlag As String
```
```

```
Rem Obtain the search name
Let searchName = UCase(txtSearchName.Text)

picDisplay.Cls
Let foundFlag = "no"
Let n = 0

Do While foundFlag = "no" And n < fNumberOfNames
  Let n = n + 1
  If searchName = UCase(fNames(n)) Then
    Let foundFlag = "yes"
  End If
Loop

If foundFlag = "yes" Then
  picDisplay.Print "Mark is "; fMarks(n)
Else
  picDisplay.Print "Name does not exist"
End If

End Sub

Private Sub cmdSortOnMark_Click()
  Rem This sorts the arrays into name order and then outputs the details

  Dim passNum As Integer
  Dim i As Integer
  Dim tempName As String
  Dim tempMark As Single

  For passNum = 1 To fNumberOfNames - 1
   For i = 1 To fNumberOfNames - passNum
    If fMarks(i) > fMarks(i + 1) Then
      Rem swap names
      tempName = fNames(i)
      fNames(i) = fNames(i + 1)
      fNames(i + 1) = tempName
      Rem Swap marks
      tempMark = fMarks(i)
      fMarks(i) = fMarks(i + 1)
      fMarks(i + 1) = tempMark
    End If
   Next i
  Next passNum

  Rem Now display the details again
  Call OutputDetails

End Sub

Private Sub cmdSortOnName_Click()
  Rem This sorts the arrays into name order and then outputs the details

  Dim passNum As Integer
  Dim i As Integer
  Dim tempName As String
  Dim tempMark As Single

  For passNum = 1 To fNumberOfNames - 1
   For i = 1 To fNumberOfNames - passNum
    If fNames(i) > fNames(i + 1) Then
      Rem swap names
      tempName = fNames(i)
      fNames(i) = fNames(i + 1)
      fNames(i + 1) = tempName
      Rem Swap marks
      tempMark = fMarks(i)
      fMarks(i) = fMarks(i + 1)
      fMarks(i + 1) = tempMark
    End If
   Next i
  Next passNum

  Rem Now display the details again
```

```
  Call OutputDetails
End Sub

Private Sub Form_Load()
  Rem Obtain the data from the file Tute9-1Data.txt

  Open "A:\00250\results.txt" For Input As #1
  Let fNumberOfNames = 0

  Do While Not EOF(1) And fNumberOfNames < 15
    Let fNumberOfNames = fNumberOfNames + 1
    Input #1, fNames(fNumberOfNames), fMarks(fNumberOfNames)
  Loop

  Close #1
End Sub

Private Sub OutputDetails()
  Rem This outputs the contents of the arrays
  Dim index As Integer

  picDisplay.Cls
  For index = 1 To fNumberOfNames
    picDisplay.Print fNames(index), fMarks(index)
  Next index
End Sub
```

Problem 18: CORT Method 3 (all lines needed, some lines to key-in)

Problem Description

Write a program to do the following:

- Allow users to enter student names and marks into textboxes, click on a button, and add to a text file called marks.txt. The file does not necessarily exist.
- On clicking a button, two new files should be created called low.txt and high.txt. These should contain details of students who obtained marks less than 50, and 50 or over respectively.
- On clicking appropriate buttons, the contents of the various files should be displayed in a picture box.

Examples of the expected file contents are:

> **marks.txt**
> "Mason, M.", 29
> "Brainbox, C.", 100
> "Fossey, T.", 50
> "Roy, G.", 49
> etc
>
> **low.txt**
> "Mason, M.", 29
> "Roy, G.", 49
>
> **high.txt**
> "Brainbox, C.", 100
> "Fossey, T.", 50

Possible Lines of Code and Part-complete Solution

Possible Lines	Part Complete Solution

`*********************************************`
`**Use the following in cmdAddToFile_Click`
`*********************************************`
`Open App.Path & "\marks.txt" For Append As #1`
`Open App.Path & "\marks.txt" For Output As #1`
`Open App.Path & "\marks.txt" For Input As #1`
`Write #1, studentName, studentMark`
`Close #1`
`Let txtName.Text = ""`
`Let txtMark.Text = ""`
`txtName.Cls`
`txtMark.Cls`
`txtName.SetFocus`
`*********************************************`
`**Use the following in cmdCreateFiles_Click`
`*********************************************`
`Open App.Path & "\marks.txt" For Output As #1`
`Open App.Path & "\marks.txt" For Input As #1`
`Open App.Path & "\low.txt" For Append As #2`
`Open App.Path & "\low.txt" For Output As #2`
`Open App.Path & "\low.txt" For Input As #2`
`Open App.Path & "\high.txt" For Append As #3`
`Open App.Path & "\high.txt" For Output As #3`
`Open App.Path & "\high.txt" For Input As #3`
`Write #3, studentName, studentMark`
`Write #2, studentName, studentMark`
`Close #1`
`Close #2`
`Close #3`
	`Option Explicit`
	`Rem =============================`
	`Private Sub cmdAddToFile_Click()`
	`  Dim studentName As String`
	`  Dim studentMark As Single`
	
	`  'Get data from text boxes`
	`  Let studentName = txtName.Text`
	`  Let studentMark = Val(txtMark.Text)`
	
	`  'Output the name and mark to the file`
	
	`  'Clear the textboxes and set the focus to the`
	`txtName textbox`
	`End Sub`
	`Rem =============================`
	`Private Sub cmdCreatefiles_Click()`
	`  'Create the two files`
	`  'This assumes that marks.txt exists`
	`  Dim studentName As String`
	`  Dim studentMark As Single`
	
	`  Do While Not EOF(1)`
	`    Input #1, studentName, studentMark`
	`    If studentMark < 50 Then`
	`    Else`
	`    End If`
	`  Loop`
	
	`End Sub`
	`Rem =============================`
	`Private Sub cmdDisplayHigh_Click()`
	`  'Display sudent details for 50 or more marks`
	`  'This assumes that high.txt exists`
	`  Dim studentName As String`
	`  Dim studentMark As Single`
	
	`  Open App.Path & "\high.txt" For Input As #1`
	`  picDisplay.Cls`
	`  Do While Not EOF(1)`
	`    Input #1, studentName, studentMark`
	`    picDisplay.Print studentName, studentMark`
	`  Loop`
	`  Close #1`
	
	`End Sub`
	`Rem =============================`
	`Private Sub cmdDisplayLow_Click()`
	`  'Display sudent details for less than 50 marks`
	`  'This assumes that low.txt exists`
	
	`End Sub`
	`Rem =============================`
	`Private Sub cmdDisplayMarks_Click()`
	`  'Display all names and marks`
	`  Dim studentName As String`
	`  Dim studentMark As Single`
	
	`  Open App.Path & "\marks.txt" For Input As #1`
	`  picDisplay.Cls`
	`  Do While Not EOF(1)`

Correct Solution

```
Option Explicit

Private Sub cmdAddToFile_Click()
  Dim studentName As String
  Dim studentMark As Single

  'Get data from text boxes
  Let studentName = txtName.Text
  Let studentMark = Val(txtMark.Text)

  'Output the name and mark to the file
  Open App.Path & "\marks.txt" For Append As #1
  Write #1, studentName, studentMark
  Close #1

  'Clear the textboxes and set the focus to the txtName textbox
  Let txtName.Text = ""
  Let txtMark.Text = ""
  txtName.SetFocus
End Sub

Private Sub cmdCreatefiles_Click()
  'Create the two files
  'This assumes that marks.txt exists
  Dim studentName As String
  Dim studentMark As Single

  Open App.Path & "\marks.txt" For Input As #1
  Open App.Path & "\low.txt" For Output As #2
  Open App.Path & "\high.txt" For Output As #3

  Do While Not EOF(1)
    Input #1, studentName, studentMark
    If studentMark < 50 Then
      Write #2, studentName, studentMark
    Else
      Write #3, studentName, studentMark
    End If
  Loop
  Close #1
  Close #2
  Close #3
End Sub

Private Sub cmdDisplayHigh_Click()
  'Display sudent details for 50 or more marks
  'This assumes that high.txt exists
  Dim studentName As String
  Dim studentMark As Single

  Open App.Path & "\high.txt" For Input As #1
  picDisplay.Cls
  Do While Not EOF(1)
    Input #1, studentName, studentMark
    picDisplay.Print studentName, studentMark
  Loop
  Close #1

End Sub
```

```
Private Sub cmdDisplayLow_Click()
  'Display sudent details for less than 50 marks
  'This assumes that low.txt exists
  Dim studentName As String
  Dim studentMark As Single

  Open App.Path & "\low.txt" For Input As #1
  picDisplay.Cls
  Do While Not EOF(1)
    Input #1, studentName, studentMark
    picDisplay.Print studentName, studentMark
  Loop
  Close #1
End Sub

Private Sub cmdDisplayMarks_Click()
  'Display all names and marks
  Dim studentName As String
  Dim studentMark As Single

  Open App.Path & "\marks.txt" For Input As #1
  picDisplay.Cls
  Do While Not EOF(1)
    Input #1, studentName, studentMark
    picDisplay.Print studentName, studentMark
  Loop
  Close #1
End Sub
```